SAVE THEM ALL

ONE COACH'S QUEST

JERRY STONE

ISBN: 978-1985868953 (print)

Publishing and Design Services: MartinPublishingServices.com

DEDICATION

Where to begin…To those who raised me,
those who taught me, those who befriended me,

And especially those young men who allowed me
to do my best to teach them, when they needed a
mentor and friend during a fragile time of their life.

With special gratitude for my daughters, Stacy and
Marci, and my wife, Shirley, who realized about the
same time as myself that coaching basketball wasn't
merely a choice, but a unique opportunity granted to
me. I dedicate this, my diary, to you.

Coach Jerry Stone

4 Games in 5 Days. Too tired to smile.

NJCAA Champs 1982 "Greatest Championship Game Ever Played"

BASKETBALL PRESENTS A CHALLENGE

to execute physical skills,

to react under pressure situations,

to develop an attitude of sportsmanship, to be a part of a team,

to match all I've practiced and learned against an opponent who has the same hopes for victory.

It's the competition, the desire to be the *best*.

I LOVE THE GAME.

—JERRY STONE
McMurry College, 1964

My game-time position.

FOREWORD

My first thoughts of Coach Stone were mixed. He was very particular about how the game should be played. He taught every phase of the game, half-court and full-court, never missed a thing. My head was spinning during those first few workouts. He kept saying that there would be a time when he would get out of the way, and the team would become our team.

During high school the ball was rolled out and away we went. I had run one drill prior to that time. Most of what Coach Stone barked out was something I had never heard. It eventually all made sense and it wasn't long before I realized there was much to learn, and that if he was willing to teach me, I'd better take advantage of it.

We started with what seemed like 20 players during the fall of 1981. Midland College had been ranked number one most of last year's season. There were many guys that wanted to be a part of a winning program. But by Christmas, Coach had sent a few home and the rest couldn't handle the work and discipline that was required to be on the floor, playing in a Chaparral uniform. By Christmas we were down to 9 players.

Everyone certainly knew their role. The small number actually turned out to be an advantage—our team had real chemistry. We could read each other's minds by the time we got into the second semester. Because of that fact, there were many occasions that resulted in victory, in fact, every game we played for the remainder of the year ended with a win.

The book explains how players and coaches feel before, during, and after a game. Everyone should read it. He is honest in his approach to the game—Coach Stone has loved this game from early childhood. Many times he would remind us that the game of basketball was bigger than us or himself. And that we should have respect for it, in other words, play the game "the right way". He wanted us to have pride in the way we played while always putting the team first.

Much of Coach's personal coaching philosophy is scattered throughout the book. Reading it reminded me how thorough our practices were. There was much emphasis on fundamentals, but there were also things like never letting our opponent know we're tired, understanding clock management, and realizing what our opponent depended on—then taking it away.

We often played only five guys during a game—much was done to allow those five to stay on the floor, things like playing zone, stalling, and holding for one shot. What was interesting was the amount of time we spent working on man-to-man defense, so that if needed, we could play it and play it well. Actually, we were a very versatile team. I believe Coach Stone was greatly influenced by the type players he had, and used them perfectly— we five starters knew a lot about basketball after going through a season at Midland.

Our season started slow, losing three of the first five games. But by early December, we began a streak that never stopped. Coach's greatest asset was his ability to motivate. Much of the habit of winning that we developed came from his skill as a motivator—it was like he was still a player. He hated to lose—it spilled over to his team.

The memories of the two years I spent at Midland College will always remain with me. They were special.

Coach Stone and I have remained good friends throughout the years.

He has had many kind words for me, as I have for him. We've played golf—we're still very competitive. He insists on receiving strokes—he still likes winning.

I hope you enjoy the book—believe me, the cast and the script join to make great reading.

SPUD WEBB

Spud Webb, 1981-83, First Team All-American

ENDORSEMENTS

Rick Penny McMurry University all-time leading scorer:

The depth of Coach Stone's teaching has only been revealed after reading his book. He is brilliant. Reading his book has been fantastic. I want others to know what he has to offer.

Nolan Richardson Tulsa University, Arkansas University:

I have coached over 40 years and I can honestly say that Jerry's book is the best coaching book I have ever read. This book should be considered required reading for players and coaches at any level. I could not put it down. Jerry illustrates the true feelings of a player and coach through the process of learning and teaching the fundamentals of basketball.

Ricky Grace Oklahoma University, Perth, Australia Wildcats; Australian Olympic Team 2000:

Before Coach Stone entered my life I was an immature kid. Two years under his influence at Midland College allowed me to have all the tools necessary on and off the court to become a man. Eighty percent of what I know about basketball came from him. Basketball and the life lessons spoken about in this book continue to guide me these 40 years later.

Todd Duncan-Head Coach, Lubbock Christian University:

Playing for Coach Stone was one of the best things that has ever happened to me. His ability to teach, relate, and inspire is second to none. I'm thankful for the impact he has had on my life and countless others.

Spud Webb-N. C. State, Atlanta Hawks;1986 NBA Slam Dunk Champ:

He taught me the game. He was a great teacher of fundamentals which I carried into North Carolina State and later into the NBA. Nothing was overlooked. What I especially learned from Coach Stone was poise and never giving up. He knew how to get into our hearts and minds—it was why we won.

Hershel Kimbrell-Head Coach, 31 years McMurry University, 1959-90:

Jerry had one of the best athletic and compassionate hearts I ever coached. I think it would be beneficial for every young coach and even the parents of young athletes to read this book.

Nathan Doudney-Texas Tech, Gonzaga:

I have been fortunate to play for several great coaches in my career...I would put Coach Stone up there with any I have been around. His passion for his players and the game of basketball shine through in his book.

Josh Naylor—Texas State University, All-Conference player; Executive Pastor of Renew Life Church:

Jerry Stone has the unique ability to inspire and lead each individual player without compromising his standards and vision for the group. He has mastered the art of motivating the individual and the team through his practical and creative leadership approach.

Coach Stone's influence has shaped me into a better "coach" and leader in my life, and I believe this book will do exactly that for you.

Reggie Franklin—SMU, Globetrotters, NMMI Coach, Athletes Director:

Jerry Stone is the best coach I have ever been around. He leaves nothing to chance, practicing everything thoroughly until it's right. Coach Stone is demanding but fair—his humor topped off the pleasure I enjoyed as his assistant. His book illustrates the thoughts I have expressed.

WHY THE TITLE

"…Toward the end of our visit, Hall of Fame Coach Dave Whitney looked at me as if to say, 'Young man, don't miss out on what I'm about to tell you.' Very softly, but with sincere conviction, he said, 'You know, Coach, I just believe you can *save every boy*.' "

Save every boy…Dave Whitney's words shot straight to my heart. I knew exactly what and why he said it—I needed no interpretation.

CONTENTS

The only team to be totally unranked.
The 1982 Midland College/Miami-Dade title game has been
described as the greatest NJCAA Basketball Tournament
title game ever played. And that's with just 8 players—March 1982.

PROLOGUE

I gathered my team during a time-out to set a play for a five-foot-seven, 135-pound freshman point guard named Spud Webb.

At this moment in time, freshman Spud Webb was little-known. Basketball fans in Dallas had heard of him—a few had seen him. Now, during the winding down of one week in March of 1982 at the National Junior College Athletic Association Tournament in Hutchinson, Kansas, there were a few thousand newly acquired followers who couldn't believe what they had been seeing for the past five days. This five-foot-seven guy had been dunking, blocking shots, stealing the ball—actually stealing the show—all week long, and never changing his expression throughout all of it.

For us to win the championship, he had to make the shot. It seemed like a great deal of weight to place on one tiny set of shoulders. We were down two points with less than ten seconds. Make the shot and we go into a second overtime. Miss it and we collect the second-place trophy, pick up the hamburgers, and drive all night to Midland, Texas.

No one cares about second place. Which would it be?

When our quiet, poised team left the huddle, everybody in that arena asked themselves, "Can the little guy do what we have witnessed all week one more time?" His teammates were, no doubt, less concerned than anyone. He had been doing that very thing all year long.

Michael Johnson, author of *The Juco Classic: 40 Years of the*

National Junior College Athletic Association Tournament, called our 1982 title game *the greatest NJCAA Basketball Tournament title game ever played.* During that game, I remember thinking, *"This has got to be one of the greatest games ever played in this arena."* I didn't have time to think any further. But I have since, and wouldn't argue with Michael Johnson's assessment at all.

The 1982 Midland College basketball team that made history with eight players that night understood the little things: details. They met every challenge throughout the week and needed one more win to complete the dream. From eighteen original members on the 1981–82 roster to eight remaining members, the Chaparrals put everything on the line.

The attempt to climax their magical year as champions is a story that has long been overlooked.

But the story of that team is but one chapter of my life. I always knew I would coach, and I always knew it would be basketball. There was no sudden defining moment during high school or college when a desire to be a coach struck me. What I observed and analyzed as an adult, I had been observing and analyzing since grade school.

From an early age, I studied people. Attempting to read people has always been a hobby—I took up for the weakling and made friends with the unpopular. I still have great compassion for the underdog today—I always loved the little guy.

I hated losing—at my age, I'm still not fond of it.

An autobiography that intertwines more than 1,300 basketball games and fifty basketball teams (as a player and a coach) spins an endless number of incidents. What you will find in these pages are numerous references to what I consider **keys to winning**.

The daily work to that end is obvious: we all know about

"out-working our opponent." But, it takes so much more. It's the simple things that have motivated me to coach. **There is a method to becoming a winner, a method that I believe can be explained and understood. That's the good news : It's nothing mysterious. It's so basic it's often overlooked.**

Ben Hogan's *Five Lessons, The Modern Fundamentals of Golf* is the book I refer anyone to who is attempting to learn a game as complicated as golf. In his writing Mr. Hogan provides an opposite viewpoint, without hesitation, claiming anyone can consistently shoot in the low to mid-80's by simply believing and practicing the principles and guidelines he recommends.

The first time I read those words, I believed him. You get the unmistakable notion that Ben means what he says! And, how convenient that "it comes from the dirt" (his reference to basic fundamentals, from the ground up).

As I crawl through the slow-moving process of authoring an autobiography, my thoughts keep returning to Ben Hogan. Everything he says parallels my attempt at explaining how I feel about the game of basketball. I have felt these deep-seated beliefs for the game, apparently from my mother. Her actions spoke for her—she never gave me a *Rocky* speech, just an occasional bit of basketball advice.

Dad's advice centered around life, in general, but it was so seldom that I can tell you almost everything he said, to this day—I listened when my dad spoke.

Pure talent is the number one factor, but following closely are attitude and effort. To attain the latter is what I will emphasize.

This is what makes the coaching of sport so fascinating and what draws a team together. The "togetherness" we all seek isn't something that occurs automatically—chemistry is a mysterious element. When it does appear, the result is a united team which makes your season all worthwhile.

Writing this manuscript means I'm coaching again. I have stayed up half the night numerous times—it's exciting. Too much golf after retirement messed with my back. I don't like it, but there has been a positive from my partial confinement. I finally got started on a project that my Dad suggested a long time ago to complete whenever possible: writing my life story. He had always told me it was something one was obligated as a man to do. Those that follow you have the right to know who they are and where they came from.

The book is autobiographical, but because basketball was so much a part of my life, a general theme of playing and coaching the game runs throughout its pages. **I believe young players and young coaches, and even parents can learn a lot from this book.** There are many points of instruction that should be helpful. Basketball fans will relate to it also. The individually named chapters will help direct those of particular interests, but I hope you will read and enjoy the book's entirety.

There is much emphasis on the feelings and inner thoughts of the participants. I want to pass along some of those inner thoughts, allowing you to climb inside the athlete and coach's mind as the game of basketball unfolds.

Basketball has changed since I played as a kid—but not really. The style of play is changing, but the teams that are constantly winning are the teams that carry an "old-school" chip on their shoulders—and that is doing the little things right, and doing them every night.

"Old school" references seem to be losing it's respect—that's a

serious mistake, because *Old School will never go away—it speaks of long-standing principles that have proven to be true.*

This book is a reminder of why certain teams win. It seems to me that many of us are beginning to forget.

The late Jim Valvano, better known as Coach Jimmy V, said, "Never give up." That sums up a coach's plight. No doubt, most of what we know and understand comes from mistakes we've made along the way.

In the following pages, I've tried to reveal some of mine, both on and off the court, to help the reader who may struggle with the enormous responsibility of coaching. If you choose to coach at any level, brace yourself. I assure you, what those players learn won't be any more significant than what you will—and it never stops. At times, you will look back with some regret, knowing, *"I could have handled that kid or that team much better."* So, you learn and move on, never giving up. Thankfully, next year's season is right around the corner.

I have always critiqued coaching styles thoroughly. That never goes away. I've constantly studied them, asking myself if they were "connecting" with each player and what tactics would work for me. Integrity for the game was ingrained in me at a early age and remains more important than any individual achievement one might receive. When Kevin Durant of Golden State says, "Winning the MVP Award isn't as satisfying as winning the NBA Finals," he's talking about his team first—he's talking my language.

Although I played everything, basketball was always my game. It was my good fortune, at an early age, to be under the guidance of excellent adult role models, primarily, Merle Hinton and Dan Kahler. We will look at these two exceptional men up close, men who had a great amount of influence on hundreds of boys, including myself. Both are gone now.

What I have to tell—the lessons that life and the game of basketball have taught me—is my opportunity to honor them.

The heart and the conclusion of this story can only lead in one direction—**follow the Yellow-Brick Road,** it's off to Kansas we'll go. While I have nothing but pride and joy for the many teams that have allowed me to be their coach, one clearly stands apart. And that would be the magical event of March, 1982 at the National Junior College Basketball Tournament in Hutchinson, Kansas, not far from my home town. For many reasons, it's the perfect illustration of what can happen to a small unknown band of hoopsters from Texas.

Tiny, unassuming Midland College lead by the smallest piece of the puzzle, a kid named Spud (all 5-7 of him) methodically mowed down four giants during a five day mission. If you were there, you will approve of it's retelling—if you weren't, this book may grab your emotions and help explain why, to this day, the pride and enthusiasm is still alive and well, as we reminisce. Chapter 16 is no more than five pages long, devoted to Spud solely. Read it and you'll want to read everything else. (What's funny is I wrote it, and it continues to excite me as I read and edit it.)

More than once I tried to list all of those from past and present that have meant so much to me. I finally concluded that it was impossible, unless I was willing to omit someone I would not choose to.

My goal is to make the story relative to the reader—reflective, informative, and humorous. My experience of forty-plus years of coaching qualifies me to do so.

"I always knew
I would coach,
and I always
knew it would be
basketball."

Jerry and Janet, The Stone Twins

I
FIRST QUARTER

MY CALLING

Mom, captain, All-American 1929, holding basketball.
Oklahoma Business College

1
LOVE AT FIRST SIGHT
DECEMBER 25, 1949

"A boy, a ball, and a dream."

—Kerry D. Marshall, *The Marvin Wood Story*

On Christmas day, a wonderful gift waited for me under the tree: a basketball goal, a net, and a leather ball for an eight-year-old. As soon as I saw the goal, something seemed wrong. Dad had made a terrible mistake. (Maybe it was Santa. What did he know about basketball?) The goal was obviously too big!

How could I possibly tell him he had been sold an oversized rim?

How embarrassing.

Not a word was uttered, but visions of an enormous rim stuck on our garage surely meant that I was about to become the laughingstock of the neighborhood. I braced myself for the ridicule. Guess what? Once it was ten feet off the ground, that rim didn't look so big.

Did you know that two basketballs placed side by side can slide through a regulation rim at the same time? You're not alone. Seems like it should be easy to hit a fifteen-footer with a goal that big. Some nights, it isn't.

At the age of eight it happened—unaware at the time, my future was staring at me while watching my mother shoot baskets, two-hand set shots from fifteen to seventeen feet. It seemed like she never missed, swishing the net time and time again. Any time I see film clips of the early years of basketball, it reminds me of the soft touch of Mother's two-hand set shots. It has always seemed harder to shoot with two hands as opposed to one. The touch and release of both hands have to be precisely the same. Mom was a pure shooter. From the moment she demonstrated her shooting skills, it infatuated me. I wasn't sure how she did it, but it was something that grabbed me and wouldn't let go.

Looking back, what I found under the tree that year was quite significant and no accident. There had never been a previous discussion regarding my receiving it. The goal was a total surprise. At the time, I wasn't even aware of the role my mother had played with the game of basketball. I do remember the genuine thrill I felt when I realized it was about to be my turn.

As it turns out, Mom was quite the player. She played at a business college in Tulsa, Oklahoma, and was actually in a semi-professional league. She was the team's leading scorer and an All-American. There were several newspaper clippings, one of which mentioned Audrey Marshall scoring forty-four points in one particular game. I think it was my aunt who first mentioned her achievements as a player to me. Mom never said a word about it, although there were occasional tips about basketball she shared with me. There were a few more clippings to verify, thankfully. She was forever preaching modesty—my dad shared the same humbleness—both most definitely endorsed it. But the love of the game was ingrained in her, although seldom was it mentioned.

Audrey White Marshall Stone passed away in November of 2004 at the age of ninety-two. During her later years we chatted as much as possible. Our phone calls, from Texas to Kansas and back, would quite often start out with something like "Well,

Larry (Bird) didn't have a good game last night," or, "Boy, Michael (Jordan) was hitting everything."

A talk with Mom always reminded me who I was.

In contrast, to understand my relationship with my father, **William E. "Bill" Stone**, you need to know a little about him. For a guy who was forced to drop out of the eighth grade to help feed his family, he did quite well. He was the district manager of the Kansas Gas and Electric Company and a member of the Kansas National Guard. At one time, he served as president of various organizations and commissions, such as the Kiwanis and the Kansas Conservation Panel. He was also a city councilman and eventually became the mayor of Ark City.

Dad wanted very much to go to college but never got the chance. Having dropped out of school early, Dad took correspondence courses to further his education. He eventually completed high school and about half of college this way. Dad never complained about it, though my mother told me much later that he had a twinge of jealously when his only son went to college for free on a basketball scholarship.

With a wife and four kids—me, my twin sister, Janet, and my two older sisters, Barbara and Carol—and so many outside activities, my dad's plate was full.

I grew up in a neighborhood that bordered the outskirts of Ark City called Sleeth Addition. The Sparks clan also lived there. They included a bunch of cousins, aunts, uncles, grandparents, and grand-kids who out-numbered everyone. **Loye Sparks** was my grade-school buddy. He had three sisters and three brothers. I had three sisters. With no brothers, "buddies" were always important in my life.

Each spring, the Sleeth Addition Elementary School Track

Meet was held. It was *the event* of the year, the only one that presented awards (ribbons). Each kid chose two individual events in which to participate. Everyone ran on a relay team. From first grade through sixth, second-place ribbons in the high jump and the seventy-five-yard dash were pinned on my chest at the meet's conclusion.

Why? Because Loye always got first place in those same events, and through blind loyalty it was my decision to enter in whatever my buddy did. He was by far our school's best athlete.

I got a first-place ribbon each year in the relay only because Loye was always grouped with slower kids to give everyone a chance to win. Being the second fastest runner in the school, the fifty-yard dash and the broad jump were mine to take if I had chosen those events.

Three first place ribbons could have been proudly displayed to all the world *every* year. It never entered my mind—I don't know for sure what that decision implied.

Loye and I spent a great deal of time visiting as we walked home from school each day. There was a little white brick church on the corner (still standing today) where we left each other each day, heading to our separate homes. Before parting, we would often sit on the church steps and talk endlessly about our future—our lives as coaches.

We were strange little kids, planning our lives in the third grade, talking about being coaches. Loye came to his senses later in life. I stuck with the coaching idea. We both did all right.

Ted Hollembeak was also a close friend throughout junior high and high school. He was my soul mate. I could always talk to Ted about anything, as he could with me. Nothing's changed. Because he was a grade above me and didn't play football, it was kind of *off and on* when it came to running around with each other. We usually made up for it during the summer. He excelled in baseball—that's where we first met.

We probably would have been inseparable if I hadn't started dating one particular girl in high school. Ted, on the other hand, started dating my twin sister, Janet (15 min. older), and they eventually married, having two kids. The son, Nathan, was killed in the Gulf War, the worst fate for any parent.

Like Loye, Ted and I have stayed connected very easily throughout the years, mainly discussing sports and politics. He knows the details of baseball; I know the details of basketball. There's much to talk about still today especially around play-off time.

My first basketball goal had been a peach basket with the bottom cut out. It was nailed to the garage, and, for a few days, it remained erect and parallel to the ground. That didn't last long. The basket gradually weakened, the front drooping down much lower than the back. The need for an arched trajectory when shooting decreased each day.

At the time, I had never heard of **Dr. James Naismith and his original *13 Rules of Basketball*.** It was only later that his significance to the game was revealed. He invented an off-season sport for the football team, an indoor sport shielded from the cold New England weather of Massachusetts. I wasn't aware that Naismith started out the same way with a peach basket, except with the bottom still in it. If a shot remained in the basket, it counted as a score. A ladder was stationed nearby so the ball could be retrieved and the game continued. Dr. Naismith's original basketball was more the size of a soccer ball.

The first basketball I ever owned was somewhat round but had laces like a football, making dribbling extremely unpredictable. If you remember laced basketballs, you've been around a few years. As a backboard, my dad bolted a square, wooden outdoor tabletop directly to the garage. Any time someone drove hard for a layup, they were forced to plant their foot on the garage door to stop their momentum. There were shoe marks all over that door.

The highlight for me was the basketball goal in a neighbor's (Arnold Thompson) backyard. There were no accessible gymnasiums in Arkansas City, Kansas. Playing on a regulation gym was just wishful thinking. You might occasionally find a gym unlocked, but not often.

Elementary schools had outdoor goals that weren't regulation height—no more than eight or nine feet—and normally were without nets. Arnold's goal was special because a big outdoor light allowed us to play well into the night. My friends and I considered this quite a treat. It was our Madison Square Garden.

Many a night I would be sent to Denson's grocery store for something and would end up at the well-lit backyard, playing basketball with whomever. Returning home one or two hours later, my parents saw all the dirt on my clothes and shoes from Arnold's dirt court. The fact they never said a word was a positive message for me.

Having outgrown Thompson's backyard, the next challenge was where to play. What we really wanted was a full court. We had to settle for one of three choices, none of which were very good. First, we could go to a grade-school yard and play with those undersized goals and no nets. The second choice was to play at one of our homes which had a single-car garage and limited court space. The best option was to go to the house of a rich kid—anybody whose dad drove a Buick or Cadillac was considered wealthy—and play on a court with a two-car-wide driveway. If there was a big, beautiful automobile parked there, we just popped the standard transmission into neutral and rolled the car out of the driveway. We were always respectful and rolled the cars back when we were finished—we wanted to return another day.

Sometimes we were forced to play with non-athletes.

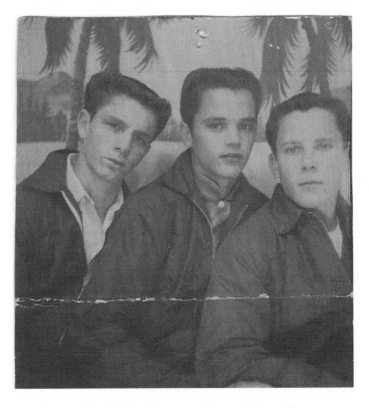

Pat, me, and Ted in our Jimmy Dean jackets

Jim Butler, trusted friend that I could count on for a vigorous one-on-one game in my private gym--there were very few I could count on.

If the kid had a nice house, a nice driveway and, therefore, a nice basketball court, it didn't matter. If he also owned a car, we really liked him. He was a shoo-in.

After two hours of our version of half-court street ball, we might go to the A&W Root Beer stand with our real good friend in his real nice car. Think we ever thought about paying for his root beer float?

Years later, another place for only myself was discovered. For the first time ever, I shall reveal *my secret gym*. Our junior high gym was built below ground level so the windows at the highest point of the gym inside were at ground level outside. One day, when no one else was around, I climbed to the top of the stands and unlocked one of the windows. Suddenly there now was a private entrance to my own private basketball court. Playing in that hot box during the summers of my high school years was delightful, although a bit isolated. It was a sanctuary limited to individual shooting and an occasional one-on-one game with a friend.

Very few people were invited to join me in my hot box. If word got out, my secret basketball court would be history. I knew to never leave the lights on because that was a dead give-a-way. The window remained unlocked for a few years so my private gym was always available to me.

Even though basketball was my obvious first choice, I'm glad to have played football. But weighing around 165 pounds didn't help. The gear we wore was a far cry from what players use today. Pop Warner leagues did not exist in our town. The first time I tried to put on a football uniform was in the seventh grade. The experience was clearly uncharted waters for most of us lowly junior high boys.

As a starting end my junior and senior years, playing on both sides of the line, my forte was a consistent level of effort. I never came off the field, even playing on all of the kicking teams.

The result was one exhausted young man who didn't have the energy to take his girl-friend to Teen Town for some rock 'n' roll dancing after the game.

Ark City had a solid football program for several years and was always ranked high in the state polls. We had quality, skilled offensive people along with a workhorse-type line.

I'm glad I stuck with it. The size of our school demanded we all play as many sports as possible. In a larger school, football would probably have passed me by, and the lessons learned from its physicality would have never been available. I may have never learned what getting knocked flat was like, or what true perseverance meant.

Blocking out, fighting through screens, and playing defense were all physical elements of the game of basketball. **They were extensions of blocking and tackling in football. I had no trouble understanding the importance of these physical and less glamorous fundamentals that were required later at the collegiate level. This was a big advantage for me.**

I didn't consider myself a tough guy off the court. But I never remember feeling intimidated on the basketball court. The few times someone did take a swipe at me (I was an annoying opponent, believe me), I never felt it. The adrenaline during the heat of battle covers up much of the pain you will feel tomorrow and the day after.

Had I not been involved with various sports, I probably would have become a librarian somewhere. ("Not that there's anything wrong with that," Seinfeld would remind us.) **The important lesson to learn was NEVER GIVE UP. Isn't that amazing? Three simple words, and your entire life is altered.** Most people didn't approach the game in that manner. It was too difficult and seldom was credit given for the effort. Sports pages basically ignored blocking in football and defending in basketball. You were on your own.

An important point I make throughout this writing is that those qualities of perseverance were already in me—I brought them to a sport and the competition revealed them. A good coach would recognize them and *cultivate* them. Strange, even though I considered most of my coaches very qualified, only two that crossed my path knew how to enhance those qualities.

One question I've often received is, "Should my son concentrate on one sport?"

My advice is, "Stay with as many sports as possible, as long as you are able to progress. There is much to learn from each sport—much correlation is involved when examining them, but every sport can teach something different.

As a youth, it was quite common to play football in the fall, basketball in the winter, and baseball in the summer. We weren't aware of it, but we were quite fortunate to play all of them.

All sports have equal forms of pressure. The similarity of golf to basketball never occurred to me until golf became so important to me later in my life. Staring at a six-foot money putt isn't much different than facing a game-ending one-and-one free-throw.

Getting knocked around in football sure made me tougher on the basketball court. And, is there any better agility program for a football player than basketball?

A fifth or sixth-grader shouldn't be deciding on one sport. At that point in his life, he most likely doesn't have a clue. Besides, his body will change a great deal in the next few years and he will be emotionally more mature.

Of course, some parents may have already planned his life and athletic career by then. If they have, I wish them luck and hope they realize what they're doing. Unfortunately, many won't until it's too late.

When it's within reason, let the kid make his own decision.

Few would argue against the positive benefits of physical fitness, especially in the form of individual or team sports.

Athletic experience influences the development of the *whole* person.

Consider the fortunate child who is allowed to participate in sports, who learns the practice of punctuality, the respect for authority and teammates, the discipline needed to reach a goal, and much more. A lot of what I'm describing cannot be taught in a classroom setting. It has to come "from the dirt," as the great golfer Ben Hogan suggested, or "on the hardwood," as the legendary basketball coach John Wooden preached.

I can't imagine missing out on it.

In high school, I played on the varsity football and basketball teams while always managing to shoot a few hoops by myself throughout the entire year. Shooting baskets outside during the winter months meant occasionally shoveling snow, often cold hands, and unpredictable ball flights. Had I gone to a large school, we would have been playing basketball inside. Football would probably have never occurred.

I'm glad it turned out as it did.

The coach I most respected in junior high school was Gene Snyder, an ex-Kansas State football player. Being a football man, he could have short-changed us. But he worked at basketball and knew the game as well as could be expected. Whether coaching football or basketball, Coach Snyder knew when and what to say to his team. He didn't over-talk or over-coach. That's a skill.

In high school, I ran the high hurdles (I ran through some of them, as well), an event my track coach—Coach Jackson, who was also our football coach—insisted I enter during every meet. Not being athletic enough to ever place in these meets but good enough to squeeze into the finals a few times was a bummer for me. Instead of hanging around waiting for the finals later that evening, I'd much rather have been up in the stands, eating a hot dog and flirting with the girls, along with all my slow friends.

One spring day in my junior year, Coach Snyder walked over to me while I was working on the high hurdles. I don't ever remember talking to him about any of the sports that I participated in, but he knew my feelings regarding basketball.

He said, "Hang in there, Jerry. This will help you in basketball." His words were very welcome. We didn't hear positive statements like that very often. The proof is that I've never forgotten his words that afternoon.

Coach Carl Jackson was different. He was a good, tough coach who didn't say much to me or anybody unless it was to criticize.

But, I will say this: he was a completely different man on game day Fridays—nothing but positives (I took note of that). The rough exterior was the mode of operation for most coaches back then (especially in football). In Jackson's case, no player questioned the method. We all feared him in a healthy way.

During football practice one day, a solid knee slammed right into my forehead. It didn't knock me out, but it definitely scrambled my brain for the next couple of days. After the blow, it was very confusing to me why we were wearing these funny practice uniforms over these funny-looking pads. As the trainer led me to the locker room, we walked past the junior college team practicing on an adjacent field. I stopped and stared and repeatedly asked, "What are they doing?" Two other persistent questions: "What's these funny pads for?" and, "Am I still going with Nancy Green?" Nancy was my girlfriend throughout high school.

Getting your bell rung has always been a part of the game

of football. Today we take collisions to the head much more seriously. Tests are conducted and a certified physician eventually decided when a player could return to the football field. If such measures had been taken back then, they would have discovered that I and many others had concussions playing football.

My case was unusual because I suffered from temporary amnesia for several days. I was concerned about everything having to do with the incident. The game of football had become a total mystery to me. I had to sit out two or three weeks before playing again but it was about three months before my memory gradually came back,totally.

After practice Coach Jackson came back to the locker room and, with his normal sarcastic tone, asked, "What's the matter with you, Stone?" Normally, I would *never* have said anything disrespectful to Coach Jackson. My condition must have felt liberating because it seemed to unlock a vault full of pent-up feelings. Combining those factors, which had been compiled since early grade school, I let it fly.

Apparently, I had a lot to say, snapping back, "I don't know what the matter is, but I'm sure it was something I did wrong. That's the only time you ever say anything to me."

My buddy, Ted Hollembeak, almost fainted.

My reaction quickly ended Coach Jackson's questioning. I'm certain he felt I had crossed the line, but experience told him to leave it alone. It always seemed to me that his never-ending sarcasm could have been tempered with some occasional praise. My outburst, no doubt, let him know that. He knew, as a two-way starter for two years, I was a good kid and worked hard for him. Certain seniors, it would seem, had earned the right to give their opinions, just not in the manner in which mine spewed out.

To Coach Jackson's credit, he didn't hold my comments against me. Not once did he badger me from that day forward. **A good coach knows when to back off.** My respect for him increased after that. We were lucky to have him. High school kids may act like they've got the world by the tail, but, truthfully, the tail is swinging a great deal of weight. They need to be encouraged. **Being critical doesn't mean you have to be negative, nor does encouragement mean you should pamper them.**

You have to remember all the insecurities you had when you were that age, and how you wanted to be approached when you were trying to prove your manhood on the athletic field. Often, it's the fear of embarrassment that's more worrisome than some form of physical discipline.

Seven Seniors, 1959, Arkansas City High School,
Bottom L-R: Stone, Hanshew, Buzzi, (Loye) Sparks.
Top L-R: Coach Valliere, Bud Stacy, Tom Gibson, Jim Haskins

Don Valliere, my basketball coach at Arkansas City High School, used to get upset with me about my offense, but not in the normal sense—he couldn't get me to shoot enough. If I missed the first two or three, that would do it for me. No more shots from Stone. It's actually easier to tone a player down than to light a fire under him. In my case, I was always worried about being called a ball hog. I'm sure my reluctance to shoot was connected to my upbringing. At home, we were taught to be modest—too much shooting would indicate a desire to receive too much attention. Go figure…

What would have been great to hear was someone saying, "Jerry, you're a great shooter. Go out there and show people what real shooting is. Don't worry about a thing." I never did hear that. Coach Valliere tried to change me but it wasn't easy. (In this day and age, this entire scenario is rather hard to believe, isn't it?).

One night, I did make sixteen out of sixteen free throws and scored twenty-eight total points against Ponca City, Oklahoma, but I never did loosen up until my sophomore year in college, when I scored thirty-one points in a junior varsity game. That game *finally* broke the ice.

Fifty years later, I visited my friend Coach Kahler who was living in Kansas City, Missouri at the time. Nothing much had changed from my perspective.

He was still someone for whom I had great respect. Like in the old days, I listened to every word as he mentioned various things, including my game and my attitude. I really started listening when he said *I was the best shooter to ever come out of Ark City.*

In my entire life, no coach had ever said anything about my shooting ability. I might have received a kind comment once in a great while, but nothing that I can remember. I played numerous basketball games as a young man and *never knew for sure if and when I should look for a shot.*

I shouldn't have had one shred of doubt regarding my role as a shooter—no good shooter should. During my junior and senior year in high school I had games where I went two-for-four or three-for-five. If I had been told I had a talent, I would have focused on it.

Before I left his home during that one visit, I told Coach Kahler about my Midland College teams in the 1980s finishing first, second, and fourth in the NJCAA Basketball Tournament. He had no idea and was genuinely thrilled to hear the news. Funny, it was sort of an afterthought, as I was walking out to my car. I'm so glad I told him—when you think about it, it seemed like a nice way to say thank you.

I never got to talk to my dear friend again. My insecurities were taken out on my opponents. The way I played basketball and the type of defense I chose to use were my ways of overcoming the fear of being embarrassed by my opponent. But, the most overriding factor was that I felt a need to prove I belonged out there.

Though I did not realize it until much later, the thought of disappointing my father was real, also. Since we did not communicate our feelings openly in our family, there was no way of directly knowing if my father was 100% proud of my accomplishments. What my dad thought of me was certainly high in the importance scale.

We needed to sit down and have a heart-to-heart at some point. We never did. It would have meant so much, a direct impact on my self-confidence.

In addition, because modesty was stressed in our home,

feeling good about oneself after having excelled in something was subconsciously frowned upon. My parents were always cautious about the effect success might have on us kids—like a little confidence. Would that have been so harmful?

They were just doing what they felt was right. Nevertheless, I believe all of the Stone kids wondered about their self-worth.

I have since realized there has to be balance. It's all right to be modest and humble but it's also OK to be proud of one's accomplishments. What children hear—or don't hear—growing up affects them later in life. **Many grown people today are still walking around trying to please their parents (dead or alive) because of the praise they needed and never received.**

What's ironic is that most of my time as a coach is spent working on the self-esteem of my players. **If they don't have proper self-esteem, it's impossible to turn them into a team of winners. It's the single most important trait a youngster needs for success. Self-esteem is everything.**

2
BEST-LAID PLANS
1949–1959

"The people who influence you
are the people who believe in you."

—Henry Drummond

At an early age, I was drawn toward athletic competition as a participant and soon thereafter as a coach. Not long after first watching my mother shoot baskets, I expanded my desires to coaching—it seemed quite natural. I was fascinated by how certain individuals had the ability to motivate people beyond their expectations. Their skill was the art of teaching.

I also was aware of those coaches who had very little feel for the player's ability to digest what the coach deemed so vital as he taught those various skills. I wanted to walk up and quietly inform him that, " All that screaming and ridicule had a negative effect on certain players." *I could see it. Why couldn't they?*

At the age of eight, I was subconsciously planning my life's goal and purpose: I would coach basketball, but not before learning everything possible from primarily two local gentlemen who could not have been more appropriately suited for a youngster like myself. Merle Hinton would deal with the preadolescent period, followed by the junior high and high school coaches, and then the ultimate, Coach Dan Kahler, at the local two-year junior college. The way I saw it, the groundwork would be laid to finish at some four-year college, probably in Kansas.

Credit goes where credit's due: it all started with Merle Hinton.

With occasional assistance from one or two volunteers, this one man, Merle Hinton, managed the all-sport summer and fall leagues for grade-school age boys. He was our only coach. Merle was perfect for the job and became a male role model during those formative years.

He was an ex-athlete who knew the fundamentals of most sports—baseball, basketball, football, and even boxing—and emphasized them. Had he not been a man of impeccable character, I'm certain his appeal would not have been felt so deep as it did for a kid from Sleeth Addition. It's hard to explain, but kids often cannot be fooled as easily as adults on subjects like character and sincerity. Ever notice?

Every Wednesday of the winter days, Junior Police met for two hours at the armory building to participate in various sports, all conducted by Merle. Junior Police was sort of a cross between the Boy Scouts and a youth center in our town, sponsored by the local VFW and the police department.

With the promise of a candy bar, we always recited this poem:

"When the One Great Scorer comes to mark against your name, He'll mark not that you won or lost, but how you played the game."

That simple verse sticks with me to this day. During one's dog-eat-dog drive to reach success, its sentiment is something that can gradually slip away from coaches and players involved in sports. **My best years of coaching occurred when I was able to inspire my teams, as the poem suggests, to "give their very best."**

That's what it ultimately boils down to—with that attitude, things just work better.

I always went straight home from Junior Police and repeated verbatim everything Merle had just preached to all of us to the younger kids in my neighborhood. I really enjoyed it. You might say I was the unofficial Junior Police ambassador for Sleeth Addition, unbeknownst to Merle.

Merle not only thoroughly taught us fundamentals of each sport from the ground up but also stressed the importance of teamwork and attitude while playing these sports. He insisted we take regular water breaks from baseball's summer heat when the prevailing attitude was the less water you drank, the better it was for your conditioning. He was ahead of his time.

During these pauses he told us stories and cited examples of positive athletic effort and attitude—stories about baseball's hustler, Enos Slaughter, or Kansas University's great miler, Glenn Cunningham, who overcame a fire that left scars over a majority of his body. He talked about certain individuals who were athletes despite wearing glasses and shouldn't be considered "sissies."

One of the activities initiated by the Junior Police was an annual "Good Citizen" contest. If they chose to participate, each of the approximately seventy-five members were asked to keep a record of all the good deeds they performed: taking out the trash, keeping your room clean, mowing the lawn, etc. Throughout the year, a parent would verify that each chore was completed with their signature on their son's scorecard. The winners received an authentic-looking metal Junior Police badge that was shiny silver and looked like the real thing. I was one of ten kids who earned one and was proud to carry it with me for years.

I'll always remember Merle Hinton's demeanor in regard to coaching. He never did anything that would encourage us to develop harmful habits or traits. He was always composed. Never did we see an act of poor sportsmanship. He never threw a fit, used a cuss word, or tried to embarrass a kid (kids are easy targets). He was the most patient person I've ever known.

We never wanted to upset Merle. His approach had a great impact on us despite the fact that few of us could measure up right away. We just needed more time.

Merle always explained *why* we did something a certain way. "If the player understands why, he won't forget it," he would say. That's so important and something I carried with me throughout my career.

Players need to know what we're doing and especially *why*. They need to take pride in being smarter than their opponent. *Being smarter gives you confidence, and confidence, in many cases, is what separates your team from theirs.* How many volunteer coaches take the time to explain that to a bunch of kids?

In the world of sports, no one stood as tall as Merle in my eyes—that is, until I met Dan Kahler, and they stood side by side.

Dan Kahler, very influential man in my life, age 26 in 1952

Coach Kahler had more influence on me than any other coach. He was the ideal mentor for me during my junior high and high school years, yet I never got to play for him. The ball bounces funny sometimes—no getting around it.

He was unique in a lot of ways. One was the fact he stayed in a small Kansas farming community for most of his adult life when his talents could have taken him almost anywhere. As a six-foot-five, handsome athlete, he excelled in basketball, football, track, golf, boxing, and karate.

He was an All-American in several of those sports. One highlight of his athletic experience was being selected as a member of the West Team in the East-West College All-Star game in Madison Square Garden. His selection was special because he came from Southwestern College in Winfield, Kansas, a small college eleven miles north of Ark City. Representing an NAIA school in such a prestigious event when all the other members were selected from NCAA Division I schools was highly unusual.

Dan Kahler had a strong intellectual side. He was a nationally known professional speaker, author, and educator. He wrote many books and articles on these subjects, anything regarding education, language, and communication. While coaching, at no time did he have trouble explaining what he wanted out of his basketball players.

Under Dan Kahler's outstanding leadership, Arkansas City Junior College (ACJC) teams were consistently strong. Year after year, I watched his squads as they went about the business of winning in a workman-like fashion. His players looked like men playing against boys. They were poised and seemed to always be in complete control with no visible change to their facial expressions throughout the game. They always looked like they were going to win—there were few exceptions. It was

Coach Kahler's calm demeanor being passed on to his team. It was right in front of them every day.

Some ACJC games were free of charge for the local high school team members. Most were not. However, since money normally was not to be found in my pockets, it was necessary to discover a way to get around this problem. Guilt was never an issue with me when it came to skirting around the price of a basketball ticket. Besides, in this case, what was fair about paying to watch a junior college team that I had watched practice so often? I could have been considered a manager if anyone ever checked the amount of time I spent observing their practices. Another factor was the very same basketball arena and court were where my games and practices were conducted.

My routine: Our high school team practice ended around 5:30 p.m. I'd mess around, shoot a little, take a shower, then head for my hideout—the men's restroom in the front lobby. (The best place to hide is where they would lest expect you to hide—about 15 feet from the ticket booth).

Normally a sack lunch had been prepared for the game later. Patiently waiting forty-five minutes or so for my chance to join the incoming flow of fans, there was only one potential hazard— the janitor. He could show up unexpectedly to clean my hiding place. He never did.

As the fans strolled in, my only strategy was to slide in with them as they headed for my favorite seating area—and that would be the front row seats of the baseline balcony, slightly off-center of the goal. These seats were located in the best spot to study the offensive and defensive patterns as they unfolded during the game.

The view of both coaches was very clear from this vantage point also—right down my alley. Why miss anything? These end-court seats were in earshot of the players, so that my buddies and I could occasionally verbally attack the opponent's best player, an effective form of distraction that was quite successful, if not sportsmanlike.

His teams played smartly, confidently, and unselfishly. It became my measuring stick for coaching later. Unbeknownst to the teams I coached later, they were prepared to play in the same mold as Dan Kahler's teams in a small town in Kansas. Small world. My only wish would have been that years later he could have sat in the stands and watched some of my games, just as I had his.

One evening, as I prepared to observe another Kahler workout, for whatever reason, the practice gear wasn't dry after being washed—all except the jock straps. While Coach Kahler was busy in his office, the manager passed out what my five-year-old daughter once proudly announced were "weenie breeches." That evening, the entire team began practice wearing only their jocks and gym shoes. Yes, it was truly quite a sight. The doors were secured, so there were no worries about the girls drill team bursting in. No one would be arrested.

There was some concern in my mind about the reaction of the highly principled Coach Kahler when he entered the court. When he did arrive, the mini-shock on his face was immediately replaced with a broad smile. He knew when to have a moment of fun. It was harmless and showed his players that he could be a regular guy with a great sense of humor—something players often wonder about during that period in their life.

Coach Kahler was the perfect model when it came to player-coach relationships. I spent a lot of time talking to him during the summer months during and after graduating from college. He answered every question.

He said that **too many rules invited unnecessary issues with the players.**

He explained that a guy just out of the military would need to be viewed differently from a high school graduate. It was obvious to him that I was serious about coaching. Prior to one of his practices, he looked straight at me and said, "You never get enough of this, do you?"

Because of my Texas location, we never were able to completely bond. Several banquets, honorary occasions, and even funerals were not attended, mainly because of the excessive distance and the lack of communication—not a chance of missing Dan Kahler's funeral, but I did. We should have had a great deal more quality time together. It's still rather difficult to realize that Coach Kahler never actually coached me. Some things are difficult to get past.

Many coaches have influenced me, primarily Gene Snyder, Carl Jackson, and Don Valliere. But Merle Hinton, Dan Kahler, and, later, Hershel Kimbrell were the ones who stood out. My assessment of them was not reached after years of reflection. I knew who they were and what they meant to me the first day we met.

My plan to become a coach had never wavered (although many tried to alter it). It was right on track. But during the spring of my senior year, it suddenly became derailed. Coach Kahler announced his retirement from coaching to become the principal at Ark City High School. **I felt betrayed**—betrayed by the man I looked up to since childhood, and a school that I had proudly graduated from. I went straight to him and basically chewed him out, enumerating all my reasons for the disappointment I felt.

Coach Kahler gave me a big smile and reminded me that things are always changing. Of course, he was right (as always, it seemed). In one quick swoop, my lifelong plan and dreams were no longer in existence—rather hard on a seventeen-year-old, who for years was certain he was in control.

I waited patiently for a call from the new coaches. It never came. Loye was gobbled up quickly by them. They were smart to sign him. He was a real sleeper.

As for me, I was crushed. Where was I going to continue playing this game for which I had so much feeling? Time, as always, heals.

During the disappointing Spring of 1959, before eventually heading to an small college in Texas, a strong urge to prove the new Arkansas City Junior College coaches wrong was very much alive in me. Ark City was my hometown, that team was my team, and that gym was my gym, having played there in all three years of high school.

I had lived in Ark City all my life and had been waiting ten years (a long time for a 17 year old) to become an ACJC Tiger. They, on the other hand, had been here *one month*. What was fair about that? It felt as though something very personal had been stolen from me. Outwardly, I handled it well, but inside things were boiling. My displeasure led me to the gym during that very spring and summer to play against the returnees and some of the new recruits.

I was all over that floor and hardly missed a shot. This continued for three or four days. I was trying very hard to prove that a mistake had been made. They got the message. It felt good when the coaches came running, hoping for a last-minute, change-of-heart signing. It continued to feel good when I reminded them that I had committed to McMurry College—it was just too late. (Deep down, ACJC was the only place I felt was meant for me, but McMurry quickly proved me wrong—all was good).

Years later, when I visited with a retired Coach Kahler, he stated emphatically that had he stayed another couple of years at ACJC, Loye and I would have definitely been instrumental in winning the big prize in Hutchinson, Kansas. He was dead serious. It was nice to hear. He would get no argument on the subject from the two Sleeth Addition boys.

With the help of **Jerol Graves,** an older high school teammate who was playing at McMurry College in Abilene, Texas, I was granted a full scholarship there—sight unseen. Jerol had somehow convinced McMurry coach Stan Burnham, the original coach, to sign me.

Leaving Arkansas City was difficult for another reason. Leaving home was always a bummer for me (I've never liked goodbyes), but going to Texas did have an exciting ring to it. What made this departure difficult, however, was the fact my twin sister had been in a horrendous automobile accident that summer. Her spine had been severely damaged. It was very delicate for several months. I left her lying in the hospital, not wanting to start my life in Abilene at that time. Everyone held their breath and prayed for many days.

Janet got through the danger period eventually. She was flat on her back for *nine* months—five in the hospital and four at home.

The surgical crew was joined later by a specialist from Wichita who viewed the spinal X-rays. His reaction was blunt: "It's a miracle Janet isn't paralyzed." He followed that with a statement all of our family remembers to this day: "That just goes to prove someone else is running this show."

My little twin has had several replacement rods throughout her adult life that support her spinal column and has always been limited regarding physical activities. Dealing constantly with pain, she's still going strong, and I've never heard her complain about the hand she was dealt. (She was tougher than all of us).

I always felt a twinge of guilt knowing that I played sports all my life with very few serious injuries. Janet was happy just to be able to take a cautious, daily walk.

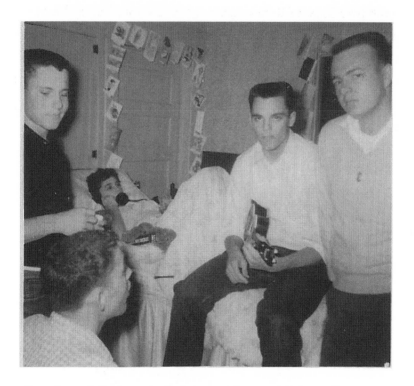

Loye (lower left), Janet (in bed), Jerry (playing ukulele), Ted (top left),
Bruce Sherwood (far right)

It was time to head south to Abilene, Texas. Dad and I took a quick trip from Ark City to my new home on the campus of McMurry College soon after I had signed the four year scholarship via the mail. He felt obligated to confirm the agreement and to check out the school for a son that hadn't been much further than 100 miles from his Kansas hometown. The campus was half-vacated—it was the middle of summer and it was Abilene, Texas, hot and dry. But it was new and exciting—a small Methodist College seemed to fit well with me.

I had no way of knowing that I would see very little of the

Sunflower State of Kansas again, when I showed up at McMurry during the upcoming fall—new friends, a new team and coach, and a new state of which to be proud. The remainder of my life would begin and continue because a coach (Dan Kahler) and one of his ex-players (Jerol Graves) made decisions effecting my immediate and subsequent long-term future. It wasn't the way I had it all planned out, but it proved to treat me kindly.

Loye Sparks

Jerry Stone and teammate Jerol Graves, both of Arkansas City,
Kansas High School and McMurry College, Abilene Texas.
Jerol was very instrumental in my tending McMurry College,
beginning the fall of 1959.

3
LEARNING TO PLAY,
PLAYING TO COACH
1959–1963

"Sports don't build character. They reveal it."
—John Wooden

Coach **Hershel Kimbrell** replaced Coach Burnham in the summer of 1959, which meant that neither Kimbrell nor I knew each other as I arrived on campus in August. We immediately agreed that, under the circumstances, a one-year agreement should replace the original four-year deal. I felt that Coach Kimbrell would extend it to three more years if I were given one year to prove my ability. (Looking back, that was no guarantee. In fact, four-year scholarships became a thing of the past with all colleges a few years later, which definitely made sense.)

Throughout this book I refer to the fear of embarrassment when an opponent basically dominates you (normally by scoring on you continuously)—he does this in front of fans, and these fans enjoy it. When this happens to you it's very difficult to join in on the fun—it gets your attention.

The fall of 1955, the eighth grade, was when my *initiation* occurred. **Michael Payne** of Wellington, Kansas turned me inside-out, as I attempted to press him full-court. I couldn't figure it out. There was no help from the coaches.

It turned out to be a simple defensive alignment adjustment that I finally figured out, myself. You shouldn't guard a man full-court if he's quicker than you or if he is a slick ball-handler (the minuses outweigh the pluses).

There is an exception: You may pick up in the back court area, but don't guard *nose to nose*. If you allow him to come straight at you, your weight will be on your heels, going straight backwards, which means you have no chance to stay in front of him. He can easily fake and go around you, either way. **You must take half of the court away from him.** Totally overplay—make him use his weaker hand as you continually *give*—keep sliding backwards (most players today still have a strong and weak hand when it comes to dribbling). **Your intention is not to steal the ball.** As he approaches his shooting area, you will have to guard more "straight-up", but you will normally have help from teammates now.

That's also why during this reading you'll hear, "And you will remember his name." You will never forget certain people—either someone you have ripped or someone who has ripped you. But when someone "Takes you to school", don't get discouraged. It's a learning opportunity. Profit from it. Study the film—discuss it with someone. Hopefully, you will have a conscientious coach who will jump right on it.

As a freshman at McMurry, I sat in the stands and watched **All-American Carlisle Strickland,** a junior at Howard Payne University, eat our team alive. He impressed me with the variety of his shots and his cool demeanor. He would be difficult to guard. The one great fear that consumed me as a player was someone going nuts while I tried to guard him. I felt it would be the same as if he walked up to me in the middle of the court, slapped me, then turned away laughing. I didn't want that to happen.

I had an entire year to get ready for Mr. Strickland.

Toward the end of my freshman year, Coach Kimbrell called me into his office. As a result of that meeting, McMurry, Kimbrell, and coaching forged a bond for my entire life. He asked me, "What would you do if I didn't renew your present scholarship? Think you can get an offer from your hometown junior college?"

I was very upset with the question and answered him rather sternly. "Yes, they had originally wanted me, but I came to Abilene, Texas, to play here at McMurry." I said a couple of other things that must have been acceptable because he started smiling.

"Just checking you out, Jerry. You are now officially a McMurry Indian."

I couldn't have been any happier if he'd said I was a Boston Celtic.

A full scholarship to play college basketball meant a lot to me.

When Coach Kimbrell spoke about competing and winning, he reeked with sincerity. When he said, "You got to want it," he believed it deep in his heart. He said it often. His message was impossible to misinterpret. Of course, if we didn't get the picture, the stands were always nearby.

When the gym was cleared, the fans were gone, and the doors were locked. The stands were still there, waiting to impress upon us all of that which one Hershel Kimbrell deemed important. It worked thoroughly, best I recall.

Coach Kimbrell's strength, however, was not the "stands." His appeal was his strong love for the game and the way he felt it should be played. That's how we bonded. The first year for Coach was my first year on campus. That year didn't count. It was "housecleaning" time for the new coach. Things fell in place by the time we got to the spring of 1960. My chance to disrupt a very good player's evening was initiated during the fall of 1960, my sophomore year.

While most players used how many points they scored as a measuring stick of success in a game, mine was how many points my man *didn't score*. **My strategy was to constantly harass on defense and let my offense take care of itself.** If I were expending every ounce of energy in an attempt to hold down a high-scoring opponent, there was little time to worry about my point production. Offensive nerves were non-existent. Offense was the furthest thing from my mind.

My shots fell effortless in the net, for the most part. It was a very important discovery for a potential future coach.

Like a great day on the golf course that comes when you least expect it, my offensive skills showed up against Howard Payne. I had twenty-one points in the first half. That never happened to me, the guy that worried 24-7 about being too selfish. I ended the night with twenty-nine for the game. I only averaged around fourteen. That wasn't the important statistic to me. **What mattered was that Carlisle Strickland only managed seven points the entire game, right there in his own backyard.**

I said nothing, but inside I was mighty proud.

I had nothing but respect for players like Carlisle Strickland— He made me a better player. All of those excellent basketball players would get a strong handshake from me if I saw them today.

And I do remember their names.

Stopping Carlisle Strickland really opened my eyes. I discovered you can play very good defense while experiencing nervousness. If you're nervous playing offense, bad things can happen: bad passes, traveling, air balls, etc. I had always been concerned about shooting too much and being a ball hog (one thing I wasn't). However, by concentrating on defense, it took away all thoughts of scoring and loosened me up. I'd look up and have eight or nine points in the first five minutes. Later on, when I coached, my players with similar issues were told, **"Think about defense and it will help your offense."**

Defense is the great equalizer. I loved playing defense because it helped my team win games. **And, it was the closest I ever got to defeating a superior athlete, at least for one night.**

If you're in a leadership role someday, you will learn from first hand experience the only thing that trumps talent is will. Sometimes will is not enough. Still, it's the best chance you've got. The team that absolutely crushes its opponent usually has both.

Since I wanted to win, I never backed off. Very few times during my relentless-type blocking in football or my harassing-type defense in basketball did I witness an opponent who wanted to continue the fight to the end of the game. Somewhere in the fourth quarter or late in the second half, I saw a change—more accurately, I *felt* a change in my opponent. It wasn't an obvious lack of competing. It was more like a *subtle shifting of gears*.

It was as if I'd received an unspoken message from him: *Okay, Stone, don't tell anybody, but I've had enough.*

Consequently, they never experience the eye of the tiger or the joy of breaking through the fatigue barrier, the very things they sing and shout about while they're drinking beer with their buddies. They don't realize their abilities are being held back because of habit and fear.

Back in the third grade, when their side started hurting, they stopped running. I understand, to a certain point, a break is necessary.

But, they didn't persevere—they gave up. They didn't get back up and finish. No big deal, you say? I disagree.

The fact is, giving up then made it easier to repeat the process the next time their side began aching, or even the next time they thought their side was about to start aching.

One of my fondest memories of grade school is getting to see the Yankees in person. IGA Grocery Stores across the state of Kansas sponsored a contest, tasking grade school kids to collect canned food labels from products sold at our local IGA. The top ten collectors from our town would join kids from all over Kansas as they shared an all-expenses paid, weeklong trip to St. Louis, Missouri. I was one of the contestants. For about two months we searched everywhere for these precious labels, looking in every home, trashcan, and the big one—the city dump. At the completion of the contest, I was one of about 300 boys and girls who were bussed from their Kansas homes to that historic city on the Mississippi River. I doubt if many of those youngsters had ever been that far from home before. I know I hadn't. The entire experience proved to be wonderful—worth every obnoxious label I tracked down. Highlights of the trip included visiting the Charles Lindberg *Spirit of St. Louis* Memorial, a ride down the Mississippi River on a gigantic riverboat and a doubleheader baseball game between the St. Louis Browns and my beloved New York Yankees.

Between the two games of the doubleheader, the teams took a thirty-minute break. Many of the players just milled around under the stands, visiting with friends and members of the opposing teams. Kids like myself were really shocked when some of them had a cigarette hanging from their mouth.

There was a three-foot chain-link fence separating the stands from the field which you could walk up to and get player autographs. Satchel Paige, who pitched one of the games for the Browns that night, signed my program. In 1951 when I saw him, he was estimated to be 45 years old. But no one knew his official age, including Satchel—he had no birth certificate. That night he demonstrated his famous windmill windup and his multiple deliveries. He threw every pitch known to mankind, many of them off-speed because of his age. Satchel continued pitching for another 15 years, ending up with the Kansas City Athletics in 1965. Even at sixty he was capable of an inning or two, although he was there primarily to draw the spectators. Many of baseball's greatest hitters, including Joe DiMaggio and Ted Williams stated that Satchel Paige was the greatest pitcher they had ever faced. He was inducted into the Baseball Hall of Fame in 1971 before dying in 1982.

What I did next in that break between games was quite thrilling. It's hard to imagine the lack of security at sporting events during the early 1950s. A skinny, ten-year-old kid could maneuver around and slip into about anywhere. I gathered up enough nerve and walked through a gate in the chain-link fence. I continued for another twenty yards, heading straight to the visiting locker room. I had only one goal—to see the Yankees up close and personal.

I believe I could have walked straight into their locker room but that wouldn't have been very smart. Instead, I waited at the door. The visiting locker room was very modest by today's standards and had only one exit. When the Yankees came out of the ballfield for the second game, they came through the door in single file. It was perfect. I touched each player's left sleeve as he passed by, quietly saying his name. I knew most of them— Joe DiMaggio, Yogi Berra, Phil Rizzuto, Billy Martin, Mickey Mantle, Hank Bauer, Whitey Ford, Vic Raschi, Allie Reynolds. They smiled at me as I looked up at them with excited eyes. I was surprised they weren't all tall. In my mind, all heroes were tall.

I don't know if any kid ever tried what I did, but I got as close as any kid—besides the batboy—to the New York Yankees. Could heaven be any better than such a moment for a ten-year-old boy? If not, touching the sleeves of Mickey Mantle, Yogi Berra, and Joe DiMaggio seemed like a close second.

Did you see the movie *Field of Dreams*? It is a story about a father and son bonding while doing something mutually important—a simple game of catch. Though *Field of Dreams* happens to focus on baseball, it could have been about any father-son bonding activity.

Were you one of the many men who were moved to tears when you saw it? If it touched you deeply, watching it probably resulted in a flood of memories. You probably played baseball as a kid and had a catch or two with your dad. Playing the game, you cultivated most of your first friendships, including one with your dad who probably introduced it to you not long after you learned to walk. It seems as though everyone played some form of baseball when they were young.

To me, baseball was something special. Playing catch with Dad enhanced it. Every boy wants to please his dad. Consequently, the simple act of playing catch with Dad was more than playing catch with a friend. It required never making a bad throw and never missing one of his. Maybe you even put a little heat on your next toss just to impress him. Whether you are aware of it nor not, your dad is probably your number one hero, and, in turn, you are a great source of pride to him. That's why you don't want to have your dad watch you sit on the bench 90% of the time in high school. He doesn't deserve that.

The greatest lesson I learned while playing football was perseverance: never give up; never go away; never show weakness or discouragement; never take a break when the play doesn't involve you; try to convince your opponent you will block him on every play. Continue to be a real pest. Both of you may be tired, but you won't give in.

By persevering, I was amazed to discover that guys who were

All-Conference, possibly All-State, didn't want it as badly as they thought they did. (It's important to note I didn't say a word during a game. A wrong word would only stir my opponent's emotions. No sense adding fuel to the fire).

I applied the principle of perseverance to guarding someone in basketball, especially in college. Nobody told me to do it. I just did it. Since my natural talent wasn't enough (I never wanted to be average), bringing something extra to a basketball game made sense. Guarding someone in a smothering fashion was also something I did out of self-concern. I didn't want to be embarrassed by a great player in front of a gym full of people. If he couldn't catch the ball, then he couldn't score. Even if he did catch it, he was often pushed away from his comfort zone. To top it off, I could wear him down by constantly forcing him to try to get open.

It's important that I explain exactly what my strategy and technique was—I do not want any misunderstandings or claims of exaggeration. My entire philosophy when it came to blocking in football and guarding (mainly denying) in basketball was not to crush the opponent. I wasn't quick or strong enough to do that.

But, I could be the most obnoxious pest around when it came to doing the job that no one noticed or gave any credence to— and those would be the very things that eventually wore the enemy down. That was the secret, and that's what you or anyone can do, if you have—**not, necessarily, the ability—but the heart.**

You will hear this a few times as you read what I have to say: **You must learn to deal with fatigue, pain, and, to some extent, injury—which you can.**

The first time I started on the varsity was during the fall of my sophomore year. I replaced a senior, Ronnie Lowe, who had to attend a funeral in his home state of Indiana.

As things evolved, I remained a starter for the rest of my career at McMurry. We played at Oklahoma City University, a location convenient for my folks, a little over two hours from my hometown, Ark City, Kansas.

My first time to start I guarded an All-American named **Larry Jones** who was the team's leading scorer just under 20 points. He later became well-known for his worldwide Feed the Children Foundation. I used all of the energy my nerves generated during this occasion and put the clamps on Larry. It was my first experiment with the *overplay-denial defense,* which I used from then on.

Coach Kimbrell had told me to stick to Jones like glue (even if he went in the stands). It worked. Larry ended up with twelve points.

Abe Lemons, who became a dear friend later, was the opposing team's coach. He loved guards who could fill it up from deep. Consequently, OCU's entire offense consisted of high picks from mainly post men.

It was possibly my toughest assignment ever, but that's why I was so indebted to football. I had to go through (over) those picks if I were going to disturb Larry Jones. Those picks felt like brick walls.

It's a little-known fact that there's something very positive about "acting" as though you're immune to the pain: *You become immune to the pain!* At least during the game. Oh, you'll feel it the next forty-eight hours, but it will be your personal "red badge of courage" of which to be proud.

Larry showed his true character after the game and went out of his way to find my parents and tell them their son was a tough player—very thoughtful.

Check this out: One thing I did that helped me totally deny my man was to convince three or four of the bench-warmers to become my personal cheerleaders, primarily during the last quarter (the last 10 minutes of the second half in college) of a game. They would yell and encourage me as I grew more and more tired of maniac guarding. Funny, but if they began watching the game and forgot their promise, you could hear me yelling at them, "Do your job!" They got a kick out of it (of course, I was dead serious) and I got renewed energy—now that's teamwork.

Stop for a minute. If I must say so myself, that was a very good idea—a group of my buddies giving me new energy. It helped me a great deal, and they had fun with it too. That's what I mean by "thinking outside the box." Don't let people scare you away from something they've never heard of or tried themselves. That's really what a lot of this is about—use your brain.

One always wants to please his parents. It took me until my junior year in college to declare to the world that I planned to coach basketball as an adult. From early childhood I knew coaching was my thing—I just couldn't get many people I respected to agree. Everywhere I turned, someone was discouraging me from my dream.

I distinctly remember the long distance conversation with my

Dad from a campus pay phone one night. It took me a while to build up enough courage to tell him. I had no idea how it would be received. The reaction from Dad was a pleasant surprise for me. No lengthy discussion, simply, "Hey, Dad, I know what I want to be."

His reply was, "Oh, really?"

"Yes. I want to coach basketball."

"Well, just be the best."

The man of a few words had struck again. Truth is, he probably had known for several years. Regardless, it was greatly appreciated by his only son.

Young or old, some things can always intimidate us—our idols.

My dad was a versatile man. He could play the piano by ear, sing on key, and work a punching bag. He loved sports and liked to fish, bowl, and play golf. When I was twelve, Dad would often include me on his Saturday morning golf outings. I don't know how he and his fellow golfers tolerated someone with my lack of ability but they did.

Years later I coached at Richardson High School, I paid my father back for those early golfing excursions. Richardson, TX, is a northern Dallas suburb located very close to the Preston Trail Golf Club where the Byron Nelson Golf Tournament was conducted annually. I hustled up free tickets every year and invited Mom and Dad down to Dallas for the event. Dad and I really got a kick out of walking along with the likes of Arnold Palmer, Jack Nicklaus, Gary Player, Lee Trevino and other top professionals. Getting autographs after their round was quite common. To us "the king" of them was always Arnold Palmer. Watching him play was like a notch below gazing at some biblical character. There was a reason Arnie had an army of followers.

One year at the tournament, I was by myself, following Arnold on his final round. On one hole, his playing partner hooked his drive into the woods. After locating the ball and analyzing the situation, he decided to hit out of the woods to get back in play without taking a penalty.

The marshalls prepared for the shot by shepherding the hundred or more mostly Arnie fans, including me, directing them to move off to the left. Instead of intermingling with the rest of the crowd, I innocently acted as though the marshalls had given us an option to back up to the right or the left. I was sure there would be other "mistaken" fans who were as clever as I was and thought I would find myself with them in the middle of the fairway—standing within a few steps of Arnold Palmer.

Guess what? No one else thought that way. I found myself alone, unbelievably standing four feet from "The King", just me and him. I could have walked away right then but I didn't. Then it dawned on me—do I say anything to *the* Arnold Palmer while he's concentrating on winning a tournament? How about a simple, "Hi"? Would it be impolite to *not* say "Hi"? When should I make my exit, before or after the shot from the woods? Should I wait until Arnold hits? I just froze.

Thank goodness Arnold Palmer was a class act. While his opponent was debating which club to use to get out of the woods, Arnie looked at me with a smile and said, "How you doing?"

My response was one word—"Fine." That was it. Only one syllable with no further reply.

We stood for what seemed an eternity waiting for the shot

from the woods. When it came, I quickly vanished before Palmer hit his shot.

Later I asked myself, "What was I thinking?" No doubt my actions would have upset most professional golfers. Of course today what I did would never be allowed. Even back then, if his caddy had been around—he probably was still in the woods after helping locate the lost ball—he would not have let me walk right up to Arnie. I was lucky. Arnold Palmer could tell that I was a dumbstruck fan who got a bit carried away. He was renowned to be a true gentleman when dealing with his enormous fan base. My experience proved it to me.

During that junior year at McMurry College, we made it to the NAIA National Tournament. It was quite a thrill. We had a very nice team but it was our first trip to the nationals and it rather over-whelmed us. It didn't help that Preston Vice couldn't play because of a sprained ankle. It was also unfortunate that our first-round opponent was the top seed, defending champion Westminster of Pennsylvania. They were not only good, but also smart.

I did a good job defensively, overplaying **Ron Galbraith, their All-American**, throughout the game. With three minutes to go, he had only eight or ten points. That's when I learned the value of the perfectly executed *backdoor cut*. It's a timing play that involves two or three players. It defies pressure and can leave the defender stranded, suddenly trailing his man. During those final two minutes, they spread us out and cut behind me twice. *That didn't* *happen to me two times during the entire year, but it happened to me twice in that two-minute span at the NAIA National Tournament.*

Why? For one reason, they were well-coached. They had never run that play one time prior to those last two minutes. Had I known about it, I wouldn't have been denying so aggressively.

They ran it perfectly—the timing was exact.

Another reason was that there was no offside defensive help. If a teammate is overplaying, his fellow teammates must be ready to cover for him on the backside, although sometimes your teammates don't see what's happening—sometimes they're too involved with their own man. Ideally, he'll see the entire floor and realize when he must help. Those two backdoor cuts sealed their victory. Sometimes pure effort isn't enough.

The positive? I was *fanatical* during my entire coaching career about using the same move against our opponents. We called it "special," compliments of **Coach Jim Gudger** of East Texas State.

I played varsity basketball at McMurry College for three years as a starter and remember only one person looking me up after a game to discuss my defense. We had just beaten Austin College in a league game where I guarded **Bobby Weddle**, a great shooter.

Bobby led the nation in free throw percentage (93 percent) and was in the top ten in field goal percentage. He was six-foot-four and had a very quick release. His shot was so pure you couldn't let him shoot. You had to prevent him from catching the ball.

This big strong player never seemed to tire. I constantly harassed him for forty minutes. Though he averaged twenty-five per game, he only got thirteen points on me. I guarded him everywhere on the court, dead or live ball, and never saw a sign of him shutting it down. I accidentally stuck a finger in his eye during a game. I quickly apologized, but he never said a word. That was his nature.

As I was heading for the locker room, an opposing gentleman whom I had never met came up to me and told me he wanted his son to meet and shake hands with a "great defensive player." I was pleased to have a parent say something like that to me. It was so rare, I've never forgotten it.

But, this illustrates what a player will face when actually contributing defense to ensure his team a victory: *NOTHING*, or very little recognition. That's why very few will pay the price. Great teams, on the other hand, have individuals who will. They are rare and enjoyable to watch.

As I guarded people during the season, I considered my contributions important, but I didn't think it was anything exceptional. All I was doing was working hard on defense so we could win.

Even though there was limited media coverage at the time, the word got out. I began to develop a reputation in our West Texas part of the world. One night while approaching the jump circle, I heard a player say, "Oh no, not you, Stone." It initially sounded like a put-down. I was thinking, *What the heck is wrong with this guy?*

He was a senior, the leading scorer for Wayland Baptist College, and he suddenly realized number 12, Jerry Stone, would be guarding him tonight. He was actually complimenting me.

Apparently, he was defeated before the game started. He got **zero points. Zero points happens rarely, but it did that night.**

Two others besides **Weddle** who never gave up late in the second period, come to mind. **Jim Reynolds,** a strong six-foot-five, 220-pound wingman from Abilene Christian University, was a lights-out shooter from long range.

He was very hard to guard because I was six-foot-one and 170 pounds. During the game, he said nothing. There I was, killing myself, while he said nothing. After the final horn sounded in one game, he held on to my handshake and tugged me toward him. Then he did say something: "You're tough, Stone."

You can't buy a compliment like that.

The third was **Marshall Proctor** of Tarleton State, who was similarly built at six-foot-four and 220 pounds. If ever there were a farm boy, he was it. ("Farm boy" as a description has a positive connotation in my mind).

He was strong as a bull, and, like the other two, never said a word during the game. The key to their endurance was their physical strength, and they never stopped competing.

To be clear, the football and basketball competition I faced as a player wasn't the highest caliber. I wasn't blocking a future All-Pro in football or denying an NBA player. I was primarily involved with exceptional small-college competition. The three players I just mentioned, however, could have played at a higher level because all were strong and pure shooters.

I certainly believe a player at that higher level could follow my denial defense guidelines with great success using the same determination and the same will to win.

How do you stay motivated to defend every game when you

know few people will recognize the effort? I came up with a unique self-motivational tool when I was a player in college.

The idea was influenced by a **Joe DiMaggio** comment when he played for the New York Yankees: **"The reason I give 100 percent every day is because I always thought that there was at least one person in the stands who had never seen me play and I didn't want to let him down."**

I knew most of the students at McMurry who never missed a home game. After asking a particular fan if he or she would be attending the game that night, I would then say, "I'm going to dedicate this game to you." I would direct my comment to someone I knew really liked basketball and our team, someone who would be sincerely excited about having a role in the game. When they realized I was dead serious they seemed to get a big kick out of it. The catch was I wouldn't promise to have a great offensive night because that could lead to forced shots and the kind of pressure you wanted to avoid as a player.

Instead, I told them to come to the game and watch me guard our opponent's best perimeter player.

The idea was to put pressure on myself to play well by personally promising someone I'd have a good game for them. It helped me to concentrate and play my very best. I knew if someone else counted on me to stop a good player, it would make my job easier because I couldn't let them down. Some may not push themselves to do something on their own but will for someone else—it's human nature.

During my senior year at McMurry College, we drove down

to Edinburg, Texas, for a one-game playoff with Pan American University to decide who would go to the **NAIA National Tournament in Kansas City.**

The main guy for Pan American was **Lucious "Luke" Jackson,** a six-foot-ten giant who didn't smile much. Later, when he was an All-NBA All-Star player, his Philadelphia 76ers teammates affectionately called him the "Animal."

Luke liked to play at the high post, near the free throw line. When a shot went up, I could usually be found in that area as a defensive guard. I was consistent in blocking out my man, but since he was a guard who seldom went to the offensive glass, I often helped block out somebody else's man. Early in the game, I asked Coach Kimbrell if he thought blocking out Jackson when he was at the high post was a good idea. He agreed.

An amazing thing happened on the free throw line in our defensive end that night. I nailed him every time the ball went up. Despite the fact that I expected severe retaliation—the kind that would require me to have chiropractic spinal adjustments immediately following the game—I persevered. To my surprise, *nothing happened.* He didn't move. **To this day, I don't understand why.**

Was he a bit lazy? Was he hurt? Did someone tell him not to get in foul trouble? Who knows? I *do know* Luke Jackson got very few offensive boards that night.

When the game ended, we had been beaten by a better team. The season was over. As we left the court, it suddenly hit me: my playing career was also over. It was my last time in a varsity uniform. I didn't want to take it off. I sat in the corner of the locker room, both hands rubbing my face, trying to conceal the flowing tears.

Though he didn't rush me, Coach Kimbrell approached me twice, saying, "Come on, Jerry. Let's go home." I appreciated his patience. He knew how I felt.

With everyone else on the bus looking forward to eating, I finally peeled off ol' number twelve. It seemed like a funeral to me.

Though we didn't win, I took something away from that game: even a six-foot-one guard can put a crimp in a future NBA post man's rebounding. It is very frustrating when a little guy ties up a big guy by immobilizing his knees and legs. Just because you may lack unusual ability, don't sell yourself short when it comes to helping your team win games. Always give as close to 100 percent as you can. **Most of your opponents won't.**

The overly competitive athlete should not be seen as someone you would never want to emulate. Competitors have many good qualities. I certainly would rather work with a person who is overzealous than one who has little or no fire. Some of those hyper-competitive qualities were possessed by me. Not many worked or trained any harder than me. Too bad weight training wasn't particularly encouraged at that time. There were very few weights in a specific weight room.

Back then, weights were for **Charles Atlas** or the ninety-pound weakling at the beach who was forever getting sand kicked in his face by a bully. My 170-pound body wasn't my greatest asset. I would have gotten hooked on weight training.

Clayton Brooks, my college roommate, was right in there with me. We were probably considered a bit different because of the dedication we demonstrated. Neither one of us would apologize for our drive to be the best guards around. We took our classes seriously and played ball. That was plenty. It kept us busy.

After being eliminated from the national tournament in 1962, Coach Kimbrell suspended the curfew. We had one night to look Kansas City over. Clayton and I celebrated with popcorn and a Coke and remained at the coliseum to see all the remaining games for that evening. Who knows where the rest of the team was? Coach walked by us with a double-take, smiled, and said, "You know, sometimes I worry about you two."

Being competitive can sometimes be a double-edged sword. If you are as dedicated to winning as Clayton and I were, good things can happen. Your life's focus, however, can become pretty narrow. At some point, you may have to deal with it. And if you have a temper or can't keep your mouth shut at the appropriate time, being competitive can be your worst enemy. If you're my age and still occasionally throw a golf club (I've actually stopped doing that), the wrong side of that double-edge is being exposed.

There was little trouble motivating myself. While playing, I seldom looked at the opponent during warm-up with one exception. There was always a glance that was given to the player who would be my assignment.

My objective was to pick up his attitude, especially if he seemed arrogant or cocky.

If he didn't show such arrogance, I created it in my mind. "*He must not be too worried about me*" (anything to psyche myself up). I would tell myself, "*Look at him. He's going to try to embarrass me tonight.*" That's all that was needed The guy didn't have a chance. He was going to be dealing with a maniac. (Call it what you want, but you must think that way.)

As mentioned before, my designated "friend in the stands" helped me stay motivated too. If your intention is sincere, it gives you an edge. Any reason to become totally focused is something to take advantage of. It gives you energy and purpose.

Coach Kimbrell and I were good for each other too. Of course, I had my coaching opinions, but we always seemed to be on the same page, especially after that freshman year. We both gave everything we had for McMurry College. I played four years for him, maintaining honor roll status throughout, then served as his graduate assistant another two years while I earned a master's degree from cross-town Hardin-Simmons University. I did my best to help him build a respectable, solid, winning basketball program at McMurry. We had some real shooters, and Coach Kimbrell knew how to use them.

Virtually, every coaching job I accepted during a four-decade period was a result of the support and recommendation of my coach at McMurry College, Hershel Kimbrell. Half of the time, I wasn't even aware of his involvement.

A few years ago, a group of us "Kimbrell Boys" got together in Abilene for a round of golf at the Abilene Country Club. Preston Vice, Dean Ingram, Marc Case, Ron Holmes, and I were joined by Tommy Estes and Coach Kimbrell, who were there to visit and watch a few holes. At one point, my turn from the tee box resulted in a drive that went nowhere. The boys got a laugh out of that. I couldn't blame them. It didn't bother me.

Well, maybe a little. Shortly thereafter, Coach Kimbrell silently motioned me over and whispered, "Do you know what you should do the next time you're on the tee box? Step up there and knock that thing right down the middle."

I looked at him. He wasn't smiling—he was dead serious. I got a kick out of that. That's why I love him. My ol' coach was still coaching. You talk about two guys who love coaching: we both do to this day. If I called him right now . . . .

Co-Captains Jerry Stone and Ross Shivers with Coach Kimbrell

II
SECOND QUARTER

MY CAREER

Indians team, Jerry 2nd from right

4
EARLY LESSONS
1963–1973

"Choose a job you love, and you'll never have to
work a day in your life."

—Confucius

My first chance to put my toe anxiously in "coaching waters" was in the fall of 1963. For me, the water was perfect—it didn't feel cold at all. I had only been waiting for twelve years to experience it. As a first-year graduate assistant at McMurry College, there were no doubts in my mind concerning my ability to handle it. Apparently, Coach Kimbrell, our head coach, also had faith in me because, while he had varsity football coaching responsibilities for the first couple of months of the basketball season, he allowed me to coach the team in his absence—total absence.

Since the squad was made up mainly of my teammates from the previous year, I'm certain they didn't appreciate everything I threw at them. Pushing them was no problem for me, because they weren't looked upon by me as teammates anymore.

Also, it wasn't like suddenly my personality changed, becoming a turncoat. They had already witnessed my fanaticism when it came to games and practice.

Not all players respect the game and understand that it is bigger than any of us. In fact, most don't. Since no one was surprised at my "all-in" attitude, I escaped most run-ins another ex-teammate might have encountered in a new "coaching" role.

Another potential sticky situation was one of the guys on the team was my roommate, Clayton Brooks, who had been born and raised there in Abilene. We first met in Indian Gym on campus during the spring of 1960. We both immediately knew there was at least one other person on earth who shared the same strong feelings for the game of basketball. Every detail about the game I had analyzed through the years, he had likewise analyzed. We talked a long time that first day. We've been talking ever since.

Clayton is a fierce competitor. He and I went at each other quite often during and after practice at McMurry. Post-practice and all alone, the one-on-one games lasted as long as possible until the last minute before the cafeteria closed. Those games were very competitive, normally ending with the ball being slammed against the floor or the wall followed by several very quiet moments. One of the participants would be sulking—the other would remain very quiet and respectful. Both hated to lose. By the time we got to the cafeteria, the ice would be broken. One of us would start a conversation, assuring the other that we were going to continue being roommates for at least one more night.

A long time later, we both coached about the same number of years. We were in touch throughout, even though our paths seldom crossed as coaches since I was at various colleges while Clayton remained at the high school level. When we did talk, it didn't take long to pick up right where we left off, trading ideas and diagrams, hoping to help each other gain a slight advantage on a future opponent.

But, during my first year of coaching, I was worried how he'd react to my new position. Like me, he was very opinionated. Fortunately, he sucked it up and fell right in line.

Clayton Brooks and Jerry Stone

I'm sure he bit his lip on a few occasions during and after practice. Since improving the team was foremost on my mind, it wasn't difficult running those guys for any misdeeds, treating practices like preseason boot camp. Clayton and I continued to communicate. No awkward comments were exchanged, though some periods of dead silence certainly did occur.

Coach Kimbrell didn't come in the gym for several days. When he did appear, he was impressed watching us work out for the first time and commented on it. I must admit, we did look good. Those guys were probably in mid-season form—anyway, they looked like it. Those complimentary remarks on my behalf forced me to disguise my grateful pride. Coach Kimbrell's trust in me was sincere. The encouragement gave me some real confidence, something all young coaches need.

Two years later, I was hired for my first bona fide teaching/coaching job in the fall of 1965. **Mexia (pronounced "ma-hair" by the locals) High School was a 2-A school in Texas, located about thirty miles east of Waco.** My salary was six thousand dollars per year, which was above average. My duties were typical for a small school: head boys' basketball coach, assistant varsity football coach, head junior varsity football coach (by myself), and junior high tennis coach.

As most people know, Texas high school football is *big*. Consequently, Texas football coaches feel they are extremely high in the pecking order, paid well, and have pressures that other coaches don't. Football programs involve a large number of kids from all the players to organizations such as cheerleaders, drill teams, spirit squads, band members, etc. As the head football coach, you are expected to win—especially at the larger schools.

If you don't, you can be fired. In most cases, head coaches in all the other sports aren't working under those type pressure conditions.

When a Texas high school athlete is good in two sports and one of them is football, conflicts arise. The biggest fear a football coach has is his star running back or quarterback will like basketball more than football. The battles for certain skilled players throughout the years in Texas are legendary. Unfortunately, the kid caught in the middle of two eager coaches is the one who may suffer and end up a disappointment to both. To me, these clashes are not worth the stress—they are to be avoided. Accepting "lesser" athletes who play basketball year round are often more beneficial to the team (and, likewise to me) than having a stud footballer. His attention is often divided, and, unfortunately, he sometimes appears to be doing the basketball coach a favor by being around. Having players in the gym who prefer to be there makes a coach's job much more enjoyable.

Texas football coaches wield much power and often also serve as the school's athletic director. If they're smart, they will try to "project" the attitude of equality in regards to all the sports teams. I understand how difficult that can be. Some try to be as fair as possible; others have a harder time.

I've witnessed, and occasionally been involved in the entire spectrum—from deflating the basketballs when the season ends to the head football's son being the best basketball player on my team. In one instance, the football coach stopped speaking to me as soon as the last football game was played. Following our basketball season, he would became friendly again.

It was all very confusing for a young, naïve basketball coach.

It's important to understand, even though it certainly didn't seem fair, it was the "law of the land" at the time. Most football coaches today look at the situation differently (of course, the courts have forced them to), and hardly a coach from either sport has a chip on his shoulder regarding the matter.

But, it's certainly understandable that any coach might covet a fine-looking athlete and feel the kid should be competing on his team. How the coach deals with the situation is what makes it interesting.

Times, however, have changed. Texas basketball coaches have held their heads up high for several years and don't feel like second-class citizens. In fact, I suspect today's young basketball coaches have a hard time relating to what I'm saying, not knowing the history of those conflicts.

My second year at Mexia, our basketball team won district. Those small-town, country boys were as good as gold—guys like our 6-5 post man, Randy Storey, and 5-11 guard, Larry Evans. Larry was a dandy, tough middle linebacker who became my point guard because of his leadership qualities. He would often have to back it down to start the offense but he rarely lost control of the ball. Though we did well, being on a team under an inexperienced, rookie coach can sometimes be annoying.

The summer of 1966 as a new teacher and coach at Mexia, I was presented the opportunity for summer employment at the **Mexia State School**. The school housed mentally, physically, and socially impaired kids, including down syndrome children, who ranged from normal dependency to absolute uncontrollable delinquency.

I had three days to decide. It took me two days before I could think clearly. This was going to be different.

The job description was to organize a physical education program for all students from elementary school through junior high school. The job was mine if I wanted it. It would be an excellent supplemental salary for two and a half months during the summer. I was to develop a complete job description with specific lesson plans, including purpose and anticipated results.

Having never been presented with this type opportunity, they gave me three days to accept or reject the job. They seemed to welcome my potential employment—everything looked good on paper.

I physically walked throughout the grounds of the State School facilities, getting a feel for what I was about to enter. I noticed immediately that this wasn't something from a movie—this was real and I would be solely responsible for how it turned out now and in the future.

By taking the job, I would be surrounded by an entire population of mentally challenged kids who were capable of anything, good and bad. Some were quite uninhibited when it came to expressing themselves. They very much enjoyed walking up and giving you a big hug when the mood struck them. Most moved around in supervised groups throughout the day while others were locked up like prisoners because of their inability to cooperate. For now, it was an uncomfortable feeling. Would I be able to treat these human beings in a caring but disciplined way, or would I need to let it go? *I was more concerned than excited.*

The problem was, by not accepting the position, it would never have felt right—I had to go for it. What transpired over the next three months was unforgettable.

It only took a short time to figure out this uncharted situation. I quickly learned that, more than anything, these kids were starving for love and attention. It didn't take a genius to imagine how seldom those two emotions were called upon during their lives. I also discovered that, for the majority, I needed to view them as unruly, not mentally deficient. They reacted favorably to good, old-fashioned discipline. *That was the biggest secret and became the key to our success.*

For example, if they misbehaved, they learned they would have to do a certain number of push-ups, etc. Although more patience was necessary, there wasn't much difference in handling them and handling normal kids. No one complained. Whatever their mental capacities, they seemed to understand my rules. In many respects, the attention they craved was like any other kid. It wouldn't be hard to imagine: neglect was a big part of their plight—they didn't mind the discipline as long as we were paying attention to them while it was being administered.

A young Baylor graduate named Judy served as my assistant. She was patient and kind to the kids (they loved her, as well as me—we were both pleasantly surprised), and she constantly commented on how effective our method of discipline was progressing.

It surprised me, too, but all I was doing was being a coach. We ended up with a productive program because of it. Miss Judy and Mr. Jerry made a good team.

Groups were divided by age and ability, and we worked with each group about an hour and a half each day. We played all kinds of games from walking like ducks to team sports such as softball and gymnastics for those who were older. The kids had no inhibitions and weren't afraid to give most anything a try. We required them to warm up with calisthenics, which helped start the day off with organization and discipline.

I never got used to the "extreme" cases who had to be locked up away from the rest of the school's population. I did my best not to walk by that area. The one time I did, I came away with two very disturbing feelings: one of physical nausea and one of pure sadness. I never went to that area again.

One day while walking the grounds, checking things out, I heard the most beautiful singing. I wondered if some of our gymnastic students were participating, sounding like a fairly polished choir. I peeked in a window and sure enough, some of them were our kids. It was an emotional moment as I listened and realized God doesn't pick and choose only the perfect ones to share something special.

When the end of summer arrived, I was ready to leave.

However, it was surprisingly difficult to say goodbye, because I knew what it would mean for the kids—there would be no more happy times in physical education. It was very possible that Mr. Jerry and Ms. Judy's classes wouldn't reassemble the following summer. I was never informed and never went back.

Early lessons have their advantages. The fireworks I went through during the early years of coaching were like a slap in the face. Though they bothered me a great deal at the time, those conflicts were a blessing in disguise. I'm actually glad I experienced them early in my career.

I can definitely say they opened my eyes to Texas football and prepared me to anticipate and deal with potential football-versus-basketball disagreements at future high school programs. In fact, I had no serious problems the remainder of my coaching career—to the best of my ability, I never allowed it. I met issues head-on and stayed aboveboard and honest. Playing golf with most of the football coaches all summer long didn't hurt matters. I also spent a great deal of time in the football fieldhouse during my off periods, constantly messing with the assistant coaches.

It didn't take long for me, however, to realize that basketball was where I belonged. My attitude wasn't anti-football—it was just pro-basketball, one that I had carried around since childhood. Whatever coaching energy and talent was in me, it needed to be expressed in a gymnasium with the sounds of bouncing basketballs and squeaking basketball shoes.

Changing jobs usually means relocation—sometimes down the road, sometimes across the country. In 1967, my next stop was at **Amarillo's Caprock High School in the Texas Panhandle.**

Texas is a big state. The city of Amarillo might as well have been Cheyenne, Wyoming. The school had a hand-full too many students for a 3-A classification which would have allowed us a much better chance of competing. Instead, Caprock was about as small a class 4-A school as existed. Coaching basketball there would be a true test. However, after coaching multiple sports, there were no complaints from me. Concentrating on one sport sounded good.

My stay at Caprock was not long. My one year there turned out good. After being picked eighth in an eight-team district preseason poll, we shocked everybody by tying for first place going into the last game of the second half of district play. I was selected "Coach of the Year" in the district. In addition, our first daughter was born. Stacy Leigh Stone was a joy—I took her everywhere I could.

I inherited a scrawny team with no bench. The only way we could win was to control the tempo of the game, be a tight-knit group, and play to our full potential. After hearing that one of my players got drunk at a party, especially after having just stated very clearly the importance of our training rules, I let him go.

The punishment may not have fit the crime perfectly, since it was a first-time infraction, but I was eager to send a clear message to the squad. **If a team has a history of losing, they will gladly continue sharing this tradition with the new coach, if you let them.** You cannot give them excuses to do so, or they'll accept it as the norm in a heartbeat. I lost no sleep giving up the kid. He became Caprock High's sacrificial lamb. To be honest, I felt bad for him—but not for my team.

When the (potential) sacrificial lamb happens to be your best player, the decision is much harder. You should try to save him somehow. But, sometimes you can't. He won't let you. You keep telling yourself, *He's so talented.*

But don't go there. You know he's got to go. Otherwise, when you're mowing the lawn next summer and reflecting on the past 8–20 season, you will be asking yourself, *Why didn't I get rid of that kid?*

That year, my entire varsity team consisted of six players. You think anybody was worried about us? We didn't win State, but in many ways we were a *Hoosier-like* squad: small, smart, and together. They gave me everything they had. As mentioned earlier, we actually finished tied for first place going into our final game after being picked dead last during pre-season. I was very proud of them. (The sacrificial lamb was, no doubt, a factor.)

One of the six players at Caprock was **Lamont Grogan,** a talented 6-5 college prospect. He was a fine athlete and a really quick leaper with a very nice touch.

He could play inside or outside. Because Lamont came from an Air Force family, he seemed rather unsettled, having experienced the typical military life moving from one place to the next. It was almost as if he were constantly looking over his shoulder, asking himself, *I wonder what's coming next?*

I didn't know what Lamont was all about. When you're a new coach, you have to get the attention of your players, making sure you're fair and consistent in the process. Of course, young people have to learn what fair and consistent means. They're always confused at first. Because I was very demanding of them, Lamont and most everyone were understandably leery of me.

When I discovered that Lamont had a stuttering problem, it helped explain why he had such a shy, down-and-out demeanor. On one of our road trips, we stopped to eat a pre-game meal. As we walked toward the restaurant, a very attractive lady walked ahead of us. We all saw her—she was hard to miss. Everyone slowed down and stared.

Not knowing I was right behind him, Lamont, with utmost conviction, said, "B-b-b-boy, I'll b-b-bet s-s-she likes to d-d-d-do it." To hear such a comment coming from such a reticent individual was hilarious. None of us could contain ourselves—it was classic. Of course, when he saw me three feet behind him, everyone *really* lost it.

Anytime you have a small squad and a player of Lamont's caliber, you always try to give him the benefit of the doubt, if possible. (In other words, don't get rid of your best player.) That's what Lamont got from me. He gave me zero problems except for one I had to correct immediately. I saw him smoking a cigarette between classes, right in the middle of our campus. He wasn't even trying to conceal it. As the product of a military family that had lived in many countries, drinking and smoking had probably become routine for Lamont.

And, as I have earlier mentioned, he was my best player, by far. Rest assured, we were going to get this worked out.

I went to him and explained in very simple terms, "Lamont, here's how this whole thing works around here. See, you hide from me, and I hide from you. OK?" He looked at me as if to say, "Gee, Coach. I'm learning so much from you." (Not exactly how you would picture a conversation concerning training rules.)

Let's be realistic. **If your discipline problem is your best player(or even worse, *your only decent player*) and he's not a thug, don't kick him off the team.** You just run the stuffings out of him, even if you have to run along beside him. If he still won't cooperate and causes more problems, you will, no doubt, be forced to let him go—reluctantly.

After a single year at Caprock, I was excited that **Richardson High School** had hired me as their head basketball coach. A northern suburb in the Dallas-Fort Worth Metroplex, Richardson, Texas, sat in the middle of a booming area adjacent to the soon-to-be sprawling city of Plano. People, cars, and homes were about to be everywhere. Several of the Dallas Cowboys lived in Richardson, including **Roger Staubach**. He and a few other Cowboys played pickup games in our gym during the spring.

Richardson High was in an upper-economic city with good students—many were children of Texas Instruments employees— and was an institution you could easily speak of with pride. RHS dwarfed the first two high schools that began my career.

For example, Caprock had 1,400 students in all four classes combined.

Richardson had 3,400 in the top three classes alone.

Every new job presents unique challenges. My first obvious one occurred when I walked into the gym in the fall of 1968 and found myself staring at thirteen seniors on the varsity squad— thirteen! None of them bad. In fact, most would have made the team on today's 5-A level.

Unfortunately, they all happened to be seniors at the same school. The problem was also that none of them were Division I caliber athletes. Too many OK players who have equal talent is not good. Had several seniors been allowed to remain on the team, a problem would have been created. Since there was no way all of them could receive enough legitimate playing time, each could claim—and rightly so—the players who were getting time on the floor were no better than themselves.

At least five needed cutting, a task no coach finds pleasant. Here I was this stranger, bringing them into my office one at a time to deliver the bad news, disrupting the lives of a bunch of boys who had probably been playing together since grade school. I don't know what hurts more—breaking up with the love of your life, being held back a grade in school, or being cut from your high school basketball team—one of three tragic events an adolescent may have to face.

Surprisingly, I didn't hear a thing in the weeks following. If parents brought it to the attention of the athletic director, Joe Simpson, I was unaware of it. My five-year span as the coach of the Eagles was a successful ride. The guys I had at Richardson made my job enjoyable and represented the school well, losing only four district games in those five years there. I was selected "Coach of the Year" three times (normally, a nice pat on the back for the guy who wins district). But, without top-notch players, the opportunities for extended playoff victories weren't real common.

The Three Amigos
L-R, Royce Cooper, Jerry Wade, and Jerry Stone

While coaching in Richardson, Jerry Wade at Lake Highlands High, Royce Cooper at J.J. Pearce, and myself were inseparable. Wade was the bold, fearless leader, and Royce and I spent a lot of time looking at each other in disbelief. That's the best way to describe our trio. We were like high school buddies; we had a great deal of fun and will cherish the memories.

Many young coaches watch NCAA games on television and see no reason why they couldn't handle a similar job at a major university. If they just had the opportunity, they believe they could give Bill Self at Kansas or Roy Williams at North Carolina a tip or two. In truth, that tip or two might be legitimately helpful. I don't know of any coach who feels he has all the answers. But the difference between all the aspects of NCAA Division I coaching and taking a high school team to state three years in a row is like night and day.

Like many high school coaches, I dreamed of coaching at a big university. Unfortunately, I had no idea how to get there. I thought the first step was to win games in high school. I believed winning a district championship four years in a row (which never happened) verified my ability to be successful at the next level. I later realized I had overrated the significance of a winning record. What you achieve in high school—or later in junior college—has little or nothing to do with your chances at a higher level. Like anywhere else, to a great extent, it's not what you know, but who you know.

If your goal is to be a college coach, you'd better get to that level ASAP. That's your first step: accepting any reasonable position available.

While I enjoyed my time coaching at Richardson High in the Metroplex with all it had to offer, I felt I would be moving to the college level soon. It didn't really matter where I started because it wouldn't take me long to move up the coaching ladder. Was I that sure of myself? For the most part, yes. To be more accurate, *I was misinformed and naïve.* I can remember thinking, *All I need is a chance.* Sometimes that isn't nearly enough.

"Be careful what you wish for. You just might get it" took on a much clearer meaning in the days and years to come.

"Be careful what you wish for. You just might get it."

Spudd Webb, dunking

5
FINDING MY PLACE
IN COLLEGE BASKETBALL
1973–1987

*"I'd rather attempt to do something great and fail
than attempt to do nothing and succeed."*

—Robert Schuller

My jump to the collegiate level came in 1973 at **Tarleton State University in Stephenville, Texas,** a town few people knew about. Stephenville was in the middle of a ranching area sixty-five miles southwest of Ft. Worth, where the locals dealt with livestock, wore boots, and, I assumed, owned and knew how to fire a rifle. My mother's father had been born in Stephenville.

I didn't feel comfortable getting my first taste of the NCAA at the Division II level. My gut feeling screamed, "Do not take it." But I felt I had to start somewhere. I'll never forget asking Vernon McDonald, head basketball coach at Southwest Texas State (now Texas State University) if he had any advice for a young coach who had just been hired by Tarleton State. My question was serious and he knew it.

However, Vern had a few coaches surrounding him at the time and enjoyed entertaining them, bless his heart. He replied, "I'd resign." I always got a kick out of Vernon, but that day I wanted to kick him. Later, I realized I should have listened.

There was nothing wrong with the town of Stephenville, the school or the people. It was just poor timing on my part. I had many things to learn—anybody having coached at this level would see this coming: First of all, the players were dealing with a coach who had zero experience with their age group and background. Second, we were simply unable to entice promising freshmen to sign with Tarleton State. Building a solid program required constantly sprinkling a few freshmen into the mix. Instead, we had to rely on mostly transfers from various backgrounds—not very promising.

Transfers are rather risky, although not always. The problem is that quite often their reason for transferring is *negative.* They were cut from their original team due to lack of ability, they got into some kind of mischief at their previous school, or they had laid out for a year or two. Occasionally, a good junior college player could be snatched up. For most transfers, however, the dream was gone. Reality had grabbed them and knocked much of the enthusiasm out of them.

I gradually figured out working with younger kids, mainly college freshmen, defined my niche. Working with players who still had dreams and were not afraid to go after them was what all coaches enjoy. That's what excited me. Trying to talk to older players—transfers—whose objective was to get a degree, get married, and get a job wasn't as inspiring. I certainly understood the importance of all of that, but, let's not forget, the reason they were on scholarship was because of basketball. Sometimes we almost found ourselves forgetting about that.

We did have a few quality players at Tarleton State. Curtis Thompson had talent, as did Richard "Space" Martin, a good, speedy point guard from Dallas who loved the game. Randy Leasley could drill today's three-pointers with ease, and Isaac Atkinson had multiple moves at the low post despite his six-foot-five size.

I also enjoyed **Robert Gill,** who turned out to be a friend for years.

We still converse off and on and enjoy each other's humor.

I didn't feel comfortable for the entire three years I was at Tarleton State. It wasn't fair to the school or the players, but I couldn't wait to get out of there. The truth was those students at Tarleton were good kids. I was the one who was out of place: there at the wrong time, coaching the wrong sport. **Heck, Tarleton State had a great rodeo team.**

Tarleton State basketball has had good success during the last twenty-five years. Universities, like everything else, move in cycles when it comes to athletic departments. Different sports are emphasized and de-emphasized. Athletic directors and coaches come and go. Budgets ebb and flow according to the make-up of administrative policies and the personalities involved.

During my time at Tarleton State, **Dave Neely** and I became soul brothers. He was the head coach at Weatherford Junior College, fifteen miles west of Fort Worth on I-20. Many times, we met and discussed our coaching woes. Exchanging philosophies and future plans helped ease the stress that invariably mounted during the season. It was nice to have a fellow coach who understood the difference between where we were and where we wanted to be.

Dave now has his own women's junior college scouting service. He includes clinics for the purpose of assisting these hopeful prospects to move on to a four year colleges been a great friend for many years—we still meet up on occasions and have lengthy telephone conversations full of laughter.

When **Gerald Stockton, the head coach of Midwestern State in Wichita Falls, Texas,** asked me to be his assistant in 1976, I jumped at the offer. The timing was perfect. Everyone needs to get away from the pressure of a head coaching position, especially during those days at Tarleton State. It was good to take a deep breath and unscramble all thoughts connected to basketball for awhile.

Basketball had a rich tradition at Midwestern and was important to the school, but feeling the lack of pressure from an assistant's viewpoint seemed mighty nice. This would be my first and only assistant role—I liked the break, but not for long.

A former player for **Hank Iba at Oklahoma A&M (now Oklahoma State),** Gerald had already been coaching for seventeen years when he became Midwestern's head coach in 1970. Without football as competition, basketball was *the* sport at Midwestern even before he arrived (They have since added football). He continued that tradition with the talent he assembled each season.

With his years of experience, he could coach his brand of Iba-style basketball blindfolded. Coach Stockton would eventually coach there twenty-four years. In fact, when you mention Midwestern basketball, you immediately think of Gerald Stockton. He cast a large shadow (in more ways than one) over that well-manicured campus. The school's basketball court is named after him.

I really enjoyed palling around with Gerald. He was a big man—six-foot-seven, around three hundred pounds—with a very deep voice. He loved people, loved to gab, and was very likeable. He knew everybody on campus and half the people in town.

As the first assistant, I had a decent rapport with the players. I had held a similar role as a grad assistant at McMurry. But I didn't like quietly watching practice while someone else developed the team and ran the show. It had been my idea to just chill for a period of time, but I was freezing. I kept wanting to have my own team again, but while at Midwestern, I was reduced to staying out of Gerald's way, which I understood.

As an assistant, you have zero ability to stamp your personality on whatever team you are involved with. I missed working with a team and everything that only a head coach can do. There's a reason for everything.

That year helped reaffirmed who I was and what I wanted to be.

I had planned to coach at Midwestern for two or three years. Everything seemed peaceful and in its place. Our second girl, Marci, was born that year. But in March of 1977, **Delnor Poss, Midland College's athletic director,** called and asked if I would come to West Texas to interview for the head coaching job with him and the **college president, Dr. Al Langford**. The previous head coach had been fired and they were looking for a replacement.

Coach Poss and I had known each other from way back. We felt free to discuss everything. There were many questions to ask, mainly because nobody knew anything about MC regarding athletics. Midland College had no history to review. The junior college had only been in existence for eight years. The basketball program had been around for two. What was the outlook for athletics? And an unknown president was about to become my boss. My friend, Athletic Director Del Poss, was going to have to help me decide. I leaned on him that first year or two—he was very helpful.

Midland College had big plans for the future, but so have a lot of other schools. What made MC different was what was happening in the area at the time. The Midland/Odessa area— called the Permian Basin or the **Petroplex**—produced 20 percent of the nation's oil. About every twenty years, new drilling methods and consumer demand result in increased activity at old and new sites. At the time, we were in one of those up cycles. Having the financial resources to expand Midland College was not going to be a problem if they so desired.

One problem continued to pull at me.

My talks with the two previous coaches and a few others pointed toward the opinion that Dr. Langford might be a man for whom you wouldn't want to work. The truth is, you cannot rely on someone else's opinion. You can listen to them, but you can't rely on everything you hear.

What applies to them may not apply to you at all. It's kind of like asking someone about a certain movie.

When I went back a week later to confirm my decision, there certainly wasn't a 100-percent conviction in my mind. As it turned out, I had no problem with Al Langford. He could be gruff and head-strong but you knew where you stood. I reported directly to Delnor anyway, and for ten years we worked beautifully together, moving upward into the top ten nationally with every team in the athletic program.

To be honest, not many people in Midland really cared about the junior college's basketball program because it was so new. Not caring doesn't mean they were against basketball; they were just sorta' neutral. Besides, in West Texas, local high school football was king.

You've heard of *Friday Night Lights?* The book, movie, and television series were based on Permian High School football in nearby Odessa. The people of Midland and Odessa directed their passion toward their high school football teams.

I didn't look at football as a rival. Football was dominant before I arrived and would continue after I departed. I had an appreciation for football—I had played it throughout high school in Kansas. As we began to have success, the people of Midland showed they could handle supporting both high school football and junior college basketball—many embraced us.

In ten years at Midland College, we won 275 games and lost only sixty-seven. We also won an NJCAA national championship, which I'll go into more detail later. Winning basketball games was fun.

However, what made coaching JC guys rewarding was being around players who had a similar passion for the game. You would think that would be automatic with any player, but it isn't.

When I was a young man, I understood what it meant choosing to play a pickup game over a Friday night date (although there were a couple exceptions). No mistake about it, I liked girls, but I *loved* basketball. That fact, in itself, made me different from most of my teammates. Later, as a recruiter, I looked for players who tended to feel as I did about basketball. (The proper phrase is "gym rats.")

The junior college kids I coached came from all parts of the country and from different backgrounds, but all had one thing in common: their love for the game. In some respects, they had too much love. Some needed to share some of that pride with their academic progress, too.

The junior college level was my niche. In my heart, I've always been a JC boy. The day after my last high school game, I had zero full scholarship offers. Like the high school kid who has the skill but not the grades, my situation was in reverse—my grades were fine, but my talent was considered good, but not exceptional. Like many of my players later at Midland College, proving myself was in order.

At first glance, most of my JC kids seemed to have less chance to succeed—it also meant, however, they had more desire to prove themselves. They cared more. I loved that atmosphere and can honestly say that after those first couple of months of "boot camp," including the departures that normally occur during the freshman year, I did love the guys who toughed it out and, in effect, pledged to come along for the ride. There was no need to fear the unknown—they just needed to follow.

The first time I met Spud Webb, I didn't know what to think. He just looked so young and small.

Basketball people in the area knew about this little guy at Wilmer-Hutchins High School—they knew he could play. Arriving at his school, there was just enough time to shake his hand before his team began practice. Spud was 5-6, slight of build, weighed only 130 pounds, wore a size six shoe, and had a quiet demeanor. He had such a youthful face he could have passed for a sixth-grader. **I felt I was shaking hands with someone who was impersonating a high school athlete.**

Before I had approached him to introduce myself, a cute little coed asked meekly, "Spud, can I tie your shoes?" He nodded as Julius Caesar would have, acknowledging his subjects while placing each foot forward, one at a time. I thought, *Oh, brother*.

Off the court, Spud was shy—not insecure, but slightly unsure and unworldly, not unlike many his age. On the court, he was the exact opposite. He felt he could do anything. He backed down from no one. To him, size was something other people talked about. He didn't see what the fuss was all about.

Years later, I realized I had seen Spud four or five years earlier than that day at his school. It was on the courts at the Highland Hills Recreation Center, which was a rich source of young talent in the south Dallas area.

I kept noticing this tiny kid bouncing all over the court with enough energy for three people. He would dart in and out, in between games or during dead balls. I was certain he had to be a grade-schooler, too young to play with the big boys—he would have to wait a few years. What struck me most was his love for the game. He was where he felt he belonged. His body language demonstrated it with every move.

Recruiting Spud was an easy decision. Despite his diminutive size, I saw his talent and noted his fierce pride. Besides, I had already learned size wasn't a concern if a player had athletic abilities, with a proper attitude. A few years later **Cullen Mayfield** thoroughly convinced me that dwelling on size was, for the most part, a waste of time—The Rule is: **If they are truly TALENTED, DO NOT WORRY ABOUT ANYTHING ELSE.**

Some of you may not believe the preceding paragraph—All I can say is, " I coached 42 years and I do."

Three years earlier, I had signed Cullen, who was another small Dallas point guard about Spud's size. He led South Oak Cliff High School to the state championship in Austin and was named the Texas Player of the Year. Most point guards are quick and good ball-handlers, but if they can't hit the perimeter shot, they can be a liability. If a point guard is not a threat from the outside, the defense can back off of him. They can double-down on the inside players and disrupt other areas of the offense. Unfortunately, the defense, at the same time, may eliminate his ability to drive—nearby teammates can sag and jam the driving lanes. A point guard's inability to shoot from outside essentially cuts his effectiveness in half. He can run the team but that's about it.

This was not an issue for Cullen or Spud—they could do it all.

Cullen was one of my first recruits, as we were just getting started at Midland College (I wish he could have been on some of those teams a few years later).

He had two fine years with MC before a calcium deposit in his thigh slowed him down during the second semester of his sophomore year. He finished his collegiate career at Midwestern State under the guidance of my former boss Coach Gerald Stockton.

In my mind, Cullen helped clear the way for recruiting smaller guards. Spud confirmed the policy—every play he concluded was more convincing than the last. Spud Webb was next in a long, continuous line of successful Dallas point guards at Midland College.

Spud loved penetrating, driving, and dunking. He was so quick, taking it to the basket was something he could do almost any time. Because of that ability, he felt no real need to stop and pop a jumper. My only concern during my evaluation of Spud was the question of his outside shooting (as I mentioned earlier, size was not a factor with me)—I just didn't know what he could do from seventeen or eighteen feet.

The spring of his senior year, Spud had yet to receive a single offer when I followed him to an all-star game in Waco specifically to evaluate his shot. The evaluation didn't take long. He hardly missed a shot (he had perfect form) during practice. In addition, he nailed several consecutive free throws during an extended session at the line. **The questions were over—no more from me.**

Two years later, **Jim Valvano at North Carolina State,** and, later still, **Mike Fratello with the Atlanta Hawks,** asked me to describe what kind of shooter Spud was. **I told them, "Believe it or not, he's pure."**

Spud was still stuck in his old habit of taking it to the basket, but was gradually learning to balance his game—he was beginning to score in a variety of ways. If the big guys were lurking around the basket, he'd stop and take a medium-range jumper. To prove my point involving his shooting ability, **Spud eventually led the NBA in free throw shooting in the 1994–95 season when he hit 93.4 percent from the line for the Sacramento Kings.**

When I first visited Spud prior to signing him, I made it clear his dunking was fine but recruiting him for his showmanship was not my intention.

I wanted to teach him to be a point guard, to lead a team, and to be a complete player. I wasn't sure what his reaction would be—maybe he thought of himself as a showman. I just knew I didn't want a showman running my team. Turned out, what I said was what he wanted to hear. **Spud wanted to be respected as a basketball player—a smart one, not a side-show.**

No problem—we were already on the same page.

While coaching at Midland College, I was lucky to be blessed with a series of top-notch point guards who were team leaders. After Spud came **Ricky Grace**, who had also graduated from Wilmer-Hutchins High School in Dallas. Ricky grew up in a moderate-income neighborhood and had a strong mother who had taught her son well. **He was a proud young man and— unlike most youngsters—knew how to disarm people in a really likable way. He was a young black male who had been**

taught to look at the world realistically but not to let it destroy any potential friendships and dreams. Consequently, he was comfortable being a natural leader, mainly leading by example. Ricky was a conscientious kid who always tried to do the things that would give us a chance to win. He also had that admirable quality of getting along with people of all backgrounds.

"Amazing Grace" was liked by everyone.

When Ricky first arrived at Midland, I really didn't know if he was going to hang in there or not because he was a bit hesitant. It took him a while to quit over-thinking and just jump in and be a tough, reactive-type player. (I was the same way as a freshman.)

Over-thinkers are usually players who care about what's going on and don't like making mistakes. There's nothing wrong with that. At some point, however, they have to let go and do what they know they can.

Ricky was discouraged by not being an important contributor during his first semester (He was actually much closer than he realized.) He almost didn't come back after the Christmas break.

Thankfully, his mother steered him back, along with some important encouragement from the mother of my assistant coach, Reggie Franklin.

I didn't know about the help of Reggie's mom until recently. Who knows how many other fires Reggie Franklin helped put out for me? Ricky became a starter midway through the second semester, and his leadership skills began emerging. He had an excellent sophomore year, was named First Team All-American, and, during his junior year, went on to play at **Oklahoma under Billy Tubbs.**

Mookie Blaylock, another outstanding guard, who came to Midland from Garland, Texas, followed Ricky to OU one year later. When Mookie was a Chaparral, he hardly said a word—at least to me. He was similar to Spud in that he didn't want to get in trouble. Since he hated running as a form of punishment, he never missed a class and was on time for all meetings and practices. He wasn't a complete loner but certainly chose his friends carefully. It always appeared to me he had a difficult time trusting people.

Mookie probably didn't know how much I appreciated his contributions to our team. We had a mutual respect which didn't need to be disturbed. **When a player is really in the groove and playing well, a coach shouldn't say much to him if he's more at ease in that environment. Show respect and get out of his way.** He seemed slightly uncomfortable talking with me, anyway, which is nothing odd for a freshmen around their new coach. I might compliment him occasionally or make a suggestion every now and then, but that was about all. My theory was, "If it ain't broke, don't fix it." We didn't engage in a lot of chit-chat. Mookie just wasn't very comfortable conversing with the "boss-man." **We had a silent unwritten agreement: he played, I coached. It worked pretty well.**

My relationship with Spud was almost the same. Some guys just don't feel relaxed around their boss. Because of their youth, they don't realize that whatever you're doing is an attempt to do what's best for them and the team. Young guys sometimes take criticism personally.

Until they get to know you, they are not aware that the constant criticism is momentary. Just tell them, "Listen and learn. I promise my plans aren't to go home tonight and dream up something to hammer you on tomorrow."

With Spud and Mookie, two future NBA players, there was hardly an issue. They both instinctively knew where the line was drawn.

One of the main reasons Mookie and I kept our distance was that we had quite a few "tough" kids on that year's team. The give-and-take of the players and the coach required a healthy, separate respect. The players, as I viewed them, were exactly what we needed to win. It was imperative that they kept their noses clean. Mookie's constant example of leadership had to be maintained—all eyes were on him. He played a paramount role in my attempt to blend the various personalities into one. **Simply put, I wanted them to, "Stay in line and do what Coach Stone says."** There were rewards awaiting.

Mookie evolved as that leader whether he realized it or not. What was unique about him was his total focus during a game. He was one of the best I've ever seen when it came to complete concentration. His loyalty to me was important. Mookie had a lot of power. I respected the fact he didn't try to abuse it. As long as he took care of business on and off the court, why worry about his quiet personality? We won many games while this private and quiet young man considered Midland College his temporary home.

Spud Webb played in the NBA for thirteen years and, at 5-7 (Spud's height has been reported as anything between 5-6 to

5-8), won the slam dunk contest at the 1986 NBA All-Star game, which suddenly vaulted him to a world-famous celebrity.

Ricky Grace played briefly with the Atlanta Hawks before migrating to Australia, where he was a member of the Perth Wildcats for twelve years, representing Australia in the 2000 Olympic Games.

He was later inducted into the Australian Basketball Hall of Fame. Not long ago, Ricky was voted the greatest point guard in the history of Western Australia.

Mookie Blaylock enjoyed thirteen years in the NBA, was twice selected to the NBA's All-Defensive First Team, twice led the league in steals, and was named an NBA All-Star in 1994.

We had our share of good shooting guards at Midland too. One was Todd Duncan of Lubbock, Texas. Todd silently went about starting for us his sophomore year in 1986–87. He was a slender combo guard who spent hours in the gym perfecting his long range jump shot and 94 percent free throw average. Todd wasn't considered an NBA "hopeful" and seemed to stay under the radar because of the many outstanding guards on our team and throughout the conference. But this quiet young man was a great asset to our team for two years. Texas Tech University recognized his shooting ability and signed him in the late spring.

I was so glad to see that happen. He played two years in his home town and is now the head basketball coach at Lubbock Christian University.

Midland College's Todd Duncan (20)

The longer I coached, the more I realized that while coaching is coaching, no two coaching jobs are alike. Many factors define a particular job, especially when considering college. It has to do with the level of play, the location of the school, the philosophy regarding the school's athletic program, the financial budget that accompanies the job, and much more.

Generally speaking, one of the greatest advantages of college coaching is the freedom a coach may have in his attempt to build a successful athletic team. How, when, and where things are done are largely left to the coach. If he's successful, he becomes very popular. If not, he may be fired. It comes with the territory.

While coaching at Midland College, during mid-February, 1986, we found ourselves in the heart of conference play with an open date, meaning we had a full week before our next game. Like always, I was getting worn down during that part of the year. I needed a break, but it was never seriously considered. When so much was at stake a couple of weeks from the playoffs, that was the last thing on my mind. . . I thought.

A day or two in Galveston or Miami kept entering my thoughts. I could feel the warm sun calling me. The truth is, by February you and your team are in need of some time off. I'd been working them out for almost seven months. Coaches are paranoid, however, during such separation periods from their teams. Unfortunately, when crunch time is near, the screws get tighter. So, it's very rare to hear of such a break—although in our case, it did no harm.

After a short conversation with my travel agent, I found myself arriving in **Cancun, Mexico** a day later. No hotel reservations were waiting for me. Like Eddie Murphy in *Beverly Hills Cop*, I walked up to the registration desk of the Sheridan Hotelon the beach and announced my name, **Jerry Stone,** just another vacationer ready to check in.

The lady at the desk looked and said there was no room reserved in my name. Since it was peak vacation time, the thought of bedding down on the beach wasn't appealing. *Think, Stone, think.* A fake concerned look on my face was quickly replaced by a confident smile (a total bluff on my part), "Oh, I must have given my full name when reserving my room—**William Stone**."

"Here it is," she said, "I thought you were coming in tomorrow." (What blind luck: the other William Stone was about to get bumped.)

Twenty minutes later, I was sucking on a piña colada and taking in the blue water and warm rays from the Caribbean sky.

I wasn't used to the beach scene—heck, I wasn't used to doing something like this. Don't you have to get permission to skip practice?

When I first walked into the clear blue water, it suddenly hit me, "If I were at home this very moment, I would be working out my team—we'd be running our 'backdoor-jumpers' drill about now." I couldn't control my excitement. Giddy as a kid skipping school, I'd pulled the whole thing off within twenty-four hours, without needing a fake note from my mother.

Three days later, I headed back to Midland, rested, ready to go, and mysteriously tanned. No one but my assistant and my secretary had been told—they were both sworn to secrecy.

While in Cancun, I parasailed, rode bicycles, checked out an Aztec pyramid, and did a lot of sleeping. The food alone was worth the trip.

Although I didn't know it at the time, 1987 would be my last year at Midland—it needed to be a good one. We entered the

NJCAA Tournament in Hutchinson, Kansas, ranked ninth with a 30–3 record.

We made it to the finals but entered the contest without our All-American and floor leader, Mookie Blaylock, who suffered a stress fracture in his foot in the latter stages of our semifinal. College of Southern Idaho beat us by one point.

Since the annual Coach of the Tournament Award is usually awarded to the winning coach, it came as a very nice surprise when I received it.

When the 1988 Division I NCAA Tournament Championship Game was played in Kansas City, Missouri, I was glued to my TV set. It was quite a duel between two teams from the Big Twelve Conference: Kansas, led by Danny Manning, and Oklahoma, which had beaten the Jayhawks twice in conference play. It was a terrific game to watch.

Though Oklahoma came up short, Mookie Blaylock tied for the Sooners' leading scorer with twenty-one points, and Ricky Grace added eight assists. In addition, Lincoln Minor, a teammate of Mookie and Ricky at Midland College, played for Kansas.

Three guards from Midland College were playing in the NCAA Division I Championship game at the same time. It was emotional watching that game.

I was told it was a first.

White jersey, 10 (Blaylock), 14 (Grace),
blue jersey, 11 middle of the lane (Lincoln Minor)

With a shooter like Nathan Doudney, smiling occurred frequently.

6
FROM DIVISION I
TO HICKORY HIGH
1987–2007

"Be careful what you ask for You just might get it."
—Aesop's Fables

Throughout the second semester of 1987, the University of Texas at Arlington had been courting me on a regular basis. It seems they needed a new men's basketball coach. You know when someone is really interested by the number of times they call. A Division I job was always my dream. Was it time to make the move? The main argument for accepting was simple: **you seldom get a chance to break into Division I as a head coach. Better take it while you can.**

From the moment it became obvious that UTA was serious, two compelling forces of tug-of-war began to grow inside me. "Plus and minus" lists began showing up in my apartment. Leave Midland—you've done all you can do here. Conversely, **don't go to a low-major program just because there's an NCAA title attached to it.**

Another analogy: You're leaving a top-ten junior college program for a Division I job that is barely alive. How about: One of the top three Juco gymnasiums in the country versus a stage? What was I thinking? Or: Leaving your friends and family (a recent divorce wasn't helping) and moving to the city, on your own, feeling very much out of place and alone.

Looking back, there were plenty of reasons, but the mistakes were mine—no one lied to me—I was naive and unfamiliar with these new surroundings. That's why it hurt and was embarrassing. Anger turned inward is not healthy.

Though we had built a successful program at Midland, I suffered a form of coaching burnout. Winning thirty games a year had become routine. No longer coaching to win, but rather coaching not to lose. I believed a Division I job with renewed energy would automatically be a rewarding position. Some are, but actually, many aren't.

I soon came to realize that the Midland job was certainly a better job for me—and that's what mattered. **As a junior college coach for ten years, there was freedom to do things at my own pace without a lot of red tape.** In our ten-team Western Junior College Athletic Association, we were free to practice every day and recruit at any time. Junior college budgets and lack of staff were the only limitations on recruiting. A true hands-on approach with our players appealed to me. Though it was a 24/7 job, your influence could definitely become meaningful.

The comfort zone I had developed at Midland never got off the ground at UTA. My particular way of doing things was impossible to duplicate there. For example, I had always planned every second of practice at Midland and made sure the plan was carried out, totally on my own. In short, the mindset becomes, *Do everything yourself, if you want it done right.* Now with two full-time assistant coaches, what was I supposed to do with them?

"One Way—My Way" had always summed up my coaching philosophy.

I especially missed my two daughters. I once watched a television show during the 80s featuring Dr. Theodore M. Hesburgh, the renown president of Notre Dame University, speaking to a huge audience at some conference.

His opening remark has always stuck with me: "Allow me to begin by saying that every one of you will go to your grave with the feeling of guilt when evaluating your ability as a parent." The guilt comes rather easily when you find yourself married to your job. While my daughters were very important to me, it seemed I spent more time with someone else's kids.

I stepped down from my head coaching position at UTA in January 1988. I had much to get straight. Having no energy, I needed the proverbial "break." The school's administration was good to me, working out a reasonable financial agreement which allowed me to finish out the year with most of my original salary. I was encouraged to drive to Kansas and sit down with my dad for some heart-to-heart. He had done everything he could to be a positive and loving father, but he was a private person who guarded against showing affection.

Evidently, this had been eating at me for years. Being a son with three sisters and no brothers, I had always wanted to be friends with my father, but that wasn't a natural thing for Dad.

During our one-on-one, he listened as I ranted, talking about how he never said he loved his four kids and how it had a negative impact on us. It felt good to get it out. After a while, as he glanced at Mom, he commented, "You know, we don't express ourselves enough around here." Then, a little later, "Well, of course I love you." At that wonderful moment a great weight was lifted from me—I was so proud of his response. I never heard it from him again, but I didn't need to.

From counseling, I actually learned it was all right to say "Thank you" when someone complimented me.

As kids, we had been sent a subliminal message from both parents: you weren't allowed to freely acknowledge anything good you had achieved.

We weren't encouraged to repay compliments with a "Thank you" because conceit could follow—rather hard to believe, but that was clearly my perception at the time. It was never stated; it was just hanging in the air. I do not believe there was ever any bad intent on their behalf.

As time went by, I slowly climbed back into society. I still lived in my apartment in Arlington and did a ton of jogging. I lost weight and felt good. Few people knew where I lived, but I still received much-appreciated letters of encouragement from my friends.

During this time, I wrote to Larry Brown, who was then with the San Antonio Spurs. It's hard to keep up with Larry, but he was a coach I'd gotten to know during my years in Midland. We had communicated off and on. He was someone who was easy to talk to. Larry loves the game like myself, and has never stopped trying to learn. There aren't many NBA coaches who I would even bother regarding something like this.

He sent me a very thoughtful reply, telling me to come down to San Antonio and visit him, watch a practice or two, and spend a little time together. I didn't follow up.

I just wasn't quite ready. But, his offer was sincere. He gave me some good advice: get out of Arlington and go visit (or live) with the ones who care about you. I needed to hear that.

I'd been stewing around in my apartment in Arlington, doing nothing other than a daily workout routine followed by a bunch of television.

Larry's letter came at the right time. It nudged me to go back to my second home, Abilene, back to West Texas.

I should mention that the University of Texas at Arlington is doing very well in men's basketball these days. With a newly built basketball arena (finally), they need not apologize for anything— I'm very happy for them.

Within four months of moving to Abilene, I began a long-distance relationship with a Kansas lady I had met two years prior. With no job in sight for me, she still accepted my marriage proposal. Now this was something of which I was sure. We told her father, who lived in Florida, about our marriage. For some reason, he didn't ask (and we didn't tell) about my current lack of employment.

Is there someone constantly looking out for us? We were married in July of 1989.

Not long after my move to Abilene, I got a call out of the blue from **Jerry Hrnciar** (pronounced Hearnshire), the golf coach and athletic director at Division II, Cameron University in Lawton, Oklahoma.

He'd contacted a few references on his own and was convinced that hiring me as their head basketball coach would be smart. *He was willing to do it sight unseen.* I found out later a high school friend of mine, **Ted Lechner**, a West Point grad living in Lawton, had pushed Hrnciar to hire me. Ted and I hadn't communicated with each other in thirty years.

Another indication of favorable luck was a strong recommendation from **Coach Don Haskins** at UTEP.

Apparently, my trips to El Paso visiting with assistant **Tim Floyd** had resulted in positive feed-back from "The Bear." You just never know.

Very few players I had at Cameron would have been able to make my Midland College teams. We still had decent teams—I was just used to top-notch players and teams, the kind you might see on TV in the future.

One player, **Carlos Mays**, a senior combo-guard from Gary, Indiana, could have played at Midland anytime, but other-wise there were only a few future NBA-caliber players running around in Division II. There were several at the junior-college level. I felt I had been to the mountaintop while coaching junior college. I liked the view much better from there.

Many people view junior college programs as unstable because of the constant evolving freshmen classes that come and go within one year or, at the most, two. But, if you're not at a solid Division II school (and there aren't many), attracting good freshmen players is next to impossible. You will experience *real turnover* as transfers float in and out. Talk about loyalty—there is very little with transfers. It didn't feel like coaching, more like supervising.

It wasn't necessary, but I'm sure I apologized way too many times to my rookie assistant coach, **Aubrey Green**, during the latter part of my stint at Cameron. It was probably difficult to understand the feelings I was trying to convey, mainly that I didn't feel comfortable being the coach of this team and school. Having gone through leaving Midland College (the school I really loved), the UTA mistake, and accepting a school that I normally would not consider, it just seemed like, "Here we go again. Someone tell me how to get out of this rut."

The problem with coaching a certain number of years is: *If you're winning, life is bearable; if you're losing, you're miserable.* It's a mistake to base your worth on how many games you win or lose, *but if you coach, you do.*

I always refer back to a quote I once read in the *Peanuts* comic strip: "It doesn't matter if you win or lose . . . until you lose."

After ten years, Coach Stone and Cameron University became weary of each other. They notified me first, but, in reality, it was a mutual decision. **Herb Jacobs, a very likeable veteran sports writer for *The Lawton Constitution*,** wanted to do a farewell interview with me. He wanted my opinion regarding the basketball state of affairs at the school.

Turning him down was difficult because he had been good to me those ten years. But I knew that whatever I said would not have mattered. More importantly, I didn't feel like voicing my opinion about a school that I hadn't given 100% to. If I had given an honest assessment of those ten years, few would have understood, believed, or cared. It just wasn't important. Their conclusion would have been, "Sour grapes—no wonder they let him go."

That same spring of 1999, I became the head basketball coach at Rockwall High School and coached the off-season practices from March through May. "Ah, new life", I thought. Rockwall is a town of forty thousand located eighteen miles east of downtown Dallas on Highway I-30. It is a very nice place to live, sitting on Lake Ray Hubbard. It remains my home today. Hired by **Mark Elam, a strong—some would say anti-basketball—football coach and athletic director, many people found my hiring surprising.**

I came directly from college with thirty-six years of basically successful coaching experience on my resume. What was the reason for coming back to coach at the high school level? Plus, why would Coach Elam hire what seemed to be a winning basketball coach?

When Coach Elam hired me, I promised two things:

1. Coming to Rockwall to build a basketball dynasty was never my intention, so there would be no problems between us regarding players and what sport in which they wanted to participate.

2. Coming from college back to high school to "retire" was, likewise, never my intention—my job would be to deal with the players, parents, media, and administration. He wouldn't have to be running back and forth putting out basketball fires. We never talked about it afterwards, and our relationship remained comfortable from the first day to the last.

I don't care who you are or how much experience you have, every new job brings a different environment along with new challenges. You can't expect a lot of immediate help from many people. Those who are eager to make your new surroundings comfortable may sometimes harbor a silent agenda. Maybe they feel there were other candidates who deserved a shot at the job and are secretly hoping for your failure.

Don't try to win the administration, faculty, students, and fans over in one big swoop. Don't make wild promises. You'll look insincere doing it (they won't believe you, anyway). If someone warns you that a certain person is not trustworthy, remember that certain person may be end up being a good friend.

You have to be patient—don't try to build Rome in six months or even a year. Wade through your difficulties always being fair, firm, and honest. Don't dwell on the number of games you need to win—that leads to possible compromises in your decision-thinking. **If you're doing your job the right way and treating people with respect, people will soon know. Word travels fast.**

When I took over the head coaching job at Rockwall High School in the spring of 1999, I found a group of half-spoiled, undisciplined guys who had no clue about playing basketball as a team. It wasn't their fault—no one had taught them (no one had made them). Considering the type of kid I had been coaching the past ten years and the plans I had for these Rockwall boys, I was certain they were not going to dig me for a while.

My biggest fear was running half of them off before they had a chance to adjust and figure out who I was and what I was trying to do. When you have an excess number of players, it's all right if some of them quit early. But if your ranks are as thin as ours were at Rockwall, you cannot afford to let any player slip away until you determine if he can contribute or not. They're not prepared for a drastic turnaround, so you have to break them down gradually. In my day as a player, we couldn't quit, period. We'd be humiliated and find ourselves lost without our buddies. What's worse, our dads would have put us to work. However, today, several options requiring less effort are waiting for anyone who doesn't want to stick it out.

Most high school or college athletes do not comprehend what it means to go full speed for an extended period of time. When faced with this requirement, today's youngsters sometimes refuse to stay the course and give themselves a chance to change.

Their idea of basketball is standing around in a zone and firing a three as soon as possible. Why not? That's about all they see these days. You must turn the soft-approach attitude around—if you don't, the season will not be enjoyable unless you happen to be loaded with talent.

For ten weeks, I worked those Rockwall kids thoroughly on fundamentals. They probably thought what they were asked to do was over the top. In truth, I held back (although, they wouldn't agree), allowing them time to adjust.

It was difficult for them to understand the importance of striving for perfection even when executing the simplest drill and *doing it every day.*

If you view this as strictly work, you will forever be missing the joy of working out. If all you do is run up and down during practice, you won't be preparing yourself for all the different looks that opponents will be throwing at you this year. **I didn't view it as work—to me it was preparation and security.**

As a player and as a coach, you must learn to find true pleasure in continuous repetition as you strive for that "perfection." It was never difficult for me—all I had to do, as a player or a coach, was focus on the immediate future, realizing that before long there would be paying customers sitting in the stands, there to watch me or my team perform. I would be combating an opponent whose sole purpose was to whip me in front of those people. **Now, why would I let that occur, if at all possible?**

During summer leagues, players are often not taught the basics of the game nor the proper mindset while playing. As a high school coach, I saw a totally different attitude from my players after they participated in a summer league. Suddenly, stars were clearly showing in their eyes and high school was not so important. When they showed up in the fall, they were somewhat burned out on basketball because they had played so many games during the summer—sometimes as many as three a day.

In order to survive, they learned to go two-thirds speed and play zone to pace themselves. And if they lost a game, who cares? There was another one in two hours.

You almost had to start from scratch to get them back on track. *It was not easy to reel them back in. I resented their new-found philosophy of showmanship.*

Suddenly, the team game disappeared—it became a *coast to coast* selfish style of street ball, and people were applauding it—influential people. From my standpoint, we were losing our beautiful team-oriented game that we had learned to love as a kid. ("Please, don't let them take it away," I thought.)

The truth is if you have a player (or players) that can advance the ball, under control, up and down the floor, I'd say, "Have at it." Just don't be careless—that's where I'd draw the line. *It wasn't the full court concept that I objected to—it was what the players viewed as a realistic chance to score once they had arrived at their basket.*

Stepping off the summer league court, back to the high school world was often difficult for both the players and the coach. I mean, "Run, Gun, and Have Fun" is intoxicating. When you look around, you can start to wonder. But, *DON'T.* There's really no substitute for fundamentals and team play. Don't get suckered in.

Early during that first year at Rockwall, we entered an eight-team tournament hosted by Wylie High School, about fifteen miles north of us. The competition was all right and we played fairly well, winning the tourney to begin what hopefully would be a successful season. However, a problem occurred during the finals. We won the game, but three of our team members each received a technical foul. *That's unheard of.* There was no reason the technicals should have occurred—we were winning the game and the calls weren't controversial. The fouls were called as a result of their smart remarks to the referees.

This incident was an example of the lack of discipline I faced the first day I arrived at Rockwall. All the work the prior spring, summer, and fall seemed to have had little effect. These guys were a mess.

Front row: Shawn Rose, Eric Moore, John Tyszko
Middle: Joseph Gonzales, Greg Hodges, David Frankenfield,
Curt Tyszko, Kevin Walker
Back: Coach Jerry Stone, Brad Harris, David Bach, Justin James,
David Walls, Nate Doudney

Their actions were unacceptable. **They were a team not used to winning and knew very little about dealing with it.**

As soon as we pulled up to our gym later that night, I told them to change to their practice gear. I heard them giggling. If steam wasn't coming out of my ears earlier, it was now. They had cheapened the image of our school and our basketball program by their actions and not one of them was aware of it.

They needed to learn a lesson. We did a lot of running—hard running—going past midnight. I'm sure I got their attention.

I never heard one word from a parent or an administrator regarding our "midnight meeting." I'm not sure why. And we never had a similar problem again.

I have several sayings I've repeated to myself over the years. **"Coaching is an endurance contest"** is one of them. Every stressful day you go through, an opposing coach is experiencing the same emotions. **Can you out-endure him?**

Another comes from Vince Lombardi: "Winning is not a sometime thing." You don't get to pick certain days to work hard and do things right. How players deal with practice is vital. The coach who can grind out tough practices on a daily basis while keeping spirits high will see progress. Constant improvement is all you can require.

The 1999–2000 Rockwall team was fun to watch. We were old-school in an era of "run, gun, and have fun." **We were the twenty-first-century version of *Hoosiers*. Rockwall High was Hickory High.**

With no shot clock, a coach's imagination is endless. We did a little bit of everything, which included holding the ball, if necessary.

The talent certainly wasn't the same as the Midland College national champs, but the style was very similar: same plays, same tempo, same five people starting throughout the year—great chemistry. Talk about *déjà vu*.

The Dallas Morning News specifically mentioned our similarity to the movie *Hoosiers*. We actually had some fans from outside of Rockwall who wrote to our team, explaining they really liked our style and came to our games whenever possible.

In *Hoosiers*, Myra Fleener (played by Barbara Hershey) says, "Basketball heroes are considered gods" in the little community of Hickory, Indiana. Basketball coach Norman Dale (played by Gene Hackman) responds with, "Most people would kill for just a few moments of being treated like a god." Her point was well taken—but, so was his.

We had similar Hickory-type players, right down to an excellent shooter named **Nathan Doudney,** our Jimmy Chitwood. **Shawn Rose** was our Ollie, a small determined substitute guard who seemed to come up with plays at the right time.

Curt Tyszko was a tough point guard who turned out to be a very fine leader.

Justin James was a six-foot-six kid who just got better every day. He might have been our overall MVP since his consistent fourth-quarter production in all facets of the game had a great deal to do with our winning.

We even had a kid with a bad attitude that came within a hair of being cut, but, as the movie portrayed, he wised up and became a solid team player.

Other than Nathan, none of them were considered Division I college prospects, but all were good team players.

I couldn't have been prouder of them. By Christmas, we were 17–1 and ranked near the top in the state. The town heard good things about us and followed us loyally all the way to the regionals in Waco. We ended up 33–2.

When a player doesn't see eye to eye with you, he may not be rebelling. It may be that he is simply not confident he can do what you're asking. Nathan Doudney, one of the players on my 1999–2000 Rock-wall High School team, wasn't a major-level athletic type but he was a major level shooter who we thought might get a look from the big boys. However, he played close to zero defense. When his defense hadn't substantially improved by the time the season started, I sat him out during the first half of an early first-semester contest.

Benching Nathan not only got *his* attention but that of the entire team.

What some coaches don't stop to think about is anybody who loves the game as much as a kid like Nathan can be made to play defense—maybe not in a fanatical way but enough to satisfy the coach. He wants to play so much that he'll do what he has to do. In Nathan's case, no coach had ever made him play defense and he *wasn't sure he could.*

Here's my point: When you are trying to make a player play defense during practice, and he's not cooperating, you may mistakenly conclude that he doesn't want to learn, so you become upset.

When the truth is he is afraid he can't do it—he's never been made to! Realizing that, your approach should be, "Come on, you can do it", encouraging him, not reprimanding him.

The problem was solved, as most are, by prioritizing drills (in this case, defensive) on a daily basis. Later when we played a game and dominated some other team with great defense, we began to see the light.

It was living proof that if we worked longer and harder than the other guy, we deserved to win and had a greater chance of doing just that.

During my first year at Rockwall High School, we played a pivotal game in the 2000 district championship against Plano

East. On paper, they were better. They actually had the game in hand. In desperation, we switched to a full-court press.

We got the ball to Nathan Doudney, and he hit a clutch three-pointer. Justin James came through in his normal fourth-quarter magic producing points and rebounds.

Finally, Shawn Rose picked off a pass and dribbled around like a rabbit trying to escape for six seconds until the horn sounded. What an amazing comeback. We were the visiting team, but our many fans stormed what looked like their home court. It became a spontaneous celebration.

The win was a special moment for that Rockwall team. Even though we had only one loss at that point for the entire season (Plano East, earlier in the season), it was the first time the guys really believed they couldn't be beat. It was finally becoming their team—a family feeling, maybe? Now we had a chance to do something. It sometimes takes a while for a team to feel that way, if at all. When it does happen, your tendency is to want to be in control. That's fine, but only to a certain point. **Allow your players to feel ownership if at all possible. Remember, you can contribute to building the vehicle, but they have to drive it.**

It was during my fourth year at Rockwall that Tim Brooks entered my life. One Saturday in the spring, a big man in his forties approached me in the club house of our local golf course. "Are you the famous Coach Stone I've been reading about the last two or three years?" he asked with a respectful smile.

I immediately began wondering where this was going. We chatted for awhile. He seemed very interested in the team, which can sometimes can be good and sometimes bad. Veteran coaches have seen quite a variety of personality from the local fan base. We're always a bit cautious.

I could have been looking at a wannabe coach, or worse, a sideline genius who would be glad to be on hand for some friendly advice during the upcoming season (whether I wanted it or not).

We both loved golf, so a friendship began to develop. He was a low handicap golfer—my main handicap was my swing.

This ex-offensive lineman with soft hands and a great short game had played football at East Texas State University, and I quickly learned that he was excellent at a game that I had only recently adopted. We mutually shared one of our good qualities: He was patient with my golf game, and I was patient with his barrage of basketball questions (which I actually enjoyed quite well).

Throughout the process of becoming friends, I realized that he was sincerely trying to learn all he could about basketball through a coach's eyes. I started calling him a "sponge." What really bonded us were all of the qualities I rave about in this book. Tim played four years of college football on two knees that would have forced most players to retire. He understands 100-percent dedication—right up my alley. Incidentally, his successful insurance agencies shouldn't surprise anyone who knows him. I couldn't have stumbled into a better friend.

Nothing's changed for fifteen years: golf, cookouts, discussions all over the map, and my integration with their family (wife Tammy, and sons Carson and Connor).

I'm like an uncle. More specifically, Tim started calling me "coach" from that first talk and it's stuck pretty much with everyone in Rockwall, allowing me to join the fraternity of retired coaches who are forever known by that simple phrase.

At the beginning of the 2003 season at Rockwall High, I decided a senior named Jason Jones and a couple of other teammates were not going to help our varsity team and varsity means the end of the line. I really didn't know Jason, and seniors that don't get to play can be risky when it comes to attitude, etc. If there are some good-looking juniors that appear primed for the varsity team, an inexperienced senior can be in an awkward spot.

It's wise for both of you to face the music now rather than later. Consequently, I brought them into my office separately to explain the situation. Jason was politely told that he was wasting his time. He looked me dead in the eye and firmly said, "You're not going to cut me. I love basketball, and I came out this year to play." His words were delivered with such force and passion, I privately thought maybe I should say, "Yes, sir." I thought, *Good night nurse. What's going on here? I'm the coach.*

Obviously, this kid was serious.

I've never made a quicker turnaround in my life. Any kid who had the guts to level me like that was someone I wanted on my team. I'm glad the young and stubborn stage of my coaching career was long gone. Jason's strong will jumped out at the right time. A kid with real determination? Sure, he can stay.

So, what do you think transpired? If Jason had been an obvious nonplayer, this story might have turned out ugly, and I wouldn't be telling it. Instead, Jason's positive spirit fueled his move up the ladder. *Wouldn't you know it, he eventually became a starter.*

He was one of those players I mention throughout this writing: usually, everyone has something they can contribute to their team, even if it's not glamorous.

As our defensive ace, he guarded our opponent's top scorer every game. The credit for his accomplishments belongs to him. I didn't have to build up his self-confidence. He already had it. **Basketball just helped bring it out.**

If a kid had some athletic ability but not enough true basketball skill, I learned to approach him from a different angle and dwelt on his character.

I would try to appeal to his exceptional desire, the kind of quality great defenders and rebounders possess. Almost every good team at every level of play has a player like that starting or coming off the bench as a sixth man.

Wichita State has the following inscription above the entrance to their basketball locker room. It speaks in very simple terms, defining the difference between great players and great teammates. It takes both to be successful.

> **"Great players help their teammates win games.**
> **Great teammates help their teammates win**
> **championships."**

When I get a chance, I enjoy telling stories similar to Jason's, stories that illustrate the preceding quotation. There have been other players I've been privileged to coach who have stepped up and demonstrated leadership qualities.

What's interesting is they all seem to view my telling their story as a necessary evil—they tolerate it. They act as though the story I'm telling is unnecessary, not nearly as significant as I'm making it out to be. Someday they will realize that most people do not possess their determination. Their modesty proves my point. They are special, and I would bet the farm they will do just fine down the road.

Double Overtime Sectional Victgory vs Dallas Carter high School,
2000 @ SMU's Moody Collosium

HALFTIME

My Coaching Career

1963–1965: McMurry University, Abilene, TX, Graduate Assistant Basketball Coach

1965–1967: Mexia H. S., Mexia, TX, Head Men's Basketball Coach / History Teacher

1967–1968: Amarillo Caprock H. S., Amarillo, TX, Head Men's Basketball Coach / History Teacher

1968–1973: Richardson H. S., Richardson, TX Head Men's Basketball Coach / History Teacher

1973–1976: Tarleton State University, Stephenville, TX, Head Men's Basketball Coach / Physical Education Instructor

1976–1977: Midwestern State University, Wichita Falls, TX Assistant Basketball Coach / Physical Education Instructor

1977–1987: Midland Junior College, Midland, TX, Head Men's Basketball Coach / Physical Education Instructor

1987–1988: University of Texas Arlington, Arlington, TX, Head Men's Basketball Coach ('87–'88)/Academic Advisor

1989–1999: Cameron University, Lawton, OK, Head Men's Basketball Coach/Physical Education Instructor

1999–2007: Rockwall H. S., Rockwall, TX Head Men's Basketball Coach

2007-2009: Rockwall Heritage Christian High School, Rockwall, TX. Head Men's Basketball Coach

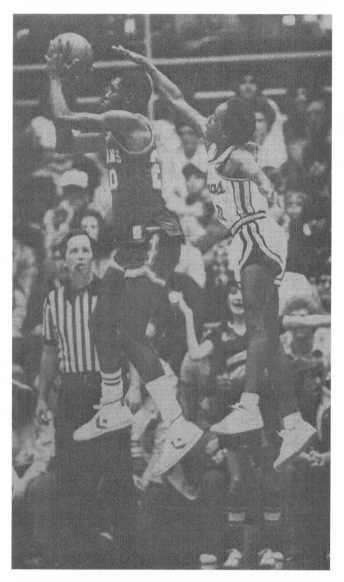

Spud Webb reaching for the block

Mookie Blaylock (left, white jersey) and
Lincoln Minor (right, white jersey)

Jerry's twin sister, Janet, their dad, and Jerry

Jerry playing cowboy

Jerry in his early days as a player

Jerry and his three sisters (Barbara, Carol, and Janet)

Midland College's Mookie Blaylock (10) crashes on top of New Mexico Junior College's Eric Kegler (20) in Hobbs, NM

III
THIRD QUARTER

COACHING ON THE COURT

7
RECRUITING

"There are no secrets to success. It's the result of preparation, hard work, and learning from failure."

—Colin Powell

The need to sign players makes it tempting to cross the line and recruit dishonestly. **Let me give you an example from my early years as a junior college coach.** Before the National Junior College Athletic Association instituted a National Letter of Intent, some clever maneuvering took place in the world of junior college recruiting. Another juco coach who had been an acquaintance of mine for many years used the following trick.

Early in the fall of the senior year, or even during the prior summer, a high school prospect would be encouraged by the juco coach to sign a scholarship agreement with his school. The coach would assure the player that there would be no problem if he changed his mind later—since the agreement would be non-binding, he would be free to sign with somebody else. There was no *National Letter of Intent* at that time, so most kids would think, "fine with me", and sign. On top of that, the coach told the kid to keep everything quiet and not tell anybody.

In junior college, most signings occur in the spring or summer immediately prior to the new school's fall semester because final grades and summer school results are, many times, still uncertain. When other junior college coaches come around to recruit the kid, not knowing he has actually signed earlier, they would suddenly receive a phone call, exclaiming, "Did you know that we have already signed him?"

The coaches who came late to the party, including myself, would back off apologetically. It never occurred to us there might be a bit of trickery involved. I never thought to ask *when* the signing took place or what the kid was told.

This happened to me by the same coach three times in two years. Each time, I informed the recruit that it wasn't ethical for me to attempt to sign him if he'd already signed elsewhere. The recruit always shot back, "But the coach told me he wouldn't hold me to it if I decided to go somewhere else." The first couple times this happened, it certainly seemed the kid was messing with me. Many did. Who would you believe, a well-respected veteran coach or an eighteen-year-old high schooler? The third time it happened, I drove to the player's house and explained to his dad what was happening. Since there was no National Letter of Intent, his son was free to go wherever he wanted. He then signed with Midland on the spot. I told him and his son to ignore whatever the other coach had said earlier and added that the coach most likely wouldn't be calling.

Again, I got a phone call from the coach who had conned the kid. As you might suspect, the conversation was different this time around—he got real quiet. After that, we remained friends—on the surface anyway—but his trick ceased to work on me. I always wondered how he felt as I apologized for interfering with his "signed" player.

He should have been apologizing to me.

Trustworthy coaches can help you a great deal. Seeking the advice of others regarding a recruit, however, is never a sure

thing. It's like asking a buddy when you're looking for a new car, "What do you think? Do you like it?" His reply, "I sure do. I'd buy it." It doesn't cost him a penny to give you an opinion, but it may cost you several pennies if his opinion is incorrect.

Your best friend—someone who would never lie to you—may not be a very good judge of talent. He may not understand the level of talent you face at your school. I've been burned by good friends who would have never intentionally wanted to hurt me (well, there was this one guy...), and once you sign a kid and involve Mom and Dad, it's very difficult to unscramble the mistake. You just need to do some backup checking before you commit. The good news is your instincts will continue to improve.

Your best opportunity to see talent in person is normally during the Christmas break, sitting in a drafty, partially heated coliseum located in some metropolitan area. There you will sit with all the other recruiting hustlers, watching high school games, one after another. Remember to bring your own Nyquil.

Coaches often tend to oversell their players. They want their players to succeed so badly they often don't tell the complete story about a recruit. It is almost like they are saying, "I'm not really sure how he'll do at your school, but if anything goes wrong, just remember, it's not going to be my fault—he was certainly a *good kid* (whatever that means) when I had him."

It was always inconceivable to me when a high school coach lied to me. Didn't he know he would be dead to me concerning recruiting any of his future players? Didn't he realize how fast a person's reputation travels? Also, it's unfortunate that a lot of high school coaches don't see junior college games. They don't realize the caliber of play involved. If they played in junior college, they usually know. Coaches don't have time to go watch other completely different levels of competition. It just takes a few years to begin to see and understand the big picture. Listening to a trusted veteran of coaching (which certainly involves recruiting) is a life saver, *if you can find one.*

Most high school coaches, along with parents, mistakenly feel if their prospect didn't get offers from a four-year program, he could ***always*** go to a junior college (I still hear that often, today). Quite the opposite is true. There are many Division I-caliber players in junior college. When I was at Midland, our scrimmages were almost exclusively against small four-year colleges. I don't remember losing to any of them. Our guys were lacking grade-point averages, not basketball ability.

Solid, reliable friendships develop over time. You learn quickly whom to trust. When you do find a reliable evaluator, treat him right and be grateful. At Midland College, I built a trust with five or six very reliable high school coaches in the Dallas/Ft. Worth area. By calling each coach periodically, I knew almost every legitimate local prospect. That's the type of help you need. It's a time and money-saver.

You learn quickly who can be believed in the coaching profession. This applies to the guys like myself doing the recruiting as well. How can a coach develop trust between himself and his player after deceiving him during his recruitment?

When you lie to a player, you are telling him he's gullible or even ignorant, and not worthy of fair treatment. You are stealing part of his dignity (remember, don't mess with a guy's dignity).

He may not have learned enough of life to explain how he feels but he knows something doesn't feel right. How are you going to be able to stand side by side with him, working to defeat the enemy? The recruit might make it through the season giving the disciplined responses of "Yes, sir" and "No, sir," but a voice inside him will be saying, "I don't trust you," and he will never reach his full potential under you.

When CBS televises the Final Four, the coach of a weaker participating team has a chance of a lifetime. If everything falls in place, he can become this year's coach of a "Cinderella" team. Suddenly, he's a prized catch for a more prestigious job, one that represents greater challenges and opportunities in every way. An increase in salary (possibly big) and a chance to recruit and coach elite players is suddenly staring at him. Schools hiring these seemingly instant success stories turn out about a 50% success rate—no one knows for sure how things will conclude.

Recruiting is the name of the game. There are hundreds of NCAA Division I, II, III, NAIA, and junior colleges frantically searching for players, knowing full well the lifeblood of their success depends on grabbing the recruit everyone else wants. Schools scramble every year, hoping to run across a "sleeper," only to have the prospect whisked away by a larger school's offer at the last second. When a kid signs with another school after you've spent half of your budget recruiting him, it hurts. It's depressing.

And if he has already verbally committed to you and your school, it's a killer.

Many of the young, enthusiastic assistants who did 90 percent of the initial recruiting of my players were quite energetic. If you had players, these eager subordinates would be all over you, pumping you up, buying you drinks and telling you everything you wanted to hear and a lot you didn't.

They would invite you to work their summer camps and give you their personal telephone number so you could call "anytime you want." Everything they did was in order to convince you that your player was top priority in their recruiting plans while failing to mention they were telling the same thing to a dozen other coaches.

How did I know? In the beginning, I was doing some of the same thing with high school coaches. It's something you learn to avoid if at all possible, but after you've been burned a few times, you start thinking about self-preservation. Kids (even their parents) that swear they'll see you in the fall, would end up in some other school. You felt betrayed and a little naive, so you started fighting back.

It didn't take long, however, to realize complete honesty was the secret to recruiting, I simply told them that I was talking to a lot of people and they were definitely interested. I only had a certain number of scholarships—first come, first serve. It was the truth, and it worked.

Though it sounds a bit shady, the four-year assistants were not con artists (well, a couple were). Most were great guys and just doing their job, mainly trying to find players. I loved being around them throughout recruiting periods. We had some late-night bull sessions I wouldn't trade.

Hearing the stories and the inside scoop regarding teams, players, and coaches were priceless. It seems the only real friends coaches have are other coaches. It's a fraternity—as long as you're not in competition with them, and even that is normally not a huge problem. When you realized the pressure these assistants were under, how they operated was understandable.

The Big Boys had slots to fill, and, although they were sometimes involved in recruiting skirmishes, their slots were often filled rather quickly with future draft picks or, at least, something very close. Sometimes their commitments came months in advance—often with amazing ease. The big programs receive recruiting help from all kinds of sources, the type most lower programs would never receive.

The lower programs were forced to settle for lesser talent. The Forrest Gump "box of chocolates" analogy would occasionally reveal itself, and they would be left with someone that could be described as a pleasant surprise or a big disappointment.

Each year when the players arrived, it was obvious most were green high school kids who had some growing up to do. With seventeen or eighteen year olds, you never knew what to expect— it was always about maturity.

Junior college talent is outstanding. JC players love the game and have worthy goals of moving on to bigger and better things. But, here's the catch: In my situation, both the kids and I had much to learn, ASAP. It was definitely a two-way street. It became obvious that tough, strong, and quick kids were what we needed to win at our level. They, on the other hand, had to quickly learn that this wasn't high school, and their off-the-court antics could result in serious trouble for them. *In short, they needed to grow up quickly.* The pleasant surprise was that the kid with the tough exterior from the tough neighborhood sometimes turned out to be one of your absolute favorites.

Example:

I really liked Kenneth "Big Time" Young. Try to follow this seemingly innocent friendly chat: One day in my office, he looked me straight in the eye and proclaimed, "You know, Coach, **I don't smoke and I don't drink, but I will steal."**

(I'll allow you a couple minutes to digest that one.)

How's that for honesty? For crying out loud, to some extent, you had to admire him. My immediate reply was, "So, that means you would steal from my office right now if I weren't standing here?"

"Oh, no, Coach. I would never steal from you," he replied with considerable concern and sincerity.

We talked further—I briefly lectured. Who knows the effect?

If I ever caught him in a "misdemeanor" lie (not a felony, mind you), he would smile and say, "No way, Coach." That usually meant some running—maybe a bunch.

I would quickly reply, "So am I going to have to worry about that now?"

He would say, "Hah." And he would mean it, *absolutely*. We would shake hands and never again would it come up.

You can look at what I've just written in a variety of ways. I usually chose to try to develop the positive and help eliminate the negative. You have a chance when they're freshmen.

I wanted Kenneth to stick it out at Midland—he had some work to do, but I felt he was worth it. He had a good heart. That's not always the case with one or two guys on your team— you know immediately. Some of them just don't fit in a college environment, and when they head home permanently, you're not surprised—recruiting doesn't always result in a success story.

After over forty years of coaching, I tend to classify people into two categories: those who have participated in athletics and those who have not. Fully aware this is an oversimplification, it's still my opinion that an ex-athlete is far ahead of the guy who hasn't dealt with the environment of sports, the required discipline, and all of the sacrifices necessary to remain on a varsity team these days.

Most young men and women with athletic backgrounds have a distinct advantage over those who don't. During the heat of competition, they've learned about themselves and others. They've learned to take the good with the bad, the wins with the losses. They've been held to standards of excellence on a daily basis, not just when they felt like it.

Many Americans—including professional athletes—are spoiled. And you don't have to be wealthy to be spoiled and self-centered. One personality trait that repeat offenders in penitentiaries have is believing, "If I want it, I take it." Should someone get stepped on in the process—tough. (They play by their own rules.)

There's no sharing, no caring, and no trust, which is exactly opposite of what most athletes learn from their involvement in sports. It's an amazing opportunity for coaches. If the players have been taught the right way and they've taken it to their hearts, athletes have a great opportunity to take these lessons and live by them for the rest of their lives.

Back to "Time":

"Big Time" was in a category by himself. To begin with, he was an exceptional athlete. After a basketball victory, he would suddenly explode into a multiple set of backflips straight down the middle of the court.

My initial reaction to seeing his post-game side-show was to call a brief one-on-one chat with him and remind him that gymnastics were for students at another place and time. The positive reaction from the fans, however, convinced me to change my mind.

From that time forward, "Time's" immediate post-game show was given an unofficial 30-40 second time slot, *provided we had won the game, of course.*

Let's face it, "Time" was basically a child who loved to demonstrate his physical skills on the playground.

I kept an eye on him while realizing the talent he possessed was real—he just couldn't keep it contained—guess you could say that he was a natural entertainer. Of course, his addictive personality was his true selling point.

These guys' endurance was equally remarkable. "Time" was the poster-boy athlete who played for me in the 1978–79 season at Midland College when our program was just getting to its feet. Beads of sweat seemed allergic to his six-foot-four, lean, athletic frame.

He was never a problem kid, though he sometimes couldn't find his classroom, which was understandable considering the Midland College campus included at least two classroom buildings—very confusing to a kid who's away from home, the tiny town of Houston, for the first time...:)

I was running him one day for that very reason. I always ran my players to a point of fatigue, then pushed a bit more if it were a disciplinary issue. Unfortunately, during this particular session, "Time" would not get tired—he could absolutely run all day. After around sixty line drills (most athletes can handle about twenty-five), he was still going strong. For a brief moment I considered suggesting he change his name to, "Never Tired Time." I kept looking for the bead of sweat, or the sign of, "OK Coach, you win." But, it didn't come.

I asked him, "You're not even tired, are you?"

He shook his head respectfully, "No sir," as he maintained a worried look that said, *I wonder what Coach's next move will be?*

My next move turned out to be ***unconditional surrender.*** "Well, I'm getting tired of you not getting tired, so get out of here." We were both heads down and grinning, as we headed for the door.

That's the way it was with Big Time Young. He ran the streets of Houston's fifth ward as a kid, yet was basically honest—go figure. Occasionally, he would volunteer too much information. Sometimes his logic was a bit puzzling—not for him, for us.

Every year, the Christmas holidays meant a nice break for all member junior colleges in the NJCAA. I very much appreciated it for several reasons. We worked long and hard during the fall— knowing a nice vacation was coming, there was no fear of a burnout prior to conference play which began in January.

There were two concerns during this period. My biggest one regarding Christmas break was: Did anyone fail to reach the requirement of passing twelve hours with a 2.0 gpa, the first semester? The other real concern was the fact there would be stragglers (or no-shows) expected to return to our campus, with legitimate excuses. That's why, if I wanted the guys to report back on December 28, I would tell them to be in Midland by

December 27, so if adjustments were necessary, we could jump on them. Some would still slither in on the twenty-ninth.

One late return was unforgettable. "Big Time" had a buddy, Carl Lee Runnels. He had also signed with us—both were from Wheatley High School in Houston, where they had won a state championship the past year. Their first Christmas break, the two of them showed up back to Midland two days late.

When I met them at the Midland Airport, they didn't know what to think. One of our managers was usually assigned to that duty. Coach Stone being there could indicate trouble.

The reality was I was just happy they had *returned*. Sometimes it wasn't just the classroom, but the entire city they couldn't seem to locate.

Straight-faced, my first comment was, "What happened to you, get snowed in?" (I was joking—snow in Houston is extremely rare.) In unison, one said yes, and the other said no.

They looked at each other. "Big Time" disgustedly snapped back, "Well, it snowed at my house."

They were both from the same neighborhood. You cannot make this stuff up.

I had always felt that junior college was a God-send for kids just like Kenneth Young, that's if the coach knows what he's doing (as a new coach, it took me about three years to get a handle on the situation—keep in mind, however, I started from ground zero). Two years of meaningful, but realistic academics, some much-needed social etiquette, and a strict daily athletic discipline—all together, these things can be very helpful for a young man like Kenneth.

Where is he now? I have no idea. I hope he has had some good breaks along the way.

As a junior college coach, I often recruited kids who were excellent on the basketball court but had not been serious about their education. You may ask, Why?" Because if they were talented and had the grades out of our school, they would go to Div I schools. Consequently, it was important that a transformation process begin as soon as possible. People don't change easily.

The sad truth was, as a junior college coach, you had to bite the bullet and go after some of your players that were probably going to have some trouble in the classroom. Setting up help in these classes was imperative.

They could do alright if they wanted it, which most did.

In most cases, it was the first time a recruit fresh out of high school had been away from home, away from his family, his old friends, that sweet little girlfriend, and all things familiar to him.

Much of what he is suddenly separated from can be a good thing. He'd realize it by the time he completed that first semester, and experienced the month-long Christmas break at home. If it required the second semester, so be it. He would be pleasantly surprised to realize that his new "home" at college wasn't such a bad place after all. There would often be a transition, sometimes a very noticeable one.

Big players were great, but always came at a high price. In many cases they were spoiled, having been treated like gods since they were in junior high. I didn't even like being around some of them. If the people around the big kid—the coaches, the parents, the peers—were level-headed, he had a very good chance to succeed. But for every person who helps keep a guy straight, there are usually three who don't.

Who is going to sit a potential NBA prospect down and tell him what he really needs to hear regarding his future—stay humble, continue learning and improving, keep up your school work, be respectful to everyone at all times? And who knows if he's even listening?

If the parents aren't available, he may listen to his grandmother. But there was no guarantee how long.

Since everyone else wants in on the spoils, they're careful not to step on his toes and continue to tell him what he wants to hear. He soon refuses to turn away from the things that can really mess him up.

The peer pressure is so powerful. I can tell you many stories of having a kid heading in the right direction, when *one weekend* with the homies will change everything back to the philosophy of the hood—he doesn't have much of a chance.

The shoes, the chains, the hair, the clothes, and sometimes even a car may become more important than the game that got him there. Above all, the *attitude* can turn—now it is serious. How many star-struck kids have gone down that road? They are too inexperienced to see things as they really are. Having been told over and over how great his future looks, it can be a shock when the future doesn't turn out as it's been forecasted. Many talented athletes have gone by the wayside because they haven't had proper guidance.

Too little parenting and sometimes too much parenting,

especially from a dad who wants to relive his athletic days through his son, can hinder a solid upbringing. Strong, level-headed family members are the kid's best chance. A kid with no role model to receive advice from is a kid with two strikes already on the scoreboard.

A strong and honest coach is their best chance. The truth is, it may be his last real chance. I tended to gravitate toward the players who had something to prove. Add that to one with a decent upbringing, and you've got a good candidate. In my experiences, Spud Webb and Ricky Grace were two excellent examples.

But, truth is there's no way to predict—I'm always surprised who stays and who goes.

I had one uncompromising motto to live by as a coach: **Never Lie to Your Players or Recruits.**

There should be no need to make that comment, but look around these days. When you violate that principle, you and your program will eventually suffer from it. When someone on your staff doesn't adhere to the same standard of truthfulness, everything you are attempting to build can fall apart.

Such an occurrence nearly wrecked a championship season.

The following are two totally different examples of dishonesty—The first is obvious. The second is a coach's feeble attempt to convince his team that they are someone that they most definitely are not.

The first, unfortunately, still remains alive and well:

The original team members on my 1981–82 squad numbered eighteen. Sixteen of them were freshmen. We signed eight or nine of them from the Delta states. High-energy athletes away from home for the first time need to stay busy. Some coaches have an ease-into-it philosophy. I didn't go that route. I wanted to get their attention before some pretty girl did. Normally, it was a close race. We began practicing immediately so idle time would not contribute to mischief. Besides we were in a race against the clock. These kids only had a semester to get it together and *grow up*. Once conference play was in full swing in January, you needed to know whom you could count on.

During one of our early practices, we were running a simple layup drill in preparation for one of Stone's "perfect" practices.

As we increased the intensity with a more advanced drill, a couple of the recruits weren't having anything to do with it. This reaction is typical for first-semester freshmen.

At that early stage, they haven't learned to rise to college basketball standards—meaning, to go twice as hard as they are accustomed to.

I was patient with them. It's hard on young guys being away from home for the first time, coming all the way to West Texas. But it was clear these two were not planning on stepping it up this morning—a rebellious look is not difficult to read.

One of the rebels was a big post man, a talented kid whose brother had once been in the NBA. While watching him for over a week, engaging everything with a "50 percent attitude", it was becoming tiresome.

Yelling out, "You need to stop acting like a baby," hit a nerve with him. His reaction was quite the opposite of what I wanted.

He remained moving at half speed, but his direction changed, straight toward me.

He was visibly shaken and not smiling. I'm here to tell you, as his six-foot-eight, 240-pound body got closer to me, he looked like anything but a baby.

I stood my ground and showed no fear (at that early in the year, you really don't know what some of your recruits are capable of). The situation was uncomfortable to say the least. He needed to understand that calling him a baby was only a coach's method of gaining his attention. I told him he obviously wasn't a baby and he had good cause to be upset with me. Unfortunately, nothing said was registering. His demeanor remained unchanged. You could hear a pin drop. (No doubt, the team was taking mental bets as to the outcome). Have you ever seen a steam locomotive slowly climbing a steep hill? He was so mad he had difficulty breathing.

I was just about to promise him a starting spot for the entire year—heck, I was ready to throw in my personal car for him to cruise around in—when he finally calmed down. Everyone was glad to see it.

My calling him a baby wasn't appropriate, but my choice of words was not the real issue behind his anger—the big man was dealing with something else. I had no idea what it was, but, with time, I was confident he would relax and fill me in. As it turned out, he never did.

We got through practice, and later went into the weight room to finish our workout. I waited until my talk could be private to reassure him all was well. Sitting down and chatting individually with all new players was a normal annual routine.

My talk with him hadn't occurred yet because a couple of his high school teammates had joined him at MC—he wasn't here on his own.

It was also assumed that his relationship with my assistant, who recruited him, was solid. He was one recruit I wasn't worried about, already having friends with which he was well acquainted. However, his mood still didn't budge after our one-on-one talk. He was very unhappy and frustrated. Something else was going on.

The next day he and two of his buddies had vanished. I never saw them again. It's not uncommon for freshmen that far from home to end up AWOL. The reasons can be numerous but usually it comes down to plain ol' homesickness. When you're away from your mama, your family, and people you know, it's easy to wonder, "What am I doing here?"

They don't realize that going through this slow, lonely first semester is like a tonic for your maturity advancement—in reality, it's one of the best experiences you can have when you look back at it . (Try telling that to a homesick freshman from Tupelo, Mississippi).

Going back home only provides temporary relief—being in a new place can be uncomfortable, but the pluses far outweigh the minuses if you can hang on.

In his case, I couldn't blame him for the frustration he felt. He had been misled during recruitment—apparently some promises had been made. By the time everything was unraveled, four or five others had departed. We never had a chance to discuss any of what had happened, so I can't honestly say what did. But, I've seen it happen many times with other schools and other coaches. It's very easy to do—an 18 year-old who's been nowhere in his life can be conned, unfortunately.

Those are the very lessons coaches have to go through—there are many—before they can comfortably feel that things are reasonably in good hands. When a player (recruit or team member) doesn't feel 100% safe and protected while in those hands, something is wrong, and needs to be corrected. The moment you become their coach, you also become a surrogate parent and mentor with other important duties, away from the basketball court.

Midland had developed a solid tradition, one that each new player was ask to keep *alive*. Most new recruits adopted it well. We coaches had pledged to their mothers to keep a close eye on their son—we did a better job after that one incident.

However, even if zero mistakes were made in the recruiting process, all those players might still have gone home. You just never know. We started the year with eighteen players and ended with nine.

My second example of dishonesty:

I'll never forget a preseason scrimmage my Midland College team had against an NAIA team one Saturday.

Even though freshmen made up 90 percent of our team while 90 percent of our opponent's roster were juniors and seniors, we gave them a thorough thumping.

Dejection filled their locker room as they dressed and awaited their coach's post-scrimmage speech. I got a glimpse of the atmosphere as I walked by on my way to the bus.

As I saw it, the coach had three options:

1. He could methodically explain what was needed for improvement.

2.   He could strongly state his disapproval with their performance.

3.   He could say nothing and drive the team home.

Instead, he went by the book (Stay Positive) and dove right into: **"Now, when we go to the nationals . . . ,"** When I glanced into their locker room, I saw disgust, frustration, and a lot of eye-rolling. After being beaten by junior college freshmen, **no player believed a word his coach said. He stood in front of his team in the preseason and, although he didn't realize it, lied to them. He lost an enormous amount of credibility that day and the season hadn't even begun.**

If a big-time college comes after one of your players and you are unsure whether he will fit in or not, what do you do? Do you keep your mouth shut?

We finished fourth in the 1985 NJCAA Tournament, losing to a strong Moberly, Missouri, team which included **Mitch Richmond**, who would move on to Kansas State before spending fourteen years in the NBA. Nobody remembers a team that finishes fourth in a tournament, but they do remember outstanding players.

Teviin Binns—to everybody he was "Yo Tev"—was tall and slender, a finesse player who preferred to play in the high post area where he could shoot more uncontested shots and play a non-physical game.

He was listed as six-foot-nine-and-a-half in the tourney program, but, after his impressive tournament, his reputation—and apparently his body—grew.

Overnight, the word got out there was a "seven-footer" who could play and was *unsigned*. A "seven-footer" doesn't necessarily mean he's seven foot—it means he's *tall*.

Here came the recruiters. When it's late—for Division I, springtime is late—it's the head coaches who take a much bigger role in the initial recruiting.

The time factor requires it. In the spring, a big man may draw scholarship offers from everywhere. Suddenly, we had North Carolina State, Maryland, Seton Hall, Missouri, St. Johns, and a bunch more, chasing after big Tev. Teviin was recruited more than any basketball player I coached in my ten years at Midland College.

One of Teviin's hot pursuers was the colorful Maryland head coach, **Lefty Driesell**. Lefty met me in his hotel room one afternoon during the 1985 Final Four in Lexington, Kentucky.

We sat down at a small table in a room that looked like three high school boys had been staying there—dirty clothes, food, and towels were everywhere. It all made sense if you knew anything about Lefty.

He was like a big ol' country boy, full of energy, whose motto was, no doubt, "Let's not sweat the small stuff." I liked him immediately—most people do.

Lefty discussed all the reasons Teviin should come to the University of Maryland: the school's location being close to Tev's New York City home. the strength of the ACC Conference, playing with NBA players in the parks in summertime, and being close to D.C., the nation's capital. While he talked, I noticed he had a card propped up behind a small lamp.

He had trouble pronouncing Teviin's name—everyone did—

and visually checked the card every time he said "Teviin," hopefully without my knowledge.

He wasn't successful. Each time he pronounced Tev's name, it sounded worse. The expression on his face was priceless. He was also doing a lousy job of peeking at his cheat notes.

If Lefty had admitted upfront how difficult it was for him to pronounce "Teviin," I would have agreed wholeheartedly. Anybody else would at some point openly laugh at himself and admit, "I'm never going to get this kid's name right." But not Lefty. He was going to plod on through. If I were in the same situation today, I would have bailed him out. However, in those early days of coaching, I was a bit cautious when engaging with such a notable character.

After twenty minutes, our interview ended. Lefty—who would eventually coach over forty years and be inducted into the Basketball Hall of Fame—had probably delivered a similar sale of his program so many times he could do it in his sleep.

We shook hands outside his room and I headed down the hall. About twenty feet away, Lefty wasn't through recruiting—I heard my name and turned around. I found myself in the middle of that award-winning Coca-Cola commercial with **Mean Joe Greene**—Joe had stopped the kid and tossed his jersey to him.

Lefty winked, and, with a smile said, "Hey, Jerry, help me out, will ya?" If he had thrown me a dirty towel, heck, I might have tried to sign, right there in the hallway.

I said, "I'll do what I can," all the time wondering what he could do with a recruit if they were together all day. It might be hard to say no to Lefty Driesell. He was a classic.

NC State, however, was also knocking. Because they had signed Spud two years earlier, they were comfortable with the Midland program and came after Tev. They saw him at his best in the recent nationals at Hutch where he had hardly missed a shot. He was a tempting find for a big school.

However, I was fearful of the route Teviin was taking. I knew him well. He was a big ol' unsure kid. I didn't know if he would fit in at North Carolina State or any top-level school. I felt his slot was at a mid-major school. But when a big-time basketball school wants you, it's virtually impossible to say no.

Mid-major schools start looking rather inept. Big-time recruiters, especially their assistants, say what the family and the kid want to hear—not lies, just the truth shaded a bit. Once the family gets involved, nobody wants to hear from the kid's former coach.

Teviin would have listened to me, but it's doubtful anyone else would have, which is quite normal.

What parents don't understand sometimes is their son has changed a great deal since high school. A junior college coach has basically raised their son the past two years and bonded with him. If he is conscientious, the juco coach will not lead their son astray.

"Yo, Tev"

I could have enlightened the State coaches regarding Tev's personality and work habits but the truth is, no one knows how a kid is going to fit in at a new school.

I certainly didn't have any foolproof information that would make the decision a no-brainer. I did tell assistant coach Tom Abetamarco of my uncertainty. He said they felt all right with him. Everybody seemed happy. I stopped worrying about it. Teviin signed with the Wolfpack and played off and on under Jim Valvano.

He was never comfortable there and slowly became a non-factor. Some players have to be constantly encouraged, almost like the way a grandmother would do it. That was Teviin. A national champion coaching friend told me if he tried to coach Tev, it wouldn't have worked out. He would have run him off within a couple of weeks.

He then added, "But you can coach him because you'll hang in there with him and bring him along."

It was true, I would be more patient with a kid like Teviin, but only because he didn't have the personality to mislead teammates—he was worth the gamble. And you can't coach a kid to be 6-9 or 6-10—they have to show up at your door that way.

Truthfully, there are never any guarantees.

8
PRACTICE

*"What you ignore in October
will haunt you in February."*
—Mike Mitchell

Throughout my career of forty-plus years, I had a slogan printed across the top of my practice schedule. It was with me during every practice. Occasionally, I pulled it out and walked over to a team member who was not giving his best that day. Without saying a word, I pointed to that slogan at the top of the schedule. It was a reminder to me and the players, **"Games are won on the practice floor."**

Enough said (rather, in this case, not said).

Positive play can be taught and learned. Winning doesn't have to wait on luck, but it's not something you can take for granted. If you prepare to win with every ounce of commitment in your body, you still may not reach the pinnacle. Too many variables await. By staying the course, however, you will discover that good things will occur—hard work does pay off, and it will for you.

There are many teaching opportunities that go unrecognized every day of the year by well-meaning people. Young athletes are waiting to be fed. But, often, we don't oblige. We seem to present the same menu that's always been served. Then we wait and hope things will work out.

When you have prepared properly, there is no need for hope.

Do not wait for anything or anybody. *"If it's to be, it's up to me."* You have to go get it, yourself.

Your sincere enthusiasm to work with each individual player for the development of a cohesive team is what must take place—the players will look to you and follow your lead. It's a tremendous responsibility. If you don't understand it, they won't. You are their teacher.

I was almost as keyed up and nervous 30 minutes before practice each day as I was 30 minutes before each game—not quite, but almost. To me practice was dead serious—it was the only real time for **learning for the players** and **teaching for me**. I wanted nothing but 100% of the players' attention—anything less, I took personal. My philosophy was, "I'm giving all I have—you had better do the same." Of course, there was always someone that didn't quite feel like it—I had no sympathy for them. They were messing up the team's plans regarding that spring trip to Hutchinson, Kansas—you know, that garden spot of our junior college basketball world.

Picture this: As the game is about to begin, your opponent walks to the jump circle. He feels an unmistakable uneasiness in the pit of his stomach. It cannot be passed off as simply butterflies. Unfortunately for him, it's more than that.

At the same time, you walk to the jump circle. Any twinge of nervousness will soon disappear. Because of consistently meaningful practices, you are prepared to win the contest. Your single compelling thought is, *Bring it on."* **That is why you**

must have good (great, if possible) practices. Because when it's game time, you may be excited, but you will know you're prepared.

Basketball encompasses skills similar to those in many other sports. A pressure free throw in basketball is very much like a pressure putt in golf. What Stephen Curry of the Golden State Warriors does from twenty-five feet on the basketball court, Jordan Spieth of Dallas, Texas, must do from twelve feet on the eighteenth green of a PGA event. A quarterback must see the entire field and read the defense as he moves his team toward the goal line much like the point guard does as he moves down the court. Tennis movements are made up of quick starts and stops plus numerous lateral slides, which are identical to movements in basketball.

Totally different. Totally the same.

Regardless of athleticism, in basketball a player and a non-player are miles apart, and it doesn't take long to distinguish between the two. If a guy can jump over the moon, but it takes him four nervous steps to do it, "Houston, we have a problem."

As famed UCLA coach John Wooden said, **"A basketball player must execute all of the skills required of any other sport, with one exception. He is required to dribble a basketball while doing so."**

In my mind, the only way to teach is the *whole-part-whole* theory of learning. Within the first three weeks of practice, our players were introduced in shell form to 75 percent of the entire offense and defense schemes we planned to use during the entire season, including our press attack, our zone attack, out-of-bounds plays, etc. With the over-view fresh in their minds, **the breakdown drills we used in practice made more sense** because the team understood how the drill related to the big picture.

How many times do young people run drills all year long and don't have a clue regarding their correlation to the overall scheme of things? Again: Details—the coach should be constantly checking where his players actually are, intellectually, and not assuming anything.

The way you practice is so important. You push and drive them further than they believe they can go, right? If you see that they are giving everything they have but are still discouraged, it may be time to walk up and say with strong conviction, "I'm very proud of your effort. You're going to be fine." They'll pause, blink, and even give you a slight smile, as they realize, "The guy that's been on my back for the last few days just paid me a compliment."

Sit down with them when possible and explain the method involved in the madness. It often does wonders for a confused first-semester freshman who feels as though he can't do anything right. I remember distinctly how confused and frustrated I was that first semester in college. I was crazy about the game and thought I was a good player—that first year made me begin to wonder. Often, a freshman just needs some reassurance.

As a coach, you need to maintain an honest connection with your players, especially since you're overseeing them so much of the time.

How you correct a player is very important.

Ask yourself, *When I stop a young, immature kid during practice to correct him, what is he going through emotionally?* You may be surprised to discover he sometimes doesn't hear a thing you're telling him. *His embarrassment and frustration distract him from what you're saying.*

I'm not saying don't embarrass him. He may *need* to be embarrassed. For some personality types, this is the best approach. He'll get over it. What I'm saying is be aware you might have to have a brief private chat with the player after practice or before practice the next day to reiterate what you were trying to tell him in the heat of the moment (when his head was spinning).

If you've been consistent with your observations, you may have already determined that he is the type who doesn't handle public criticism very well.

Explain to him that correcting him in front of the team is standard procedure and not to take it personally—you're not criticizing him personally but coaching him like everyone else on the team.

If the kid understands what is taking place, he'll feel 100 percent better. I always started practice by saying a few words. I'm not talking about the history of basketball, but just a reminder that **"What we do the next two hours here will determine what we'll be doing the last two weeks of our season." (I really like that one).**

My best practice and game talks were based on my thoughts, not Mike Krzyzewski's. Young coaches make a mistake when they read a book and then try to copy what another coach does or says. I've known coaches that even try to *sound* like some well-known coach.

It doesn't work. Your philosophy needs to come from your

beliefs and your personal feelings, straight from your heart. My brief pre-practice talk might have dealt with any subject, but the underlying theme was always *we are going to have a great practice,* with emphasis on what I believe is important.

One Saturday morning, my message didn't seem to be resonating with my '83–'84 Midland College team. It was January and cold outside—the auxiliary gym was always cold during that time of the year and that time of the day. Though they were told to do so, I'm certain the players hadn't eaten anything. Since there were no games soon and I hadn't set any curfew, I'm also sure most had been out half the night with the young ladies and hadn't had much sleep. Being cold, hungry, and sleepy didn't put them in the mood for Stone's "great" two-hour workout. Trouble was waiting right around the corner.

The vibes I received while standing in front of those fifteen basketball players were not good. What I saw was unhappy talent. Most were on full scholarships at a beautiful school with one of the most fantastic basketball facilities in the nation.

They were in a program that was annually ranked from tenth to first in the country, and often in the top five. Yet they were looking at me as though someone was abusing them.

About then was the time I viewed my team as *the enemy.* I was about to express my sincere displeasure when Alvin Dunson caught my eye. He was sitting in the group, eyes glued on Coach Stone, anxiously awaiting the "great practice" promised minutes earlier. He could hardly sit still. Here's the catch: Alvin was like that everyday.

A walk-on from Midland, this lowly freshman seldom saw the floor during a game but was genuinely thrilled just being part of the team and part of every practice. His nonstop energy prompted Reggie Franklin, my assistant, to name him "Snicker," the name of my equally hyper schnauzer at home.

I addressed my so-called "All-Americans" while pointing at Alvin and saying, "He has more character than all of you gentlemen put together" (slight exaggeration). I mentioned the consistent effort and attitude Alvin brought to the gym every day, no matter the circumstances. Whether he received playing time or not, he always had a big smile. I summed up by saying, "Alvin actually inspires me with his spirit and enthusiasm." (That was not an exaggeration. Sometimes the coach isn't real crazy about being there,either).

Whenever I talked straight from the heart like that, holding back my emotions was difficult. I've always had a soft spot for the overachiever. Everyone gave me his full attention. The sophomores had learned to sit real still when Coach Stone started in that direction. They had advised the freshmen, "When Coach gets that look, one of two things is going to happen. He's either going to get through it in a couple of minutes or he is going to throw something—so don't move."

With my message received and after a couple more reminders, we *did* have that "great practice."

But let's be realistic: the entire two hours of practice can't be a pep rally. **Certain mundane drills have to be repeated every day. Basic fundamentals can never be ignored.** There are some drills that not only do the players dislike, you may not like either.

A block-out drill in practice is not much fun, but reminding your team to block out at half-time of every game isn't much fun either. It's a waste of time. A short and lively block-out drill can be survived by everyone—that's the secret. Or maybe have them go half-speed every now and then, just to maintain the *habit* of turning into your man and keeping him from getting that offensive rebound.

Some would say that professional athletes don't need fundamental drills—they're pros. Just the opposite is true. Whether these guys know it or not, the only thing that makes many of them "professionals" is their salaries. **Don't mistake raw talent for fundamentally sound basketball players.**

The reason Michael Jordan was the elite player in the history of the game (my opinion) was that he was fortunate to be around some of the very best teachers of basketball. I'm not overlooking what he contributed himself: tremendous talent, along with the most tenacious will to win we've ever witnessed. He had the best of both worlds: his coaches, Dean Smith and Phil Jackson, and himself.

If you want to win, you have to do certain things. Just remember, the other coach may be letting things slide a bit. He may, however, be working his tail off. **Don't ever let the other coach outwork you—it's an endurance contest, remember?**

I have visited many basketball practice sessions throughout the years, including those of some elite programs such as Kansas, Duke, North Carolina State, Oklahoma, Oklahoma State, and Texas Tech, when Bob Knight was head coach. I've also watched the San Antonio Spurs practice as well as the Chicago Bulls, thanks to a friend who pulled some strings.

Here's what caught my eye:

Not every coach had a whistle or a horn going off for the purpose of moving to the next drill. A large squad, as with football, where particular offensive and defensive groups are taught specific techniques, there's a need for one basic practice clock to move everything along in organized fashion, but not so in other sports.

In basketball, all drills shouldn't be timed. Here's why: The perfect teaching moment cannot be predicted during a drill. No one knows when that incident will reveal itself. *What if it occurs at 4:58 of a 5:00 minute drill? Question—Do you really want to switch drills when the horn goes off at 5:00? No way.* Wouldn't you like an extra two or three minutes to complete your teaching point? Or to repeat something over and over? It may seem disorganized, but those extra minutes might just be your best teaching period for the day.

If the right teaching time is now, you should take the time to explain it **now**. Otherwise, what should you do? Wait until practice is over and by-pass "the moment of truth?" Should you save it until the next day so today's perfectly scheduled practice won't be interrupted?

When you are in control of the entire squad, it's much easier to practice what I have described. Sometimes we coaches do things a certain way because we've seen someone else do it that way. There's no need to, unless it's the best way.

One of my better points was not overlooking details. We wanted to be smart if at all possible. I wanted them to read and understand situations, not memorize them. If someone threw a surprise trap at us, we shouldn't be surprised very long. Our instincts should take over. Instincts are possible if they learn to observe the entire floor. Always know what's going.

My way of saying it in practice might be, "Don't look at your shoes!" (That seemed to work).

I didn't worry about over-coaching at the beginning of a season but made sure my players understood why it was going to take place. My teams expected to be stopped quite often during the early practice sessions to point out the good, the bad, and the ugly.

However, I promised them, **"When things improve—and they will—I will get out of your way."**

If I hadn't explained the reasons for the constant interruptions, they would have gone nuts. The road is long and the time is short. If your team wants to be successful, each player has to allow you to teach them every minute of every day. But, it's important that you explain what and why you do things a certain way. I think that is important—you want them to be aware.

The longer you coach, the less you will worry about your opponent. **Avoid mentioning specific names of upcoming opponents prior to your season.** No matter what your point is, the message your players receive could be, "Coach seems kinda worried about them," which, unfortunately, they will not forget.

Experience will bring you to this simple conclusion: every year, prepare your team for everything—you simply can't avoid it. If you want your team to enjoy real success—that's playoff success—you do not have the luxury of skipping over areas that aren't fun to deal with or areas that don't seem all that important. If your particular district doesn't have a team that full-court presses very well, practice five-on-seven full-court twice a week anyway. You don't know what kind of competition you'll face in the playoffs. Just like Mike Mitchell said, **"What you ignore in October will haunt you in February."**

Focusing on fundamentals during the preseason is especially important for incoming freshmen. Most have been allowed to run up and down the court with no conscience while in high school. They know little about fundamentals or team play. They're often confused and discouraged.

Sometimes, it seems as though they're not playing the game they've enjoyed their entire life. They think, *"What's with all these drills? Why does he keep stopping and talking? I just want to play. I know how to play this game."* **But, truthfully, they don't.**

They have to learn how to stop and listen, something they're not used to doing. **You'll have to train them—you'll have to understand that at this moment, they are the enemy—their attitude is trying to tear down what you're gradually building.** It takes patience. You'll wonder if it's worth it. But when your team turns out smarter than those other teams, it will make you proud.

At some point, usually around Christmas, those fundamentals will become second nature to them, a natural part of their game. By February, they won't even remember all the steps it took to get there. They'll just be having fun and winning basketball games. When a sports reporter asks one of them, "Why the successful turnaround?" he won't think about mentioning all of those fundamental drills he was forced (by YOU) to do every day in the fall. He's more likely to say, "Coach finally saw the light and started letting me shoot more."

You gotta' love 'em.

Travel can wear a team down, too. Living in Midland, Texas,

we were accustomed to long-distance trips because of our location in West Texas. As a young college coach, it didn't take me long to realize traveling—by whatever means—was important, especially in the non-conference portion of the season. A traveling team has obstacles a home team doesn't. It can also make the team a stronger unit. That's the main reason a coach will subject his team to it. A more mature, experienced team has an easier time handling the road. A coach with a young, unproven team may not want to venture out too far, too early. **The road can also destroy confidence.**

Early games and tournaments are an excellent opportunity for coaches to get a glimpse of the type team they may have. What adjustments seem necessary will jump out at you—that's why you drive the van to East Texas and play in an eight team scrimmage all day Saturday in October. A few non-conference games can reveal surprising results too.

Against different competition, coaches can identity the team members who are "practice" players and those who are "game" players. Bench warmers may demonstrate a side no one knew existed. During an early game, it isn't uncommon for a head coach to whisper in an assistant's ear, "I've never seen that before," or, "Where'd that come from?" Something happens to a certain type of player when the lights come on. It's as though he's been energized by some video game force he played while traveling on the school bus to the game. At the same time, someone who shines during practice may disappear when confronted with actual game pressure.

As games are played, starting lineups and substitution rotations change. **Winning early games is nice, but figuring out who**

needs to be on the floor for the upcoming conference play is what's important.

The team you put on the court during preseason may look quite different by midseason. Every team has its own chemistry and personality. If it turns out positive, you can be grateful. In actuality, you have little control over it. If it happens, it seems to happen on its own.

Despite the possibility of burnout, anyone who coaches or plays the game of basketball comes to understand that **practice is a sanctuary, a safe haven from what's going on outside the gym.** By concentrating on the game they love, coaches and players can escape female problems, money problems, schoolwork, grades, and all the troubles of the world for a couple of hours. There is no better example of this than what happened to our team on November 22, 1963.

I was a graduate student at McMurry College when we got the news that **President John F. Kennedy** had been assassinated in Dallas, Texas. The initial mood on campus was shock. It soon turned to fear as rumors spread that **Texas Governor John Connally,** who was also shot, had died, and that **Vice President Lyndon Johnson** had suffered a heart attack. Confusion reigned.

The world seemed to be coming to an end.

Events scheduled for that night were canceled. Football games were either moved or completely canceled. I was supposed to sing with another student in a talent show that night, but it was canceled. I'll have to admit, there was a certain amount of relief because we weren't prepared. Basketball practice always took place at 3:00 p.m., and I was sure it would be canceled. I was wrong.

When I heard practice was still on, my first thought was

that Coach Hershel Kimbrell was being coldhearted. Cynical is the best way to describe my feelings when he had our athletic director, Pete Shotwell, talk to us beforehand.

Shotwell was a retired football coach who had become a Texas legend by taking three different high schools—Abilene, Breckenridge, and Longview—to the Texas State Championship and winning, a feat that has yet to be equaled.

Mr. "Shot," as we called him, made his address to us short and simple: "What do you think President Kennedy would want you to do? Just stop everything and sit around depressed?"

I didn't know about practicing—I was questioning it in my mind. Later, I realized the two coaches were right. After running up and down the court like a herd of antelope, we all felt too tired to worry about it at that moment. When practice ended, a quiet peace was in the air. We all felt that everything was going to keep going. Everything was going to be all right—another lesson learned.

My favorite method of getting players' attention was utilizing **Coach Stone's "line drill"** (inherited from Coach Kimbrell). It was used throughout my coaching career and it never failed me. It was the only drill we used that didn't involve a basketball. It was fast, efficient, and economical—it was tough, but fair.

Originally, the line drill was used for conditioning. It gradually evolved into a strenuous disciplinary drill. **It seems that each year, every team has to be shown that their coach means what he says. It's vital that a team get that message as early as**

possible. Just make sure all your ducks are lined up first. Usually, one such session is enough.

The drill was essentially a nonstop sprint from baseline to baseline with a few turns in between, always sprinting, not running. There is a difference. Each sprint had to be completed with every line touched, and each sprint was timed.

I controlled the watch, and if I saw great effort, the exact time didn't matter to me. If the effort was lacking, more running would be required. I just wanted them tired. The entire scenario was a test concerning effort and attitude, a trait that the team had to develop and learn to live by if winning was going to take place.

Consequently, it didn't matter to me how many sprints were initially run. All I was looking for was the "breaking point." I wanted to see what they would do when the gorilla was firmly clinging to their backs. After more running and occasional bouts of protesting, they would end up pretty well spent, wishing they were anywhere but there.

Now was when they needed to hear from me. As their coach, I needed to know what to say and how to say it. These times are priceless. It's important to take advantage. Find the middle ground between toughness and understanding. Sometimes they need to simply be reminded why they were having to run, while other times they need to be scolded. If the effort was there, perhaps a compliment was in order. But, be assured, **they will always take note of how you treat them during these uncomfortable moments. They're dead tired and you've got the hammer. If you say to me, "It's just not my personality to be mean," stop right there. You're not being mean; you're being fair and you're being firm.** If you really care, you won't allow these young men to miss out on the joy of 100-percent dedication.

There won't seem like much joy at the time, but it's actually a positive experience. And, as I keep saying, "Someday, they will thank you over and over."

While they recuperate, mention an appropriate story, one that gives additional support to all of which you are attempting to communicate. I would have them all sit up against the wall to assure they were listening.

Something like: In the fall of 1992, after a Kansas University basketball workout (the second one that day), I watched a few of the Jayhawk players running extra sprints as a result of mistakes charted by managers during that practice. By the way, no one died of lack of oxygen—in either practice.

One of those running was a seven-foot post man from Duncanville, Texas, named **Greg Ostertag**. Unfortunately, he had a lot to do, which is hard on big men. Without one word from the coaching staff, who had already left the floor—something of which I don't approve. Why? Because the moment the head coach vacates the scene, it's importance decreases 50%. If the players have to stay late, a coach has to accompany him, if possible. And the higher up the coaching ladder, the more meaningful it is (think about that one). Sometimes it can't be helped, but when a leader acts as though he, "feels your pain", and routinely heads for the door as you begin running the required 100 laps, how can he feel your pain running when he's driving his new car out of the parking lot? *All I'm saying is share the good and the bad with your team as much as you can, especially when they're young.* Later on, when they begin to mature, it won't matter so much.

Two teammate guards joined big Greg, spontaneously running

and verbally encouraging him during the ordeal. As far as I could tell, no one had instructed them to assist their teammate. Their sole purpose was to *help* him get through the day. I would wager that those two teammates wouldn't have thought of that gesture during their first year at Kansas University. I would bet they grew into that type maturity. *Oh, the things you learn in athletics.*

It was a thoughtful example of leadership. Those are the type opportunities that can lead to positive team unity. That's what you're looking for from your players: while they're dead tired, they're thinking about how a teammate is doing. That's unselfishness—it's called leadership. Don't mistake this situation as a minor incident.

By the way, no outsider is in the gym during line drill type sessions. This is a family matter. No one gets to sit in the stands and laugh at our expense. And I won't be putting on a show for some of the boosters who like to pop in to watch the coach embarrass his players. Truth is, I never enjoyed that part of coaching at all—but, it had to be done—I had to learn that. **I didn't like spanking my two daughters, either.**

Somewhere during the preseason workouts of athletes, players need to successfully experience that point where pain and perseverance shake hands with one another. For me, this is the drill that helped accomplished that.

In terms of building courage and confidence, timing line drills may be the single most important activity you lead them through during the entire year.

The players may not realize it at the time—they seldom do.

Consider this: Who usually wins the highly contested event when all else is even? Isn't it usually the best conditioned athlete, the tough guy who's learned to never give up?

After completing the line drill, the guys were free to stagger back to the dorm. I found it interesting that about a third of them ended up in my office instead. Why, after all the running and lecturing from me, did these same worn out young men just happen to "drop by" before heading to their rooms? The typical response was something like, "Just to chat." That spoke volumes to me.

I did not believe their main reason was to butter me up—their crime had been absolved. Instead, I always felt they were really saying, "I'm with you on this one, Coach. You're doing what you said you'd do. I've never had to run like that. I didn't really know if I could." Having successfully completed the line drills gave them pride and confidence. They were thinking, *You know what? I think we're going to be tough this year, and I want to be a part of it.* What had seemed like a negative was turning into a positive.

One more thought: it kills me to see a kid quit before he's pushed through the barrier that some well-intended person, at some time, had placed in this youngster's subconscious. You know, the adult who said, "When you're tired, young man, stop! You might hurt yourself." How much better it sounds when that same kid pushes himself to the limit and realizes, "And just think: I was about to quit."

While playing golf these past few years, at some point my playing partners would discover I had coached all my life. Most enjoyed discussing their athletic days. (I'd usually rather concentrate on golf.) They would become excited, remembering the great times with their teammates and coaches. Most males love sports—no getting around it.

What's interesting is that the previous line-drill discussion and all of its ramifications is *exactly* what they loved to talk about. Each one had a similar story and relished the chance to tell it. It's because they were so grateful they went through the hardship and survived. It gave them confidence. It made them proud—it still does. (Sometimes, the spouse struggles with this a bit.)

Practice sessions should not be unpleasant experiences, nor should they be like recess in grade school. Though there is plenty of hard work that needs to be done, the players should have real joy in what they do. Some days, this is impossible. However, if you can create *small feats of accomplishment* in your practices, or at least put them in a position where you can say, "Great job fellas, great job," they will be more productive. **They need to look forward to tomorrow's practice.**

If something funny happens in practice, have a brief good laugh, but don't prolong it. There's a big difference between being happy and being silly. Your players need to learn the difference.

The younger they are, the greater the challenge. In fact, with young players, don't even let it get started. Young kids, especially if they're in junior high or even high school, can create an atmosphere of silliness that hangs around a practice too long. Immature kids can instigate such moods without even trying. Having fun without becoming silly is very difficult for them.

When you join in their fun, you send a false signal. It may take you half of the practice to get them refocused. They just don't know when to quit.

You will quickly learn not to go there.

In contrast, if you want to see chemistry in action, picture the 1982 NJCAA championship team. They were unique. That team of eighteen players had shrunk down to nine by Christmas time and finished the tournament with only eight. These guys knew each other like the back of their hands. They very much knew their roles and proved their toughness many times throughout the 1981–82 season. When I say tough, I mean mentally tough. These guys were finesse players, not physical specimens.

This was the most versatile team I ever coached during my entire forty-plus-year career. They could press, fast break, and spread out and stall with Spud Webb out front with the ball.

They could free-lance, run numerous offensive plays with interchangeable positions, and force zone defenses to come out. They could also run several different defenses, full-court and half-court. To top it off, Spud was virtually impossible to trap anywhere on the court. This team was smart, which made them confident and poised under pressure.

I worked the '82 team very hard, even practicing twice a day on weekends in the fall. I just about wore them out, and they, in turn, almost did the same to me.

Some of the players may have thought those practices were overdoing it, but I felt that if everyone survived those sessions, they would be hard to beat. Even though, to this day, Spud Webb half-jokingly says I took five years off his professional career with my preseason workouts on a tartan-surface court, I believe the players were proud of what they went through. Because of all the workouts, they felt they could go all day, which was important since you had to win four games in five days to claim the NJCAA National Tournament title.

The ultimate reward for that group of guys was four wins and a championship in Hutch. Those kids were always out-manned. But it proved the boot camp they survived during the fall was all worth it. And again, I didn't concoct anything that created their beautiful chemistry. It was in their DNA.

In many ways, I was their biggest fan.

9
DEFENSE

"You can't wait for inspiration.
You have to go after it with a club."

—Jack London

To love defense, you have to have a competitive nature as part of your DNA, and *I loved playing defense.* Defense is the great equalizer. I loved disrupting a good player's evening on the court, especially one who was arrogant or highly regarded. A chip was on my shoulder, and, most of the time, it was an asset. Glancing at the opposite end of the court while warming up, I tried to develop a touch of animosity (to say the least) toward the guy who was to be my man. It was just my way of being ready every time I suited up and he never knew it. It really wasn't personal . . . well, maybe a little.

A secret: The first five minutes of the game is vital. Much of the atmosphere is established during that time. The best approach is to completely shut him out, then never back off. You can have your man frustrated real quick. He will start to feel out of sync and irritated. Do not take your foot off his neck.

Don Valliere, my high school basketball coach at Arkansas City High, should get a good amount of credit for my love of the defensive side of basketball. I enjoyed guarding people before entering high school, but Coach Valliere confirmed its importance. He was not only the first coach, but really the *only* coach, I had who possessed a passion for defense.

Coach Valliere was an excellent fundamental coach and taught me a great deal about the techniques of individual and team defense. The individual motivation came from me. It must come from within you if it's going to succeed throughout the year.

We all have certain personality traits that, in all likelihood, came from our youth. The chip on my shoulder was a result of two distinct occurrences in my life: the lack of affection (real or perceived) by my parents and the uncomfortable fact that I was lucky to even be playing basketball in college, a game that meant so much to me which had almost betrayed me after my senior year in high school. I couldn't even get my local junior college interested in me.

Consequently, as a college player and during most of my forty-plus years of coaching, I was highly concerned with proving that I belonged. I completely understand this now, and when one understands it, he can smile at himself. **It's not life or death. You can get through the highs and lows of coaching.**

If you don't understand it, this "must win" obsession can bring on a certain amount of misery to yourself and those around you—it can also, temporarily, bring great joy to your life. A few of those years may bring this same euphoria to an entire community or state, for that matter.

One night, while playing for McMurry College, we found ourselves at Midwestern State University in an important conference game with playoff implications. That night I used a tactic that I wouldn't consider advisable. As we lined up at the jump circle, I walked up to my man, and, almost nose-to-nose, without a word, said nothing. I planted my foot squarely on his toe and looked him in the eye.—**I do not know why I did it—it wasn't planned.**

Johnny Carroll was a well-built, six-foot-four, 210-pound, very athletic power forward. He was an excellent player and could have retaliated with a great game, along with an elbow to my gut anytime during the night. I was fortunate that he didn't. Looking back, one could call it an example of "friendly intimidation." What he projected, as we looked at each other for about three seconds, was a puzzled expression. He was confused—**then he blinked.**

Advantage Stone.

I'm not sure I can account for my actions. I do know that prior to the tip-off, I thought to myself, "*This guy is good. He's bigger and stronger and has the ability to crush me.*" In a split second, I decided to put up a friendly front, as if to say, "You don't scare me."

Call it naivety, but, on the basketball court during my entire career, I never was afraid of my opponent's retaliation. Let's face it: a college basketball game is not considered a dangerous setting for amateur athletes. You can play aggressively as long as you keep it clean. *There's a fine line between aggressiveness and poor sportsmanship—my behavior that night was debatable.*

You must decide for yourself how your actions will be judged. Just remember to never back down from *aggressive play*—you cannot be afraid to win.

I played with confidence that night and we had success, winning a big game on the road. I didn't allow Johnny to get going—he was a non-factor. It's important to understand, however, that one game is only one game. During a basketball season, there's no time to gloat over any one victory.

Developing poise and overall awareness—seeing the big picture—are important factors for any team's success. I mention awareness because many players spend a great deal of time involved in a sport but cannot draw one single play accurately on the chalk board. If you ask them about the basic alignments and assignments of others on the team, they can't tell you.

During a game, who is doing the scoring on the opposing team? How is he scoring? The players I remember who were able to answer those types of questions were few in number.

Coaches must train their team to be coaches on the floor. The players should always have their minds zeroed in on what's taking place on the floor, not how pretty they look in their uniforms.

Can you answer this: What is the most significant segment of your opponent's game plan that you can disrupt, thereby hampering their chances of victory? What's the one thing they rely on offensively and defensively? Think about it: Why should the players be unaware of those questions and the answers to them? **Educate them. Help them be the smartest team on the floor.**

There are so many possibilities to aid in snagging a victory—just look around. I have never been able to understand how a young man could play this relatively simple game all of his life and be so unaware of the actions around him.

In every endeavor, knowledge is power. Everyone would agree. Athletes who observe and respond have obvious advantages over their adversaries.

Players shouldn't have to wait for their coach to point out what's going on in a game. You should know why your team has failed to score the last three times down the floor. Your coach shouldn't have to call a time-out and explain everything that's happening. Ignoring the coach's instruction is not what I'm suggesting. Rather, be aware of what and why he's giving such instruction. Help your coach and team win the game.

One simple example: This occurred when my man (their top scorer) repeated a particular maneuver in a college game in which I played. With-in a short period of time, I noticed a trend. After my opponent received the initial pass from the point guard, he always returned it and immediately crossed to the other side to screen a teammate. It was their normal method of initiating much of their offense. It became clear that every time he screened away, he basically took himself out of that series, offensively. As I've often mentioned, I loved denying my man the ball on defense.

But in this case, allowing him to catch it amounted to his *disappearing* to the other side of the floor, giving him almost no chance to score. I didn't do this every play throughout the night. I didn't want him to figure out what was happening. He and his coach never noticed or made any adjustment, helping us to win.

I should say that swinging the ball to the off-side is very common now, meaning the teammates on the opposite side of the floor are very much involved with most teams.

That was just a simple illustration of paying attention to what was taking place. Some teams might not present an opportunity such as that, but most do. **Every team has a weakness that can be exploited. Be on the lookout for it.** Don't wait for somebody else to point it out. But also don't declare "the sky is falling" on the other hand.

Another excellent example of observing and reacting is one particular game in which we were one point ahead with around ten seconds remaining. I was certain the opposing team was prepared to throw the ball in from the mid-court area to their All-American. There would be little we could do to stop him (by all accounts, he was NBA-bound). He was good enough to get open, head toward the goal, and finish it off with a field goal or a couple of free-throws.

We huddled up. I didn't believe any two of our players could contain him, so how about three? I felt he had one big flaw that might allow my strategy to work: *this guy was arrogant and selfish.* I was pretty well-convinced he would not give up the ball, no matter what. My players liked the idea immediately. *Without fouling, I wanted him aggressively triple-teamed the second the ball hit his hands—**without fouling!***

I did not want him having room to square-up and face the basket. He was capable of beating all three of our defenders.

Well, I assume you know I wouldn't be telling this if it hadn't worked.

He couldn't believe what hit him. He forced a drive (as I felt he would), lost the ball, and we won the game.

It worked perfectly. The risk factor did make it exciting.

I should explain: I am not here to tell "war stories."

My purpose in relating the individual triumphs of guarding certain players is twofold: Anyone with average abilities can contribute mightily to the success of their team if they **never accept fatigue and observe what's going on.**

There is such a thing as one's "second wind", which you've heard about forever—you *can* push through barriers that have always stopped you in the past. And likewise, don't ever let anyone discourage you from who you are deep down. If you persevere (there's that word again), much can be accomplished.

Remember, "It only takes *you* to believe it." An occasional boost of confidence from someone certainly helps, but it may not come very often. **Everything you need is inside of you.** Lean on your *spiritual* side.

That's what's inside you. Did you not know? I didn't for years, but it's never too late.

When someone, even someone that loves you, says, "You're probably not really cut out for this," you can respond one of two ways: Hang your head and tell yourself, "*I guess they're probably right*", or you can realize what's been said, and allow it to be used as a *springboard* that inspires you to prove just the opposite.

When I first mentioned my intention of writing this autobiography to a coaching friend of mine around ten years ago, another coach happened to overhear and ask me, "So, you're going to write a book about your life, huh?" **He couldn't control his laughter.** He had barely known me at Rockwall High School, nothing prior. *That image never left my mind.* There were days when I thought this entire project was a waste of time, and then I remembered his words and his attitude. Need I say more?

Consider this: Do you think Spud Webb could speak to this? Can you imagine how many times he heard, directly or indirectly, "What are you doing out here?"

This is not a Hollywood script we're dealing with or some magical dream. It's you, or your son, or your team that needs to know what is real and what isn't—what he or she is capable of doing. And what you experience as a player, a parent, or a coach when you see or feel the joy that subsequently, follows, will be quite enough to keep you focused on the prize.

I feel obligated to pass on what I have learned, and that's why this book is so important to me.

The definition of "total-denial defense" or "maniac defense" is a 100% commitment of one man sticking to a player whom the opposing team depends on, usually for scoring.

This will greatly decrease their chances of winning. A big part of the strategy is to let the player know this early in the contest, (by your actions, not your words.)

"I'm going to drive you nuts for forty minutes. You will not be prepared for my tenacity. I'll get tired, but you will too, and because I do this every night, it won't bother me. I'm anxious to see how you will react to it. Good luck, my friend."

These are the keys to **total-denial defense:**

1.   **Except for rare occasions, don't try full-court denial defense.** There's too much room for your man to get open or for him to be screened by a teammate. However,

don't wait too long. Start guarding him seriously (3/4 pressure) by the time he gets to mid-court. Personally, I would stay nearby all the time, anywhere on the court, during dead balls or live balls. During a timeout, I would try to be waiting for him as he broke from his huddle. **Think that didn't get on his nerves? Fight through screens.** *If he's dribbling in his shooting range, go over the top of the screen, not behind.* Going behind gives him too many additional opportunities.

2.   **Keep in mind, everyone on your team is not denying his own man.** You will receive help from them, on and off the ball.

3.   **Try to *never switch*. Switching means your man may be free for a while.** When I played defense and switched, by the time I got back to guarding my man, he might be feeling comfortable. I never wanted him to have any positive feelings that entire night.

4.   I wanted him to wish he had never suited up for the game. (He could have faked an injury.) It made my job twice as hard when he returned to me after some weak-hearted teammate had let him get happy again. **I basically had to start all over.**

Coaches should keep an eye open for that "sleeper," the kid whom we all have hidden within our team, ready to contribute. He's ready to be your *maniac defender*. There's always a guy who doesn't seem to have any outstanding offensive basketball skills, but during practice each day the team he's on *always seems to win*. That's your man! It won't be difficult for him, and he'll love doing it. As their coach, you've got to give him a chance. It's been my experience that he often completes the puzzle, helping to create the "chemistry" we coaches are always attempting to discover.

That first fall semester at Richardson, 1968, as I previously stated, we simply had too many seniors. Some decent players ended up being cut, a case of being at the wrong place at the wrong time. One particular player, **Joe Longino,** posed a problem for me, as well as himself.

He was 5'8" senior, possessing average speed and quickness. In a normal year he would have been an asset to one of my teams—his great love of the game was demonstrated largely through his defensive play. I felt that his playing time, however, would be very limited.

I ask him to help me with coaching—he did, and with the same great attitude. I must admit if I were placed in that position today, I would decide differently. Kids with that type attitude seem to find a place to fit in, if given a chance.

Years later, as the athletic director at Rockwall High School, 1999, he took the first steps in getting me hired as the head basketball coach at the high school. As the new athletic director, Mark Elam confirmed it shortly thereafter, while Joe took up new duties as a junior high principal.

I always encouraged young players to experiment with this defense during practice. We had a "maniac" defensive drill to help players become comfortable with the denial position. No one allowed his man to catch the ball. I stood to one side and threw rather weak passes to four moving offensive men. I wasn't allowed to throw a lob or a "bullet" cross-court pass. It was specifically a "deny and recover" drill. If you knocked it away, your teammates cheered. If he caught it, you ran a sprint, up and back. You begin to understand that you are capable of controlling your opponent, "killing the giant." It's an excellent confidence-builder. The secret? Accepting fatigue and pain—something of which anyone's capable.

Here's what you can count on: After an actual game, when playing in this manner, you will be tired—and happy. Your opponent will also be tired—but he won't be happy. **Plus, he will remember your name.**

One of the best defensive players I coached at Midland College was **Vernon Coleman,** a six-foot-two, strong, tough competitor from Paschal High School in Fort Worth. He was very aggressive and loved to play defense. He could have been a defensive cornerback, or perhaps even a middle linebacker for some college football team.

It's rare to have a basketball player with a football mentality on your team. Football-tough kids usually lack true basketball skills unless they are exceptional athletes. Despite what some people believe, basketball is a physical game, especially at the collegiate level. Consequently, I love kids like Vernon Coleman.

Vernon had the stamina and drive to play defense. He enjoyed making a great scorer suffer. He had a way of destroying an opponent's offense because he seemed to be everywhere. This guy loved his job. When he guarded people, he actually smiled.

Vernon's value to the team was exemplified when he was selected the MVP of the 1985 Region V Tournament based strictly on his defense. Very rarely do defensive efforts receive that kind of recognition.

Perhaps the best thing about Vernon was his dad. Geno was a big man who looked you in the eye and told it like it was. My assistant Reggie Franklin and I liked him immediately after hearing him say, "Now, if you ever have any trouble with my son, just let me know." That's like music to a coach's ears.

I never had one ounce of trouble with Vernon. I wish we'd had a couple of Vernons every year. He had the perfect disposition for athletics. He loved to compete and hated to lose. Vernon ended up going to Wisconsin-Eau Claire, an NCAA Division II school, on scholarship and did well. They liked him for the same reasons we did at Midland. He now coaches in the Flower Mound school district in DFW. I'll bet his guys hustle.

When I coached at Midland, we used multiple defenses. As we prepared for different defenses during preseason, I believed it was smart to add them to our arsenal. Besides being able to apply them ourselves, we weren't caught off guard or confused by them when an opponent used a particular one against us. In the middle of a three-day tournament, preparation time is limited. In our case, there were very few times the defense we faced wasn't one we actually used ourselves, or hadn't already seen in a game.

Most trapping defenses require solid trapping techniques and proper retreating angles. However, once you learn them, almost any full-court or three-quarter-court press can be taught. If you have plenty of quickness on your squad, those presses can sure make you smile.

To close out games at Midland, we used a unique half-court matchup defense we called "13." If our opponent was behind with time running out, "13" presented them a look with which they were not familiar. Simply put, it was a defense that was very difficult to penetrate. Thirteen was often a savior. Most of the time, we only used it when we were ahead. If we were behind, all they had to do was spread it out and play keep-away.

The 1987 NJCAA Tournament quarter-final game against our old nemesis, San Jacinto, was one of the greatest contests I've ever seen at any level. (The Ravens had kept Midland from reaching the tournament in 1983 and 1986 in interregional playoffs.) Coaching in it made it even better. No. 1 San Jac, the two-time defending national champs, were 34–0 and riding a record 71 game winning streak.

Our Midland College Chaparrals were 31–3 and ranked No. 9. Both teams from Texas were loaded with Division I talent, including a few who would later go on to play in the NBA.

This game rivaled the '82 Championship game. The game was close throughout with several lead changes. With twelve seconds to go, we held a one-point lead. San Jac had the ball on the sideline at their end of the court.

We huddled up at our bench and tried to figure out the best way to prevent the Ravens from scoring. Percentage-wise, the safe bet was to go straight up man-to-man. Almost every coach does this because it leaves no doubt about who's defending who, as well as clarifying rebounding responsibilities. Since man-to-man would be the normal call and what San Jac would expect,

I decided to go with our unorthodox matchup defense "13" because we had run it all year in similar situations and had experienced much success with it.

I was about to mention this in the huddle when a need to be cautious grabbed me. San Jacinto was so talented it was a risk to leave anyone unguarded. Consequently, I changed my mind, telling the players to play man-to-man.

Billy Ray Smith, a freshman from South Garland, Texas, who had said about six words to me all year, interrupted me. (His mama had raised him to be reserved, but he wasn't that night.) Completely out of character, he butted in by saying, **"No, Coach. Run Thirteen."** I'm not sure Billy understood all the points of strategy involved, but the look on his face and the force with which he'd made the suggestion gave me no other choice. I immediately agreed.

In our "13" defense, **Lincoln Minor** stole the ball and took it to the other end of the court. Lincoln always liked to add a bit of flare to his game, so I was half-expecting him to miss a dunk attempt that would bounce high off the rim and into the hands of a San Jac player who would put up a half-court shot to beat us at the buzzer.

Instead, Lincoln made a basic layup any junior high kid would take. The Ravens immediately called for a timeout, which they didn't have. Todd Duncan, as always, casually (without ever taking a dribble, as was his style) hit two technical foul free throws to sew up the Chaparral win.

Every time I see Billy these days, I remind him of how he spoke up at the right time.

Defensive strategy at Rockwall High:

Sometimes you have to employ a defense that will contain an outstanding scorer who no one individual on your team can handle by himself.

My 1999–2000 Rockwall High School team had just beaten a good Dallas Skyline squad in a sectional game and were about to face **Dallas Carter High School**, the third-ranked team in the state, at Moody Coliseum on the SMU campus.

Carter High had some fine talent, including some who would become Division I players. Among them was **Andre Emmett**, a six-foot-five, 225pound star who would later set the NCAA Division I, Big 12 individual scoring record while playing for **Bob Knight at Texas Tech.**

Disrupting Emmett's normal offensive routine wasn't possible with one man. We decided to go with a **box-and-one defense**, which allowed the middle defender to face-guard Emmett using any legal tactic possible to slow him down while the others on the perimeter of the box helped out when needed.

The goal of the middle defender was twofold: do not let Andre Emmett comfortably catch the ball and limit his dribble penetration. *In essence, be an absolute pest.*

I used five-foot-nine sub Sean Rose and six-foot-three Brad Harris to defend Emmett in the box-and-one. When one got winded, the other took over for a while.

There are four important points I stressed to my players when dealing with a quicker opponent: (All instruction is in general terms)

1. **When denying the pass of someone with real quickness, give yourself a little more cushion.** Do not

overplay as much with someone who can burn you going back door. (This is important.)

2. **When guarding a ball handler, realize that your first responsibility is to contain him, not to steal the ball.**

3. Avoid reaching against a good ball handler. You can flip at the ball with your trail hand, as long as the direction of the flip coincides with the direction you are moving.

4. **He is definitely quicker, so be content with never allowing him to dribble around you**. Always anticipate moving backward. Give a little more room than normal.

The strategies were successful that night. Emmett only managed twelve points, which had to have affected his teammates' morale since he was the heart of their team.

The game went into two overtimes before we won. It was a major upset.

Afterward, I remember feeling very fortunate and saying to myself, "I sure don't want to play them again." I thought about how this Rockwall team had transformed during the year. In the preseason, it was literally me or them. They did a lot of complaining to their parents because they couldn't figure out why I was so darn picky about everything.

However, they began to figure out by the second half of the season that it was going to take everybody being on the same page, playing smart with poise to beat our opponents.

By Christmas, we were pretty solid and beginning to understand how to win and not just how to play well. That night against Carter High, the kids showed some early nerves, then settled down and played some very savvy basketball.

We looked like a team with a purpose and played well together.

It was the only way we could come out ahead. Today, I see players who want the easy way out. They want everyone to notice what they do individually. Sometimes they use antics designed to get everyone's attention.

I understand a brief emotional display, but "pointing to the sky" and pounding on one's chest after something as magnificent as making a three-pointer seems like a stretch.

Shouldn't he be looking for his man or surveying the floor as he retreats to a defensive predetermined area? The point is the second you score, you are on defense.

Playing defense seldom brings proper recognition your way. In fact, there may be only two people who will be aware when you have done a good job defending: *you and the guy you guarded.*

If your defense helps your team win a game, but you receive little recognition for your effort, will the team-win be enough for you?

Great defense is about more than great hustle. People tend to equate good defense with that very thing. When your parents yell, "That's OK, good hustle", several times during a game, that could be a red flag. Hustling is only half of it. An out-of-control hustler is going to get in foul trouble and/or make numerous mistakes that hurt his team. If a young player hasn't had that explained, he may become confused and discouraged. Quite often, unfortunately, that is the case.

Playing good defense means discipline. It involves moving at angles, knowing where the ball is at all times in relationship to your man, knowing how to get around screens, always staying balanced, knowing when to be nose-to-nose while guarding someone, and when to temporarily give (if in doubt, move backward) to maintain defensive angles and containment. The battle is won as a result of the accumulative individual skirmishes that occur during the course of a game. It's up to the coach to see it gets done.

A lot of coaches don't feel totally comfortable demanding the necessary effort from their players when it comes to defense because, if the truth were known, (don't tell anybody) *they never did it themselves. They actually do not know how it feels.*

Don't feel like doing the work, Coach? Hey, get them into a zone. They'll like that. That's what they've been doing all summer during AAU games.

I had a junior varsity coach who occasionally sat down and drank a Coke during our practice. What do you think we thought of him? It wasn't good—in this case however, a short discussion was all that was necessary. He wasn't even aware of the message he was sending.

Playing half-court backyard basketball (that's about all we had) has advantages and disadvantages for developing one's game. Full-court play helps acquaint you with making outlet passes for fast breaks, filling lanes, three-on-twos, two-on-ones, and defensive transitions. We didn't have much of that.

However, half-court basketball demands you learn how to play one-on-one offensively and defensively. You become accustomed to the triple threat—shoot, pass, or drive—and the pull-up jumper. Half-court backyard basketball taught me many fundamentals.

Most importantly, it requires you learn how to block out. When we played in someone's backyard or driveway growing up, there was no big post man hanging around the basket to take care of rebounding.

Blocking out during rebounding is the last phase of defense.

Blocking out is a lost art today. To me, it is the most underrated skill in basketball. It is a skill that can determine who wins and who loses, yet it's seldom mentioned by commentators. Effort and perseverance is necessary to keep your opponent off the boards (that may explain it).

A player who is pinned by his defender has difficulty maneuvering to get into rebound position. If he is consistently blocked out, he may become worried about getting hurt (though it very seldom happens). After a while, he quits trying—it just takes too much effort to battle for the rebound.

I once had a well-known Division I coach come to Midland for the purpose of evaluating Spud's junior-college play. He hung around, watching two pre-season tournament games. We did a lot of visiting. I asked him what he felt Spud should improve on in order to play at the next level. He said that Spud's defense was too inconsistent and that, because of his size, he should be stuck to his man like glue for forty minutes. I didn't say much (I would now), but the truth is, my thoughts were a bit different.

I've always felt there are times when a little man, closely guarding the passer, will be taken advantage of by easily throwing over him. Because of Spud's size, I felt he needed to be totally unpredictable. I wanted him to mix up his pressure defense and play it instinctively.

Spud always gave his opponent false security for the first five to ten minutes of the game. He was sizing him up. Halfway through the first period, Spud pretty much knew what was available and what wasn't. He had been observing. He was always a pass or two ahead of everyone else.

I would have done him an injustice had I insisted on him playing basketball the "normal" way. *Spud Webb wasn't normal.*

There was one more important factor that one might overlook. Versus presses—versus everything—Spud had to handle the ball 99.9 percent of the time for us. Unfortunately, he was our only ball handler. His playing denial defense would have worn him down. We couldn't afford that.

Tuesday, March 3, 1987
Midland Reporter-Telegram

Lincoln Minor, seeming to be everywhere

Another such player was **Lincoln Minor**, who played for me at Midland College before signing with Kansas University in 1987.

Every once in a while during a game, if the opposing point guard brought the ball up the court deliberately, Lincoln would trail him while constantly flicking at the ball. Since nobody guards the point guard from behind, the dribbler was not prepared for this tactic. He would become uncomfortable and have difficulty concentrating while his attention was drawn to Lincoln and his long arms.

This was all Lincoln's idea. I didn't discourage it, but he was told not to overdo it and to realize that the back court was the only time for this unusual maneuver. It was one of many creative maneuvers Lincoln and his teammates were allowed to do. This is a great example of allowing your players to think and create. Defenses can be fun—smart fun, not stupid fun.

If you can get your players to carefully observe (most don't, initially), they can play intelligently. *Some players have great instinct and timing.* They know exactly when to fly off and double-team the ball, basically on their own. (Just the mere threat of this surprise attack can unnerve a team at times.) These types of players can help you win. *Always maintain that only certain individuals are allowed to participate in this, and only at certain times.* The best I had at that was probably Mookie, Spud, and Ricky Grace.

The single factor that makes me most proud is when I look out on the floor and see a smart team wearing our school

colors. That means all of the detailed hours of practice have not been wasted.

It's a thing of beauty.

One Sunday morning during the summer of 1963, driving from my Kansas home to Cushing, Oklahoma, an idea struck. The trip took me through Oklahoma State University in Stillwater, where **Henry "Hank" Iba**, Oklahoma's version of Kentucky legend Adolph Rupp, coached successfully for thirty-six years. Everyone referred to him as "Mr. Iba." On the spur of the moment, I looked his name up in a public phone book (you do remember phone booths, don't you?) and was surprised to find it listed. I called his number and was even more surprised when he answered. Unbelievable.

I explained my position as a graduate assistant at McMurry College and wondered if we could join up sometime and talk basketball. When he snapped back, "Where and when?" It was one of those deals when you felt compelled to ask, "Is this really Coach Hank Iba?"

Pushing it a bit, I answered, "Because I'm just now passing through, this very moment would be perfect for me."

Well, I guess it was my day because he came back with, "I'll be at my office in ten minutes." As I hung up the phone, I thought, "*This can't be this easy.*" Our conversation lasted for almost two hours.

Afterward, Coach Iba gave me game film to study the following week. There were no DVDs or videotape back then. The next Sunday, I drove back to Stillwater, where we met again in his office. Our discussion centered on questions I had after studying his tapes.

This was repeated four or five times that summer—just Mr. Iba and myself in his big office. It was hard to believe he was being so generous with his time since he really didn't know me.

Mr. Iba had a reputation for being very stern. I had always pictured him as having a bulldog demeanor: someone who would never say good things about his players and who would never smile. That image was totally wrong. I felt honored to be in the presence of this basketball icon. I was treated with great hospitality.

When Coach Iba learned I had played against **Luke Jackson** of **Pan American University** in Edinburg, Texas, he really got interested. He was preparing for the upcoming 1964 Olympics and was in the process of assembling our USA basketball team, which, at the time, did not include professional players. He wanted to know my thoughts about Luke. I could see no reason to omit big Luke from consideration because he was very intimidating, and a rugged defender and rebounder. Coach Iba eventually did choose Luke on that '64 team, along with Larry Brown, Bill Bradley, Jim Barnes, and Walt Hazard. They won the gold.

Years later, while at the 1988 Final Four in Seattle, I ran into Mr. Iba in the lobby of the Sheraton Hotel, the official headquarters of the NCAA that week. I politely approached him and initiated a conversation intended to be a brief "Thank you" for all those talks we had so many years ago. He abruptly interrupted me, spun around, and left me standing there.

I had heard his mental state was wavering. He probably thought I was just somebody messing with him. All I wanted to do was tell him how impressed I was that he took time to talk about the game of basketball with a complete stranger and how he had helped so many others in his lifetime. I just wanted to say, "Thank you, Coach."

I still remember much of what Coach Iba told me in our meetings. One thing he said was that a coach can always have a solid man-to-man defensive team by applying ball pressure and offside team defensive rules. He smiled and added, "Then tell them they're good."

It was an insightful comment from a man whose teams were noted for their defense: **"If you tell them they're good after they've been working hard at it, they will start believing it and will work even harder."**

Prior to our meeting, my impression of Hank Iba was a rough old man who would be impatient. I felt that after twenty or thirty minutes visiting with this man, it would be time to bolt out of there.

He was *nothing* like that. Once again, more proof that success is not accidental. He was quite the gentleman.

During my early coaching days, picking up the phone and calling certain successful coaches was rather routine for me. Whether it was my home or theirs—in fact, anywhere. To this day, it's one of my favorite things: to help a young coach avoid some of the pitfalls I've experienced is a pleasure (this book is primarily for that reason). Not many young coaches take the time and effort to reach out to veterans of the sport, people with experience.

I've never understood why. It always looked to me as a great opportunity to learn.

10
OFFENSE

"Great players help teammates win games,
Great teammates help teammates win
championships."

—Wichita State locker room

I recently watched a team win a state championship game in which both teams played the same style. It's difficult to be critical of a program that consistently heads to the Texas state playoffs every year, but basketballs and bodies were flying all over the place, almost like the way ants scatter when one steps on their bed. Together, the two teams committed over fifty turnovers before they finished the third quarter. By that time, I got tired of counting. Though it was ugly, no one seemed to mind. It was I score, you score.

After the game, I bumped into an ex-coaching acquaintance of mine who let me know how much he enjoyed watching the game. My response was, "Really?" We didn't visit much after I barked my reply. Maybe I was too blunt. Watching a game like that didn't make me happy.

My problem is I'm a purist when it comes to the game of basketball. In my mind, the game was not created to encourage kids to shoot air balls, commit charges, or turn their man loose for easy layups.

If everybody's running and dunking with no challenge from the defense, I get restless and a little upset. I can't help it.

It's a beautiful team game, not a demolition derby—

anyway, it's not supposed to be. As John Wooden said shortly before his passing at the age of ninety-nine, "The best basketball isn't being played at the college level these days" (He could have added high school, too). Today's players and fans seem to think running and shooting quick threes is the way the game must be played. If you emphasize anything besides quick-shooting, full-court basketball, you're old-school and out of touch.

There's no intent here to bad-mouth basketball at any level. It's just my opinion that basketball has a distinct air of selfishness and arrogance when everything about the game becomes "me, me, me." In my way of thinking, it teaches the wrong thing, period. I keep asking myself, *What are the kids learning?*

Every time I start thinking that the game has possibly passed me by in some way, the following observation comes to mind: you can enjoy any style that suits you, but take a look at who ends up in the NCAA Final Four and the NBA Finals.

Most of the good teams run, but they also know what to do when they get to the other end of the court—and it doesn't mean jacking it up right away. They also play good, solid team defense. If patience and teamwork is considered old-school, let's have some more old-school.

What **Stephen Curry** and the Golden State Warriors did in the 2015 NBA Finals would seem to discredit my opinion regarding quick, long-range shooting.

Curry demonstrated what most would label as the greatest exhibition of shooting in the history of the league. It was like he was someone from another planet. Because his teammates, notably **Klay Thompson**, fit the scheme provided by **Coach Steve Kerr**, Golden State had the ability and chemistry to turn the league upside down in one short year.

When you have shooters like Curry, Thompson, and now **Kevin Durant**, it's easy to throw out some of the rules. **However, if you look close, you'll see the Warriors do many other things besides shoot well:** they move the ball, get loose balls, and play very good team defense. In other words, nobody's throwing out any rules. **Golden State is verifying them.** That has much to do with explaining their phenomenal winning the last few years. And, because of that, backing Golden State isn't difficult at all for an old-school coach like me.

Caution: When a team is on fire from outside, the average fan gets excited. The question is: Is it smart? That strategy may be fine for one game, but does it work over the course of a season? Out-of-control, emotional decision-making on the court may give the fans a great show for one game, but it also gives them false hope.

The house wins in Vegas because it knows how to figure odds. Good, solid percentage defense and shot selection wins out over the long haul almost every time. Playing consistently hard and smart gets you to the finish line: the playoffs. Generally speaking, why do you think the Spurs of the NBA and the Patriots of the NFL are always hanging around at season's end?

By the way, **the coaches of these *consistent* post-season winning teams are, in my opinion, not given near the credit they deserve.**

Watch what happens to winning programs when a Popovich or a Belichick retires. How about Jimmy Johnson's departure from the mighty Dallas Cowboys? That didn't take long—straight to the bottom. And they haven't been back since. I hear people struggling to figure out the reasons teams drop out of the picture so quickly. To me, it's plain as day.

It's not just the players that determine victory—the guy coaching the players has something to do with it too! It's also the guy (s) in the front office, selecting the coach. There are NBA basketball players today who still don't understand why the extremely talented team they play for cannot bring home the trophy. Their coaches often allow the "stars" to run the show— give them the ball and get out of their way. The remaining four stand and watch. If he needs you, he'll let you know (slight exaggeration, possibly). Take a look at what's been happening on a number of teams today, **although I am glad to say that number is diminishing,** *the "team concept" is slowly returning.*

There has been a lot of one-on-one, create-your-own-shot maneuvers. Some are comfortable with that; others aren't. Kevin Durant can score just about every way possible, but what's so comforting to Kevin playing for the Warriors, as opposed to the Oklahoma City Thunder, is that *he doesn't have to score every night for them to win. He doesn't have to score every night—he can rebound and play defense.* He also doesn't have to figure out how he's supposed to play with his previous outstanding teammate, Russell Westbrook. He is now on a real team: there are one or two offensive options every time he looks up, not the single one that screams out, "If you don't make your next shot, we're going to lose!"

Most NBA players are young men with absolutely no coaching experience. How are they supposed to know how to coach. People think coaching is fairly simple—well, it's not. It takes years to become a good coach. Even the great ones—John Wooden is the best example—went a long time before producing winning records.

I realize the local volunteer coach figures he can coach anytime and anywhere—wrong again. Just because you played some ball as a kid doesn't mean you're ready to take on an entire team for an entire year against strong competition. But you will never understand what I mean until a legitimate opportunity presents itself and you are introduced to all kinds of factors that you are not familiar with, mistakes that are waiting to happen—every job is more involved than one realizes.

It's important to understand that it's not the selfishness of a player that upsets me—it's the fact that coaches allow players to play that way.

I believe it's the coach's responsibility to lay the foundation and create a winning atmosphere. Let the individual stars shine *within the coach's system.* The fans may not know how it works and the sportscasters are often unaware, and as mentioned before, even the players don't necessarily know why things work better.

Team concept is the answer, if it's allowed to develop. (I can't stop mentioning the "San Antonio Spurs"). The teams that seem to always end up in the top echelon aren't there by accident. Even so-called "individual" sports have a big-picture, team approach.

Consider golf: The Ryder Cup's *lesser* player quite often wins his team the trophy by upsetting the obvious favorite on the last day. Baseball produces countless unexpected heroes during playoff time each year.

The little-known second baseman gets a game-winning hit or makes an outstanding catch.

In basketball, it's a mistake to invite pressure by constantly

setting specific individual goals, especially a certain number of points.

How many times does a lesser-known team member (a non-starter, a role player, etc.) end up being the hero in the final game? True teams produce such endings. With true team philosophy as the trademark of an organization, a bench warmer that is used sparingly during the regular season can step in for an injured starter and play "lights out". As a member of the **team,** *he has been prepared for the unexpected and he's ready when it occurs.* The less pressure you create, the easier it is to deal with it when it arrives.

In fact, you may not even consider it pressure at the time. Your reaction just takes over and, before you know it, you're shaking hands and signing autographs.

Basketball should involve everybody with some type of organized flow in the offense (perhaps just exchanging, or swinging the ball) **during play**. Otherwise, the players end up getting in each other's way. Too often, what I see is very little screening, backdoor cutting, and continuous ball movement. When everything stops, the outcome is normally unsuccessful.

I'm not implying that good players should be tied down to restricted and predictable movement when they play. There should always be a certain amount of freedom to suit individual abilities. While observing good teams at practice, I saw no hesitation by these coaches when it came to that type freedom.

There is a fine line, however, and it's my opinion that careless shooting and passing is on the rise. I just prefer the "well-oiled machine" look of a true team as opposed to "Let's get out of Joe's way so he can do his thing."

The former encourages togetherness; the latter suggests "me, me, me" and can lead to dissension.

My teams were encouraged to look to run first. Getting a quick uncontested shot off the break was ideal. But once it was determined that the break wasn't available, it was imperative that we knew how to correctly flow into our half-court offense.

One of our sets was a high-low one we used in two ways. It became one of our many quick-hitting plays, set up strictly to feed the low post. We called it "A game." *It was also used a second way—a rather unique secondary offense:* Anytime a play *fizzled* during our regular offensive scheme, but we maintained possession of the ball, we automatically went into the basic high-low set ("A" game) with an emphasis on ball reversal as we looked inside, attempting to feed the low post. There was no need to call out the play—as I mentioned earlier, it was automatic. This quite often caught the other team napping. The body language of the receiving low post helped to make it work. An occasional, "Set it up!" by the passer didn't hurt either.

The reason it's smart to check inside after an unsuccessful play is because defenses, especially the big-men defenders, tend to let up. It isn't uncommon to see the defense lose their concentration when they sense their opponent has failed to execute a play successfully. They feel a quick rest is in order, just a couple of seconds. I've seen it happen again and again. That's when you can strike if you're prepared. At the same time, the offense keeps things moving. You seldom have to slow down and start over.

By the way, if you have a postman that is not very efficient and you prefer him to shoot only sparingly, instruct him to play with that understanding. *Using him as a relay passer is very common within a good team philosophy.* The offside perimeter players will have to learn to "spot-up" as they attempt to receive a pass.

Eighty percent of our half-court offense was made up of a series of quick-hitting plays designed to keep the ball moving and to allow my best shooters to do just that—shoot!

I always considered it a compliment when coaches asked me about our "motion offense," even though it wasn't one. It was actually a "pattern offense" that looked very similar to motion because we rarely stopped to reset.

As a coach, I preferred pattern basketball for many reasons, one being that a specific play could be called during the game or a specific player could be called on to score. Another advantage is that at any time during the season, a new play could be easily added.

The constant motion of our offense also allowed a sub-par player to get out of trouble. When he found himself with the ball in an uncomfortable spot, namely the point-guard position, his predetermined *"favorite" play* kicked in automatically.

It was used to help relieve unwanted pressure on this weaker team mate. We never had to waste time getting the ball back into the point guard's hands (that's a relief).

His teammates knew what he was about to run so there was no hesitation, no decision to make. The "uncomfortable" player surely did appreciate this offensive wrinkle. As the season progressed, there was no need to call or signal a play— it was already in motion. **To me, it was the ideal offense.** The development of the system evolved over several years.

It was an efficient approach to a multi-purpose offense that was easy to teach and hard to defend.

Like blocking out goes unnoticed when it comes to defense, passing is often overlooked for its value on offense.

One of the best players to ever come through McMurry College—perhaps the best—was **Preston Vice** (although many would give that honor to Rick Penny, the record-holder in almost every scoring category in the team's history).

Coach Kimbrell had coached Preston at Garland, a high school in a suburb of Dallas, and when he took the McMurry job, Preston followed him the next year.

I've always said Preston was the best passer I've seen anywhere, anytime. "Feeder" might be a better description for Preston than "passer." He was not an ESPN-highlight passer.

He was a precision passer who could get the ball to whomever at any time, when and where they wanted it, with no frills. He had a unique skill few possess at any level. Red Auerbach would have loved him.

While watching Preston feed the post, I noticed the key ingredient to his success: he always looked like he was going to do anything but what he was going to do.

He occupied his defender with the constant threat of driving or shooting, anything other than passing. You couldn't tell what he was seeing or thinking. To compound his opponent's problem, Preston could do everything with either hand: dribble, make behind-the-back passes, feed the post area, etc.

Because he was a pure shooter with a very quick release on

his jump shot, whoever guarded him never knew what to expect. When your defensive opponent is continually worried about multiple possibilities, passing lanes open up because the defense must stay down, play conservatively, and be prepared for anything.

Few coaches know how to teach good passing—I was one of them until halfway throughout my coaching career. The skill is more complex than you might think.

The process is not a step-one, step-two function. It's a continuous blending of all steps involved in an apparent drive, a shot, or any offensive move that suggests anything but a pass. The pass must be made during the process of faking something else, not after.

While all of these things are happening, it's important to remember that passes are successful if the target is not directly to your teammate; the target should be opposite your teammate's defensive man. *Throw the ball where your teammate will be, not where he is.* When coaches set up passing drills, they should be sure the passer has the freedom to drive or shoot during these drills. Otherwise, it's not realistic. I will repeat, **"A great passer always appears as though the last thing he's going to do is pass."**

I guess you can tell I'm a Preston Vice fan. He was a very likable guy who always had a big smile. He was never moody and never got excited about anything. He was always on an even keel emotionally.

I play golf with him occasionally now and, true to form, a bad shot doesn't alter his disposition at all. He could have been a race car driver, a pilot, or even an astronaut. He could beat you on the court and at the poker table. Well, not at the poker table in my case, because I wouldn't play him.

One thing Preston wasn't good at was cross-country running. During the offseason we were supposed to lift weights, run stands, or run cross-country to keep in shape. When it came to Preston's offseason training, it was nonexistent. We would go on a three-or four-mile run every other day, and, as we rounded the first corner, when clearly out of the coaches' sight, Preston would sit down comfortably on the curb and say, "See you boys later."

No one ever ratted on him. We all liked him. If anyone could skip this offseason stuff and get away with it, it would be Vice. And if fanatical Jerry Stone didn't mind, you know the others found it acceptable. We didn't feel that way about anybody else, however. Just Vice.

As McMurry's leading scorer with 17.7 points per game his sophomore year, Preston Vice was selected NAIA All-District. He duplicated the honor the next two years. As a junior he led the team with a 22.9 average and was named a second-team NAIAAll-American.

Preston's biggest honor came in the selection as a member of the *First Team* (five players) *All-Texas College Team* his last two years—an honor that went to the best five collegiate players in the state, including those from all the major universities.

Joining Preston were four notables: Jim "Bad News" Barnes of Texas Western, Lucious "The Animal" Jackson of Pan American, John Henry Young of Midwestern State, and John Savage of North Texas State.

While passing is a necessity, the object of offense is to put points on the board. Having someone on your squad who can adequately shoot the ball sure makes meeting this objective a lot easier. **The plays seem to work better—ever notice? Plus, the coach looks like he knows what he's doing.**

I always liked that part.

Now, allow me to say this: **contrary to what you may hear, I believe "pure" shooters are born.** I'm not saying that practice won't improve your shooting. I'm talking about "pure shooters." Practice certainly solidifies it, but I believe people are born with "touch." Small children with unusual gifted talent, whether it's sports, science, or the arts, are born with it the majority of the time.

During my junior year at McMurry College, we had three or four "pure" shooters—that's very unusual. The best of them was **Toby Burkhardt,** a strong, talented, six-foot-six Indiana boy who once made eleven out of eleven shots in the first half, all jumpers from the corner.

I always wondered why he wasn't playing for a bigger program. He wasn't a troublemaker. In fact, he was the nicest guy on the team. My guess was he might have been too nice. Everybody liked big Toby.

My freshman year we had a six-foot-three junior guard named **Bobby Driver—what a great name for a basketball player—** who really sparked our team. This guy could play. He wasn't just a shooter. He was that and more. He was a scorer. Bobby had the ability to drive straight at a defender, then instinctively slash around him for a wide open layup. It drove me crazy trying to guard him in practice. But I will say this: the experience I received guarding Driver was priceless. It was a move that is very common today but wasn't in the 60s.

He was the first basketball player I saw who used the now-popular "teardrop" layup. Bobby was about thirty years ahead of his time when it came to scoring. He could have played at a higher level. (By the way, I learned to steer a great driver like Bobby in one direction until he got to his particular shooting range. Then, I'd have to square up when we were in that area.)

Lance Stephens was another pure shooter, a six-foot-six Canadian who possessed a variety of shots, inside and out (hook shots, included), and, get this, *with either hand.* If we needed a winning basket, we learned to get the ball to Lance.

Clayton and I were somewhere in all of that—we both could shoot too.

When you have a great shooter, teach him the system, then leave him alone. Let him do his thing. Coach Kimbrell understood this—a few coaches I had didn't.

If the shooter has a bad night, don't look at him like he did something wrong. As long as he continues to take good shots, your demeanor should let him know that he has little to worry about. A great player needs to always feel his coach is 100 percent behind him.

A budding shooter and his teammates should also learn this as soon as he can: "**Let the shot come to you.**" If you only remember and coach that one thing, it will have been worth my time writing this book. *When the player stops constantly "hunting" for his shot during his attempt to become the hero of the night and* *allows it to simply appear on its own, he will shoot it and it will go in at a much better rate.*

Then, his shooting average and percentage will increase. Add *defensive concentration* to his game strategy and he will be a true basketball player. Now, if you can get his teammates to play with the same philosophy, you will have a solid team and an enjoyable year.`

But, beware, confident shooters are confident, sometimes cocky people. It's a fine line. They can change on you very quickly if you're not careful, especially in high school with Mom, Dad, and Uncle Joe coaching them on the side.

Outsiders can cause real damage without your being aware until it's grown into a bona fide problem. Remember to keep that thumb ready—the one you use to clamp down on him once in a while. It's your team, not his (or his father's).

Here's an extreme example: Immediately following a high school regional playoff game, I had a couple of my friends ask me, "Who was the spectator talking *in your huddle* during a time-out?" I was so involved with the few seconds a coach has that I didn't even notice. He was giving advice to his god-son in our huddle! How's that for parental interference?

In the heat of a playoff game, in my huddle! I cannot imagine what would have happened if I had seen what was going on.

As long as your stud maintains the good attitude required of every player, his teammates should have no issues with him shooting more than anybody else. Ideally, they all want to win and should recognize he can make it happen for them. But that would be relying on a false assumption like, "My teammates are mature and incapable of being jealous." We might ought to rethink that one. Chances are, your players won't see it quite like you do.

Even if they do agree, there's still a likelihood their parents won't. Some players are very aware of the number of shots they take as compared to the number their teammates put up. Jealously and dissension can pop up very easily. Along with playing time, this shooting issue will eat at a team more than anything.

Whether you're coaching the neighborhood peewee team or the San Antonio Spurs, playing time and who's shooting will be your two biggest issues.

Who's doing the shooting will be discussed by almost everyone after the game and the discussions won't necessarily be friendly. You have to stay on top of the situation. It's the one factor that can rip a team apart.

But sometimes you get lucky.

When I coached at Richardson High during the late 60s and early 70s, I had a slender, six-foot-three two guard who was not only my best shooter but close to the purest shooter I have ever seen. He understood my previous advice regarding shot selection.

I do not remember a single bad shot from **Rick Penny**. (The truth is, if you don't occasionally have a *bad shot,* you're not shooting enough.)

I would put Rick's shooting up against most anyone. Stephen Curry at Golden State is the better player, but his superior athletic ability is the reason. They both have the same pure shooting delivery and touch.

I realize I sound like a proud parent, but Rick Penny was truly special. You can develop a shooter with endless hours of work, but, as I said before, pure shooting is a gift. Rick is now in his fifties and can play two or three rounds of golf a year and still shoot close to even par with *absolutely no practice.*

Rick Penny became an NAIA All-American at McMurry and finished his collegiate career as the leading scorer in school history with 2,296 points. In his senior year, he led all guards in the nation, hitting 60.9 percent of his shots while averaging 24.4 points per game. He was invited to try out with the San Antonio Spurs before choosing to go into coaching. He coached a handful of Texas high schools, the last of which was Brady.

He and his wife, Jane, now live in Brownwood, Texas, since his retirement in 2000. Rick now teaches his "One Motion Shooting" in clinics and through videos.

Even though he is retired, Rick can still shoot. His "One Motion Basketball" website lists evidence of Rick's exceptional shooting ability:

988 of 1,000 free throws – age 56

490 free throws in a row – age 50

97 of 100 3pt. shots (top of the circle),
56 in a row – age 50

1,774 of 2,000 3pt. shots (top of circle) – age 50

77 of 100 NBA 3pt. shots – age 50

Today, I would have had numerous scoring opportunities within that system for Rick. At Rockwall thirty years later, **Nathan Doudney** took advantage of my updated offensive version of the game. I learned from my experience coaching Rick, so when Nathan came along, I handled him differently. He certainly embodied all that I emphasized for a real shooter like himself. This team was not physically Division I talented. They needed all the gimmicks and distractions they could find. The use of screens, multiple sets, changing of tempo—you name it—helped them to confuse the opponent. And, sometimes that wasn't enough, but it was most of the time—and it sure was fun.

At the 5-A level in Texas, a coach can be hands-on throughout the school year. I was with them *every* day. There was plenty of time to introduce whatever I wanted to involving any particular offensive or defensive scheme. Besides, some years it became obvious that we would be starting the same five and have only one or two subs.

With very little depth on the bench, we learned to read each other quickly and gelled sooner than normal. Consequently, I could add offensive plays and defenses in a much shorter time period than it would normally require. It wasn't difficult to add or adjust something, sometimes even the day before a game. It also wasn't difficult to know who should be shooting. However, how you sell it is important.

Very seldom did I say a certain play was for Nathan (although, it's funny how it seemed to work out that way). We actually had fairly balanced scoring. Our offense was made up of quick-hitting plays, using a maximum of two or three passes (unless we were delaying), with all five players being involved.

But the system gave Nathan plenty of chances to shoot. You definitely would say our offense went through him.

During the 1999–00 season, some of the guys were mumbling about **Nathan Doudney**. Nathan was a very confident, pure-shooting two guard. I had no problem with a pure shooter on the team. To them, his shooting was becoming too domineering. They had a right to inquire—I had an obligation to explain.

One day in the locker room before practice, I told the team they were going to participate in a little experiment. First, I told them to look around the room and fix in their minds where each of their teammates were seated. I then asked everyone to close their eyes. Finally, I said, "On the count of three with your eyes still shut, point to the one teammate you would want to take the potential game-winning shot."

After they had done so, I told them to continue pointing and to open their eyes. From my vantage point, every one of them were pointing at Nathan. I reminded them that we all had our strengths and Nathan's was shooting.

It would be stubborn of them to ignore the obvious. I also promised to keep Nathan under control (knowing he believed any shot was a good shot) and to insist that he improve on his defense.

As the season progressed Nate kept looking for his shots, which I had no trouble with, and, of course, surprised none of his teammates.

Rick Penny

Coach Stone during a time out.

IV
FOURTH QUARTER

COACHING OFF THE COURT

My assistant, Reggie Franklin and I were friends first;
everything else was secondary. The partnership was irreplaceable.

11
RACE

"To teach is to touch a life forever."
—Nicki Brook

For me, the greatest athlete in the world, the greatest runner, the greatest boxer, the greatest basketball player, and the greatest football player were all minorities. Their minority status never crossed my mind while growing up. Jim Thorpe, Jesse Owens, Joe Lewis, Wilt Chamberlain, and Jim Brown seemed like my friends, my heroes. There were others, of all races, but who cared?

I just recently discovered three scrapbooks that had escaped me for a little less than 60 years—I had given up on finding these childhood treasures that had been pasted together by mixing all-purpose flour and water. Every time a family moves, items such as these seem to remain in one of three places: the attic, the basement, or the garage. It's living proof that human beings did occupy these walls where, in my case, one sports-minded fanatic was certain his most prized possessions were lost forever.

Newspaper photos and articles hadn't been altered—they were just as my memories had projected. I was once again reconnected to those priceless childhood days that we all hold onto.

Two local guys of color I admired as a youngster were also my heroes: **Russell Towles and Curtis Adams.** Russell was a tremendous black athlete and nobody messed with him. He was very likable, but his off-the-field activities kept him from furthering his athletic and academic career past high school. They were quite a pair on the football field. They looked like twins out there, built low to the ground, very stout and very agile, and provided many a thrill for the locals.

Curtis and I connected because of his vocal talent. He knew the words to all the **Platters's** songs and, as he sang, I jotted them down. Both were five years older than me, and treated me like a kid brother. I felt protected by them.

Because of my shooting abilities, they picked me over some of the older guys, and my esteem was greatly enhanced when Russell Towles, the toughest cat in town, started calling me "Star" after noticing my shooting skills on the court.

When I was growing up in my small (everything's relative; it didn't seem small to me) Kansas hometown, there were some inconsistencies regarding different races that we hardly noticed. When you're young, you seldom question what you find. You see no need. You do what adults say to do—most of the time, anyway. You repeat what you hear at home as though it's gospel. When you're young, you haven't had enough personal experiences to develop your own ideas. In my home, I never heard one word about race, so I had no idea how my parents viewed racial issues. Race in my house seemed almost nonexistent, or perhaps neutral, if that's possible.

Only a few black families lived in our town, maybe seven percent of the total population. Latinos numbered about the same. I participated in school and athletic events with black friends. We visited each other's home, but not often. Their home locations prevented frequent visits more than anything.

Though our public schools were integrated, other parts of our society weren't. There were separate swimming pools, but I never saw one black person using either. Most of my black friends, and, later, my players, didn't like to swim because they had never learned how. Nowhere were signs posted saying "Colored served in the rear" as you might see in some other towns, but most eating establishments were, I assume, off-limits to blacks. I actually don't know. Nothing dealing with race was official that we were aware of, but I'm sure there were unwritten rules regulating the daily activities in our town.

In a small Kansas town in the fifties, "segregation" was an unknown entity to me. Blacks simply chose to go where they were comfortable. Keep in mind, we're talking about *one* town in *one* state. The churches served separate races, even though there was no city ordinance requiring it. It was like the **Chilocco Indian Reservation** just across the Oklahoma border south of Ark City. As far as we youngsters knew, the Chilocco Indians were living where they were supposed to because that's where they had always lived, at least during our limited lifetime.

Summer baseball was integrated, but not many black players joined the mostly white teams. My impression was, if you were a good black player, there was little objection to your playing on a white team. Since there was also an adult black league, you might be more comfortable playing with black teammates regardless of your ability.

But, actually I don't remember one racial incident while growing up in that town. I do remember black kids standing up for themselves if the climate began changing against them. My theory, looking back, is there were few blacks, meaning few tension, and, therefore few incidents.

It's a theory—as I've said, I really don't know.

The black teams played a completely different schedule

throughout the summer. Their games were played primarily on Sunday afternoons and lasted forever. Food was prepared ahead of time, and the game became quite an event, almost like a giant family reunion.

They seemed to have twice as much fun as the white folks during these Sunday afternoon games. I know because I kept the scoreboard in center field for every game played during summer, regardless of age or race.

Not much was said in our community regarding race, integration, segregation, civil rights, etc. There was little or no conflict in our town because blacks were in the extreme minority. I don't, however, remember seeing blacks with a negative demeanor as though they carried a second-class label deep in their psyches. It seemed we all got along. But what did I know? They may have felt a great deal of sensitivity and learned to keep it inside. My issues were different. I was a kid and I was white. I had the luxury of not having to think about racial injustices.

Not many whites shunned away from using the N-word, but only when talking among themselves.

Whether anyone considered it or not, the word was disrespectful. Saying "negro" seemed inoffensive much the same way "black" is used today. The term "colored people" was very common.

I remember thinking those words were descriptive, not derogatory. (It's interesting, but the first time I heard someone sarcastically ask, "What color?" a whole different thought process was introduced to me).

Of course, if you were black, the truth is *it was all offensive.* Though some were, most whites were not mean-spirited, just indifferent and naive, me among them.

My first awakening to a different way of life occurred one day when **my close friend Ted Hollembeak** and I listened to **James Judie.**

He was a teammate of ours who angrily poured out his frustrations regarding his being one of only seven or eight black athletes on all of the athletic teams in high school. I distinctly remember his feelings summed up in the lament, "Why has God chosen me to be black?"

Ted and I were speechless.

It didn't come as a complete surprise to us when James Judie, as an adult, committed suicide. Ted took the incident much harder than me. They had been closer as friends—same grade schools and same proximity to neighborhoods and summer activities. I lived on the edge of town. Downtown Ark City seemed a long way off as a grade-schooler.

When I started my junior college coaching career a few years later, I realized most of my players were going to be disadvantaged black kids. A poor black kid I wasn't. Not coming from a ghetto or a black neighborhood, this Mr. White Boy from a Kansas farming community had a few things to learn about the world.

My college team, McMurry in Abilene, Texas, had two or three blacks, but, generally speaking, Abilene and the entire state of Texas was slow to completely integrate.

Not having grown up around many black athletes, it was important to educate myself in regards to the backgrounds and inner feelings of these athletes who shared my love for basketball. Suddenly, they were calling me "Coach."

To be the best possible coach, I wanted to understand how the young black athlete differed, if any, from his white counterpart. I had a lot to learn and needed to know right now.

What did I do? I talked to as many black coaches as possible. Two men who were most influential were Nolan Richardson and Andy Stoglin. I went to El Paso each year to recruit and visit with Tim Floyd, a UTEP first assistant under Coach Don "The Bear" Haskins.

El Paso was a very friendly city on the Mexican border. Because of its isolation, the high school coaches greeted any college recruiter with open arms.

I first met Nolan there in August, 1977. I was joined by a few onlookers during an informal UTEP basketball practice at the Special Events Center in downtown El Paso—Nolan was one of them. Neither one of us knew the other. I told him that coaching at Midland Junior College was why I was recruiting in the El Paso area. He allowed that coaching at one of the local high schools was alright, but his ultimate goal was to get into college.

Some people immediately grab your attention—Nolan was one of them.

Timing is hard to decipher sometimes—not more than 30 minutes after shaking hands with this impressive figure, I got a call from Sid Simpson, athletic director at Western Texas Junior College in Snyder, Texas, about 90 miles from Midland.

Both of our schools were in the powerful Western Junior College Athletic Conference.

Coach Simpson wanted to know if I knew of any last-second potential head coach candidates that might be available—it was early fall and his coach, Mike Mitchell had suddenly headed for greener pastures. I said, "You might not believe me, but I am presently in El Paso and I just met your man about a half an hour ago."

Coach Simpson had been an assistant coach under my coach, Hershel Kimbrell at McMurry when I was a player there a few years prior—we knew and trusted each other implicitly.

He said he would call Nolan immediately. Coach Gerald Myers at Texas Tech (with the help of his assistant, Rob Evans—a man I highly respected and enjoyed being around) had made the same type recommendation recently to Coach Simpson.

I guess if some things are meant to be, it doesn't take a genius to comprehend the inevitable. I eventually met his wife, Rose, and his best friend Andy Stoglin. I felt I had known all three for a long time.

Nolan was the basketball coach at El Paso Bowie High School. Andy later became his assistant at Tulsa University. In 1981 they won the NIT. Andy went on to be a head coach at Southern University and Jackson State, while Nolan moved on to the University of Arkansas, where he won an NCAA Tournament in 1994. Before his success at the Division I level, I faced Nolan many times (too many for my resume) at Midland, when he coached at Western Texas College, winning the NJCAA title in980.

Both were very proud black men who graduated from UTEP after playing for Haskins.

Never having been timid when it comes to asking questions, Nolan and Andy got bombarded with many questions that were stored up in me. I would pose questions regarding the differences and similarities between the black and white races when it came to athletic issues. They couldn't figure me out. Was I serious, asking all of these racial questions?

They were suspicious of my motives. The topics I brought up were very important to them—but they were important to me too. I wanted to know *now*.

After I hammered them with questions over a period of time, they turned to me one day and said, "We've decided that you're different."

"What are you saying", I asked? (I had no idea where this was headed.)

"You really do want to learn and you really do care," was their quick reply.

My reply, "Why do you think I've been hanging around here for all this time? I really am trying to learn."

This was a significant moment for me. From the perspective of my two black friends, I came to realize whites don't know, or don't take the time to learn, what blacks instinctively do from the first second of introduction to **anyone that has white skin—it's called self-preservation.**

Blacks have to constantly survey and analyze their surroundings—they don't enjoy it, but it would be foolish not to take a quick (and, hopefully, accurate) read—it takes about two seconds.

I'm positive that most white people **DO NOT** carry some deep-seated hatred around for non-white individuals—they simply find themselves "on edge."

I believe the average white American and black American finds themselves uncomfortable when they find out they are the race that is in the minority at any given moment. **They're just dealing in unfamiliar territory.** But, by walking in someone else's shoes for a brief period (listening and learning), it isn't so difficult accepting a completely different viewpoint.

The truth is, with a small amount of civil conversation, the conclusion can easily be, "Yeah, I can see why a young person living in poverty would feel the need to think that way—hey, I would too."

Another point to remember (and often, we don't) is when we speak of white people or black people, discussing our opinions of either race, we have to consider who we're specifically analyzing—all races have a variety of opinionated individuals which, if not careful, we will quote as a majority of that race. We violate this a great deal.

Both Nolan and Andy were patient with me and addressed some sensitive issues. Andy wanted me to see through the eyes of a poor black kid. As a child, he didn't like the ridicule directed his way because he had one pair of pants to wear—*one pair*. He explained that good kids in dirt-poor environments learned to steal and had no problem justifying their actions. I stayed in El Paso longer than I intended, asking question after question, as they likewise did when I gave them a chance. **We both expressed our views, but we also both listened to the other's.**

I hate stealing. In my mind, it ranks one notch below murder. Stealing destroys trust, and without trust a basketball team or any relationship can't survive.

So, does that mean two grown men can't talk about the issues young people deal with according to where they've come from and what they are dealt? That's the very reason I stayed as long as I did—it was a highly educational visit for Coach Stone.

If a freshman entering college hasn't learned these things, he needs to quickly. With the proper guidance, a kid with nothing can still remain honest and trustworthy. It may be difficult, but there are too many examples of successes coming out of poverty. In almost every instance, however, the kid has had a mentor or a good role model.

Without guidance from home, how would we have handled Andy's situation? A coach is in a position to help change that way of thinking in the first semester.

I was surprised at the speed in which any player accustomed to that type thinking could change. A few heart-to-heart discussions did wonders. They just needed to hear it from someone they trusted.

The flip side of the education received from Andy and others was that it taught me to eliminate potential recruits. Some mountains are too high to climb—you have to consider percentages. I learned to have a much more critical eye when meeting candidates.

Hundreds of times you watch a kid play and think, *Man, that kid's got talent. Look at that move!* But you learn to ask trustworthy people pertinent questions before taking a risk—and recruiting is a risk, for the coach and the recruit. More importantly, your own instincts are what you will learn to obey. The ability to sort out these questions takes experience and will determine how successful your program will become. **Even the best programs misjudge prospects. It keeps everyone humble.**

Nolan and Andy honored me with their trust. The more we talked, the more I realized how rare it was for them to say what they did.

As I continued to talk with Afro-American coaches during the weeks to come, one particular comment kept emerging: **"Stop worrying about a player's race—just coach."**

That sounds good, but it isn't that simple—not if you want a chance at developing real togetherness and a team based on complete trust in each other. As a young white coach who had little experience with black players, I wasn't capable of "just coaching" these guys.

That came later. I had too much to learn, as did they. We both came from a different place. Whether that was good or bad could be debated. We just needed to eliminate fear and doubt for the time being. We needed to realize that we both wanted the same thing. All of that takes time, but it's very possible to do.

I wouldn't trade for all that I learned during those early years with my black teams.

Consider the following:

The players on your team may have cars and some may not. Those who don't will constantly need rides. Some players will have both parents at home and some will have one or none. Some will make the dean's list while others will only have a sixth-grade reading level. It will greatly benefit you to know everything you can about your multifaceted team.

Black athletes with outstanding grade point averages who end up at Stanford or Duke in their attractive cars are referred to as *Afro-Americans*. So too are the black athletes with poor grades and no cars who end up at Podunk Junior College. ***What do you want to bet these two groups have several things that are not in common?***

I've learned that sometimes the only thing in common between one particular twenty-one-year-old black male and another twenty-one-year-old black male is their skin color—and even that can differ greatly. The way the two think about things may be 180 degrees apart. Coaches must get to know their players as individuals above all other criteria.

All other aspects of race are important and will be revealed at their proper time, but for now, get to know the individual as a human being. Everything else will usually fall into place.

The coach and his individual players cannot have any type of obstacle between themselves as they approach the opponent. Until loyalty has been established, you may constantly be disappointed. Things just won't feel right. Many teams go through the entire season unaware of this fact. Their patent explanation is, *"We just didn't seem to have it this year."*

When teaching my first American history class during those first years of high school coaching, an occasional film was selected to show the class regarding some historical event. One was a documentary on the Third Reich and the Nazi concentration camps. This was a situation when race was, without question, a vital factor. It never entered my mind that some of my students were Jewish.

Had I been conscious of this fact, a very uncomfortable experience for these few students could have been avoided. As the film revealed the horrors of that nightmare, those few students sat frozen at their desks, eventually bursting out of that uncomfortable room, Coach Stone's government class. I couldn't have been more regretful. In this case, the race issue wasn't just important—it was everything. Another lesson learned by a young teacher/coach.

Athletics—even the simple activity of running—knocks down a lot of barriers. With all the preparation it takes to successfully compete in athletics, you don't have time to dwell on differences.

These days, the color of someone's skin is not the most

important thing that crosses your mind—we're talking junior college now.

I've observed during the course of my career that, after working intently with a new team, I really had to stop and think when someone asked me, "How many black guys do you have on your team this year?" In fact, now days, race has little to do with recruiting. Quotas are a thing of the past (there are exceptions).

Coaches want players! Schools want to win. Prospects can be black, purple, white, or green for all they care. In this way, athletics has been a major factor in bringing the races together.

Coaches get a real break when it comes to racial issues the average citizen faces. We can go in the gym, lock the door, and teach eager kids who want to please the coach. We are a group of like-minded people trying to reach a goal. To achieve success, cooperation and teamwork are required. It may take a few confrontations and a lot of patience, but, somewhere down the line, most everyone will understand and buy into the premise.

One of my first high school principals once told me, "You coaches are lucky. You don't have to deal with unmotivated students like the regular faculty." That's not entirely true. A coach is constantly involved with motivating his players to a higher status. There are also a number of issues a coach has to deal with that most classroom teachers wouldn't go near because they don't have the type personality to cope with them.

Athletes on the field are different from students in the classroom. If they are males, testosterone is fueling their actions. In the heat of competition, disagreements occur and fights occasionally break out. Teachers in an advanced English or math class will likely never have to deal with these types of issues.

The same teachers may seldom have to raise their voices. If a coach never raises his voice and never shows his masculine side, his players will gobble him up (the manner in which he shows that side is important). Once again, the two coaches I felt undersood this best were Coaches Hinton and Kahler. The playing field requires a more exacting type of discipline than is needed in the classroom.

In addition, coaches deal with many more facets of a child's life than the classroom teacher. His relationship with the student doesn't end when the bell rings. That's why so many assistant and head principals come from the coaching pool in a school district. They've received solid training for dealing with the school administration, media, parents, and students.

Because of the cooperation and teamwork involved in basketball, communication of the players is far more advanced than that of the average student. Before taking the job at Midland College, I spent a year as an assistant for Gerald Stockton at Midwestern State University.

One of my duties was to scout future opponents. In one of my typical scouting reports to the team, besides detailing each player's tendencies, descriptions of them as black or white were common.

This was standard procedure so our players would be able to recognize and identify their defensive assignments quickly.

Standard procedure was about to change.

Gerald was a good man. Later that evening, after practice, he told me not to mention whether a player was black or white while giving a report in the future. I had been there long enough to know our guys knew I had no hang-ups about a person's skin color. I am also quite sure not one black kid on that entire squad ever gave it a second thought.

I felt Gerald was making way too much out of the issue. He was being noble (we all like feeling noble, occasionally), but not realistic.

I told him, "Come on, these guys are college basketball players." However, after some discussion, I agreed to follow my boss's wishes—he was much bigger. He also signed my checks.

My next report was not delivered as smoothly. I kept hesitating, making sure I complied with Gerald's request. It didn't take long for the players to figure out what was going on. Some began snickering—I was trying not to. Gerald was sitting in the back of the room unaware of what the players and I were dealing with. He couldn't see their faces, but I could. It seemed to never end.

I don't know when I changed back to my normal way of delivering scouting reports, but it happened soon thereafter, probably following a brief discussion with the big man.

It's important to note that my comments concerning race happened four decades ago. Much has changed, but much hasn't. The color of one's skin is insignificant in much of society today. The positive progress dealing with race relations is absolutely indisputable.

But, let me ask you this: Do you realize how many white

people at this moment have never had any meaningful acquaintances with members of other races and vice versa? Any socializing, home visitations, etc.? I'm not stating any negative, positive, or neutral conclusions.

I'm just saying, "Do you realize with all of the progress that is proclaimed these days, isn't it odd that, with the microscope drawn in tightly, the view often appears very similar to days gone by?" Why?

Now that requires a complex discussion—for another time.

Racial issues can tear teams up in no time. These issues have to be dealt with quickly. The coach, no matter his personality, is perceived as the team's leader and is expected to protect each player's well-being.

Coaches have a real opportunity to teach in these situations. **If you don't feel comfortable, you need to get comfortable.**

The potential for progress in this area is unlimited. As a coach, you are in an enviable position. Talk about "Coaching is much more than X's and O's." The truth is, a normal athletic team has less racial issues than anywhere. They work for a common goal every day. They don't have the time, energy, or reason to dislike their teammates to any real degree. That other team is enough to dislike.

I used to compete against a very fine black coach. We liked and respected each other, but on the court he was a very effective intimidator who scared the heck out of the referees. While protesting a call against his team, he would sometimes yell, "It's because I'm black."

What's interesting is there were times when I believed him. I'm sure if you examined his life story, it would reveal a great deal of prejudice directed his way, but what was I supposed to do? Ignore something perfectly obvious to anyone no more than three feet away?

Was I supposed to allow my team to be the victim of the referee's intimidation? I felt it was definitely giving our opponent an advantage. I finally had enough.

One night I retaliated. When a call went against us, I screamed at the referee, "It's because I'm white!!" My adversary and I were both standing near mid-court—no way he could have missed it.

The look on his face was priceless (actually, the look on the referee's faces were equally priceless).

I definitely wanted them to do some serious reevaluating. The coach was speechless. I didn't know what his reaction would be, but I just wanted to stand up for my team and try leveling the playing field. I wanted them to know the white guy wanted to win too.

The only thing better for me would have been a sneak wink or a slight smile from him, which I wasn't going to get in the middle of a game. I just wanted him to know how I was feeling. (We laugh about it these days. I finally did get that smile).

Sometimes, coaches try to get their team fired up, to get them mad, by creating an atmosphere of "It's us against the world." I've used it myself. Sometimes it's appropriate. I'm not an authority, just an observer. I'm also white, not black. But, it doesn't matter what color I am, there's still an obligation for me to protect my team (90% are black in jr. college) and also must teach them to be strong and reflect the treatment they are going to receive at times.

It may be difficult, but turning the other cheek is sometimes what's needed. **It's a delicate balance.**

One more point: **Often we make things worse when bending over backwards, feeling obligated to demonstrate our love for our fellow man, especially one of the opposite race.**

We end up looking foolish proving that we possess no racial prejudice, when the truth is we are simply *out of our element— and by going out of our way to demonstrate it, we sometimes end up looking rather foolish.* We haven't been around other races and we're slightly uncomfortable—and that's all there is to it, nothing more.

It's true for any race—just be politely quiet and respectful. Observe and learn—it won't be a problem for very long.

The opposite race, whoever that may be, can spot insincerity in a minute. I went through those issues early in my coaching career. So, I'm not preaching, nor am I judging.

I was thrown into college recruiting and suddenly felt a bit out of place. It was awkward walking into a black home and not feeling completely comfortable—not any different than the first time my black players walked into a white person's home. (Some of my black freshmen players later told me that one of their mother's last minute instructions was to not go into a white booster-club family's home—it wouldn't be polite).

Those issues were resolved in no time. Everyone realized we were all on the same side—Midland College! We all just had to learn to take a deep breath and be ourselves. Don't force it. Things tend to lighten up. It seems to me that trust takes more time to develop than any human emotion. And trust is what we're all looking for here. It's what every team must have before it can reach it's true potential.

And while all of this is going on, the coach has to see the big picture—he can't protect his new batch of children, coming in as freshmen each year. He has to throw them out into the arena, providing numerous opportunities to grow and learn—it's difficult and it's wonderful. It's what they'll talk about ten years from now and twenty years from now. And you'll be surprised and proud.

The truth is, many freshmen athletes, black or white, are spoiled, selfish, and have a lot to learn. They must deal emotionally with race as they see it, and they must learn to push through the physical pain on the field or the court when their bodies want to stop.

They've never had to take it to a higher level. Most will hang in there and gradually move forward. When they go home at the Christmas break and see their old teammates who are still in high school, they notice the difference immediately. **They wonder, "Did I play that weakly just one year ago? Did I act like that?"**

They begin to realize the fierce competition and discipline they face every day in college has benefited them. Their confidence increases accordingly, and they have more enthusiasm and more pride in themselves, their team, and their new school.

Their parents also notice the difference. When these young men return to school from their break, they think differently and realize that they have developed a sense of pride in their new second home.

This scenario didn't happen for all the kids I coached in college. Some kids didn't want to be taught—they already knew everything. For the first few weeks of every season, I made trips to the bus station to wish them luck as they headed home.

What's interesting is that almost every kid said the same thing as he departed: "You were right, Coach," or, "I learned a lot here." At that moment, they were sincere. They had no reason to blow smoke.

How ironic that they would sound honest and mature just before getting on a bus to go home. I always hoped that they had gained from the lessons they had learned and that they would land on both feet and get a second chance somewhere else.

However, the reality was that there wasn't much hope it would occur.

One spring, while coaching at Tarleton State, I was asked to speak at an annual coach's clinic held at the East Texas State University campus.

About one hundred and fifty coaches attended. My hour-long talk centered on my views on being white while coaching young black kids. It was a bold topic, but I decided to have at it (that was the route I usually took—much more interesting.)

I focused on breaking down barriers—both black/white ones and coach/player ones. By attempting to build real trust through communication, a subject that needed constant attention. **Like it or not, most black kids start out not trusting their white coach, with the possible exception of a well-known, successful coach.**

They may play for him, but they won't be comfortable until the coach reaches out to them and establishes some kind of personal connection with them. This connection must be a two-way street between coach and player, but it's the coach who must lead the way.

It's so easy to remain aloof while barking out orders to a group of hopeful young athletes. The reality is that it's also *impersonal and hollow* to the kid who wants to learn everything about the game he has loved since childhood.

A coach can choose to treat everybody the same no matter their differences. He can mimic an Army sergeant. It's a more objective and easier way of dealing with youngsters, but it's far less productive.

When you read about an extremely hard-nosed *successful* coach who puts his team through the ringer every day, read a little further. So often, we discover that this same coach has another side: he cares about where a kid came from and where he's going.

He has a completely unknown persona—that's what rounds out his tough side. That's why his players stand by him. It can have a lot to do with why he's successful.

The player who's interviewed after a victorious season (if given the time to respond), invariably mentions the coach as a father-figure. He's described as a tough, fair gentleman who always places his team above everything else.

That's what we all want in a coach. While speaking during my time allotment, I asked the coaches if they had ever had a coach who was basically a bully, and I reminded them of General Dwight D. Eisenhower's quote which appropriately concluded my thoughts: **"You don't lead by hitting people over the head—that's assault, not leadership."**

During my talk, the room was noticeably quiet. I thought it went well but didn't know for certain how anyone viewed what they had just heard. I had no doubt, however, that many coaches questioned my thoughts and felt that "bonding" sounded weak.

I realize when you express opinions outside the box, criticism will follow. Anything that deviates from "the way we've always done it" usually causes discomfort. But, to me, it was worth it. I always thought what they heard might have provoked some to consider (or reconsider) their approach in dealing with young athletes.

About two months after the clinic, **a shipment containing eighty pair of Converse shoes arrived at my office.** They were all sizes and in our school colors.

The gift came with no mention of the sender's name. For a couple of days, I tried to figure out where to send them because the post office had surely made a mistake. The correct school colors had me wondering, however.

Then I remembered my speech at the clinic.

Normally, the various shoe companies—Nike, Converse, Reebok, Adidas, etc.—send representatives to every major basketball event.

Prior to speaking, I had visited with an elderly gentleman who worked for Converse. Actually, we had visited during other clinics throughout the country many times. No doubt, we had introduced ourselves to each other, but I never caught his name. He was a soft-spoken, likable man whom I always looked forward to visiting.

Later, it hit me: he was John McLendon, an ex-collegiate coach who broke down color barriers, becoming the first black member of the NCAA Basketball Hall of Fame.

Coach McLendon received his tutoring under Dr. James Naismith at Kansas University before later becoming the head coach at Cleveland State University, the first black coach at a predominately white, major university.

He was also the first black head coach for any professional athletic team when he took charge of the Cleveland Pipers in the American Basketball Association (ABA). Coach McLendon heard my speech and must have approved with eighty pair of shoes. With such a significant legacy associated with his name, justification for my clinic subject seemed apparent. *I had John McClendon's blessing.* That's all I needed.

I learned a lesson from that experience: *always* introduce yourself and have your new acquaintance do likewise. Sometimes the enthusiasm of a conversation overshadows the most important ingredient: the person's name with whom you're conversing.

Coach McLendon died of cancer in 1999 in Cleveland Heights, Ohio.

What I'd give to visit with him now. Can you imagine the stories?

Thank you, Coach McClendon. The time I spent with you was very enjoyable—it was a privilege.

I first met Reggie Franklin when he played for the New Mexico Military Institute, one of the teams in the WJCAC with our Midland College team. After spending ten or fifteen minutes talking to him, I had a positive feeling he could be a potential assistant coach someday if he wanted.

After NMMI, Reggie attended SMU in Dallas, then spent a couple of years with the Harlem Globetrotters. From basketball, he moved into the insurance business. Like many others who have been away from the smell of the gym too long, he wanted to return.

Six years after first meeting Reggie, Dave Campbell, his junior college coach, called me suggesting I call soon-to-be Coach Franklin. Dave thought Reggie was ready to get into coaching. After a brief conversation which detailed my reasons for choosing him as an assistant, he agreed with no hesitation.

My intent was to hire him at Midland College prior to Christmas 1981. However, he was unable to take the position until the following March, when he drove up from Houston and joined me on the bench for the first game of the NJCAA Tournament in Hutchinson, Kansas.

It was Reggie's first coaching experience. He barely knew the players' names. Five days later, we had won all four games and captured the national championship. When the final horn sounded, we shook hands and smiled.

I told him, "You know, it doesn't always play out like this." Together, we did our best to build a strong basketball program at Midland. In the process we slid into a great friendship.

The main reason we clicked could be traced to our basic personalities. I was obsessed with playing the game a certain way.

Right or wrong, good or bad, I wanted to control the practice sessions—I just couldn't help it. Although there was much to learn, I was going to learn while being the person in charge.

Because Reggie knew his own strengths and limitations, he gladly stepped back and tried to soak up all he could. We worked well together. He was always given the liberty to express his opinion, and he knew how and when to do it. He listened to me and I listened to him. He gave me a lot of behind-the-scenes support that he didn't mention until later. That's the way it should be. We both contributed as much as possible. We were much more effective together than we would have been separately.

Our combined professional success had much to do with a close friendship. It seemed we could read each other's minds. Always consumed with coaching, he was able to pull me away from my head-coaching headaches and get me into a more jovial place. Consequently, we had fun together. Recruiting players or scouting other teams was much more enjoyable when we went together. I knew at some point he would be anxious to coach his own team. If I had it my way, we would have been co-coaches for a long period of time.

Reggie also helped bridge the generation and racial gap for me. He was in charge of the athletic living quarters and was able to extinguish fires that broke out among the players before they affected the team.

He liked recruiting, which I didn't. He always dressed nicely and conducted himself in a professional manner. Moms and grammas loved him, which didn't hurt one bit. When entering the picture, hoping to seal the deal on a recruit, I frequently discovered it was already sealed.

The reality was that an unknown white coach from West Texas coming for their son caused concern within some black families.

You couldn't blame them.

Having Reggie with me gave relief in those situations. We always shot straight with them, and soon my being white wasn't an issue.

Because I understood how they felt, serious tension never arose when discussing the future plans of their boy. Once they got to know me and were presented with our successful record at Midland, the wall came down.

However, I'm sure it happened much quicker because a black coach was standing next to the white coach. It would be nice if someday that were not an issue. Athletics is a very positive force toward that end—that issue is almost non-existence these days.

I don't consider myself a white crusader fighting for the rights of black basketball players. Looking into the face of a kid, black or white, I see myself. If the same desire to be great is in his eyes, we're on the same page. Nothing to do with culture or his skin color—I'm looking into his eyes, trying to read his heart—it's exciting.

Now all we have to do is go to work.

Reggie as a Globetrotter

Lance McCain. Hurt but still able to help.

12
ATTITUDE

"If it's to be, it's up to me."
—Nolan Richardson

Without question, a proper attitude is what allows someone to have a chance to succeed in anything. Young players must learn to overcome the negative intangibles. Like demons bouncing around inside the player's head, these thoughts can impede the possibility of success. They encourage a player to "disappear" in the heat of battle. They plant feelings of "let someone else take the shot" or "I can't stop that guy." Thoughts like these must be eliminated, but it won't happen overnight.

One of the first steps in the process of learning how to win as opposed to learning how to play is *enduring pain and fatigue*. So much of sports is dealing with attitude. *You are not going to die.* By learning to deal with the physical contact and pain in football, I discovered it was possible to have a psychological advantage over my opponent which would wear him down. It was carried over to basketball. **I told myself, "Anytime I feel pain or fatigue, my opponent will never know."**

No one ever knows for sure how you're feeling when you get hit. It may hurt, but your opponent doesn't know that. He needs to think that the guy across from him can go all day. **What's beautiful about this scheme is, during the process of**

convincing your opponent that you are the Energizer Bunny, you convince yourself.

If you're lucky when coaching, you'll have a player who already has that wonderful quality of *never giving up* when he walks in the door. **He had it before you ever met him.** For the others, there is good news and bad news.

The good news is a player who doesn't seem to have it actually does; he just doesn't know it yet. You can make a believer out of him. You may have to experiment with different methods. You'll push him to become a different person. As much as you can, you need to do it now, not next year.

The bad news is, there are some who don't have it and never will. That's when the coach must step up. One of the major duties of a head coach is knowing when to hold 'em and when to fold 'em. It's always a difficult task to break the bad news to a young man who's dreamed of being involved in a sport he loves. But, let's be honest, quite often, deep down, he knows his coach is right: he's not as good or interested as he used to be. And if he's honest with himself, he never did *love* it enough. He may have just enjoyed being with the fellas. Competition didn't really get him all that excited.

Another approach: when dealing with a talented team member who had never bought into the 100-percent idea, I would seriously approach him with, "Do you realize my opinion of your athletic ability is way up here?" I'd hold my hand up, about head-high.

He didn't know what to think, but it sounded good to him so far.

Now came the tough part. I would then say, "The only problem is your attitude is about here." I'd hold my hand down, about knee-high.

"You hurt our team every day with your selfishness, and you're not even aware of it. It's all going to stop very soon, or you won't be with us much longer." Two things are now possible: a big confrontation in the middle of practice is avoided, and it's now his choice. The ball is now in his court. See what he does with it.

After revealing your sincere admiration for him while also revealing your disappointment in him, **how can he continue to remain the same?** Most get the message, but some are incapable. You may have to bid them farewell. A good player with a bad attitude will contradict everything you try to build.

Jackie Phinnessee could have been that way, but he wasn't allowed to. He was a specimen at six-foot-five and 220 pounds—the closet thing to Muhammad Ali I've ever seen. You wouldn't want to get in a scuffle with Jackie. Pound for pound, Spud Webb was obviously the greatest athlete I've ever been around, but Jackie Phinnessee was a close second. I recruited him out of the Army. With all his power and skill he had one undeniable flaw—his immaturity and quick temper were a constant, potential problem. I loved the guy (maybe if I had been his roommate, I wouldn't have felt that way). But I was his coach, and he tried very hard to do the right thing. There were some good days and some not-so-good days.

One incident stands out. We were in the middle of the 1983 Midland College season, the year following our championship run.

During a hard-fought conference game, Jackie became very upset over what he thought was a touch-foul he had been assessed. Things hadn't been going well for him—I could see the kettle beginning to boil.

As the players and referees all moved toward the other basket to shoot the free throws, Jackie was slowly trailing along mumbling to himself about the injustice that had just been handed him.

As he began to walk by our bench, I felt if anything was going to settle him down and curtail his increasingly negative response (which could be anything from extreme profanity to a well-placed punch at an opponent's nose), it was going to have to be me, ASAP.

I stepped onto the court in front of him asking, "Jackie, are you all right?"

He looked right through me. He didn't even see me.

A different tactic…let's see. I then placed the palm of each hand on the sides of his face and asked, "Jackie, you know I love you, don't you?"

Still, no response. The second time I asked, he blinked, looked at me, and calmly replied, "Yes."

I continued, "Do you love me?"

"Yes," he answered without hesitation. (Progress, perhaps?).

With my hands still on his face, standing on the court in front of a few thousand fans, I quietly said, "Then I want you to do something for me—understand we are about to win an important game, unless you go off as you've been known to do in the past. Got it?" In a flash, his reply was, "Yes sir, Coach. I'm cool."

Just like that, it was over. Whether anybody understood or not (which you cannot worry about), it was very real—it was the best way to handle Jackie Phinnessee while he was about to do something he would regret. The reason it was effective was because I meant every word of it, and Jackie knew it.

My point is this: it's imperative that you try to figure out each player, the sooner the better.

Had I yelled at Jackie during his original state of mind, he probably would have verbally replied in a manner we both would have regretted. You have to figure things out for yourself and become the leader you were hired to be. Throughout the year I had been giving Jackie little tidbits of praise whenever possible—something to counteract the occasional disciplinary actions. That's why Jackie trusted me and eventually heard what I was saying. **Most of these guys are just big kids—we can't forget that.** That's why I continually emphasize that *teaching* X's and O's are important in coaching, but no more important than *learning personalities and emotional makeups.*

Anyone who has coached a few years has interesting, sometimes unexplainable stories to tell. One of mine doesn't even deal with one of my players. It happened in the spring of 1985 when I coached an all-star game in Waco.

The two teams were made up of twelve sophomores, each from the two NJCAA regions, primarily from Texas—Region V (Western Texas and Eastern New Mexico) and Region XIV

(Eastern Texas and Western Louisiana). I had the Region V squad.

Players end up in junior college for many reasons. But one commonality they share is proving they are capable of playing at an upper-level school. There are over five hundred two-year schools, called junior colleges or community colleges, throughout the country with athletes hoping to go to a top four-year program. They've ended up at this junior college in a small town a long way from home to play ball for two years and maintain adequate grades.

They are hoping for a basketball scholarship so they can further their careers in a sport they've dreamed about and played all their lives. About a third of these all-star kids in Waco had yet to sign with anyone for their upcoming junior year and needed to shine in front of the scouts over the next two days. This was a serious, scary time for them.

As their coaches, we were allowed two workouts with which to get acquainted—it was our only chance to appraise them as players and see how they conducted themselves during the off-time. One of my players from Ranger Junior College wasn't doing too well. He was what coaches call a "tweener," a player lacking the quickness and ball-handling skills needed to be a true guard while being too short to play inside.

He might have been a good athlete, but he was caught in between what four-year coaches were fond of. No one was interested in him. He had heard nothing from any four-year school and his body language showed it.

Talking with him before boarding the bus to return to our hotel after our second workout, I told him it wasn't too late for him. But his moping around wasn't going to help his cause.

It didn't seem to be getting through to him so out of nowhere came, "Get on the bus and you'll see that before we make it back to the hotel, something will happen that will make you realize how lucky you are."

Who knows—it just came out. (You may notice—there will be no mention of a sudden scholarship offer—that's what he wanted to hear).

As we drove back to the hotel, a glimpse in my rearview mirror revealed a half-dazed, troubled young man. His future was a question mark. I thought, *Lord, please give this boy a sign.* Nearing the hotel, my mind was turning over possibilities—something had to surface. How about, "See, we made it back to the hotel without an accident." Good grief, that couldn't be the sign. What was I going to do?

While I was deep in thought, **it happened right before my eyes.**

Two blocks from our hotel, we came upon an elderly bag lady waiting for the street light to change. (Need I say more?) When it did, we watched her amble across the street at a very slow, shaky pace, pushing an old beat-up grocery cart, no doubt filled with everything she owned—old clothes, shoes, pots, pans, etc. It got very quiet. It was one of those "But for the grace of God, that could be my mother" moments. I looked in my rearview mirror again. Downcast had turned to joy for one young man. This kid from Ranger could hardly sit still. He had seen the "sign" before it had even registered with me. The whole thing was wonderful.

I have no idea if that experience stuck with him. I don't even know how his scholarship chances turned out. But he was a different person during the rest of the weekend. I'm sure he learned something that day—I know I did: **If you ask someone else to expect a sign, you shouldn't be surprised if one appears.**

When you're away from the gym and see one of your players, stop him and talk a little basketball, at least the "attitude" phase of it. It will help solidify what he's been hearing all week. Not only may the light suddenly click on in his head, but he'll appreciate your enthusiasm and dedication and be motivated to work harder.

Even if you only give him five minutes, he'll be pleased you singled him out and gave him some extra individual time. When your players realize how important it is to you, it will become more important to them. (It's all a form of brainwashing, but it still remains in the realm of honesty.)

I recall a player on one of my last Rockwall teams who was always respectful to me but, at the same time, worried me. Rockwall is a small town, and a couple of people who were in the know said he had associates who were not good influences.

One day after practice, while other players were shooting on their own, I sat down with him under one of the baskets, our backs against the wall. (For some reason, this is always a great place to talk to a player.) I leveled with him. I reminded him of the many temptations he was presently facing and that he would continue to feel pressure to follow the wrong path. I told him he had to be strong and do what was right no matter who was telling him differently. (In this case, it was an older brother.) He had to continue to be the good citizen I saw every day in the gym.

I recently found out that that young man is now a preacher at a local church. Is that cool or what? Was it my talk? Who knows?

It might have helped. It certainly didn't hurt. But that's not the issue. In this case, basketball opened the door to that conversation. I'm just proud to hear he's doing well.

Quite often, when young players hear what every coach talks about—trusting and caring for each other, being a team—**they actually do not know what that means**. They think they do. They agree that it sounds good, but, like a lot of people, they've never cared much about anyone but themselves. They've never seriously thought about being part of a team.

I believe, as their coach, you must break it down when you tell them what you expect. Give specific examples. **Remember, imagine you're talking to third-graders**.

Don't assume anything. When something happens in practice or while the team is watching last night's game film, and a beautifully unselfish play occurs, point it out. Make a big deal out of it. Run it back. Do it again. Explain that what you've just observed is how to play basketball.

From the first time he dribbles a basketball, a child inherently believes the ball belongs to him. He doesn't want to share it because if he throws it to his brother, he may not get it back.

The selfish attitude begins then and doesn't change until the kid's lucky enough to have a coach who insists that his brother (teammate) throw the darn thing back.

The road always presented problems—a lot of things can happen. You had to be strong. When any type of poor sportsmanship is mentioned, I always think of an anecdote regarding **Knute Rockne, the legendary football coach at Notre Dame.** At halftime of one game, Rockne's best defensive lineman complained bitterly that the opponent lined up across from him was playing extremely dirty—grabbing, holding, and occasionally slugging him during their constant battle within the line of scrimmage.

Coach Rockne trusted what his player said and gave him advice which has become one of my favorite quotes: **"Contain yourself until the game is well in hand. And then, if your adversary insists on the illusion that he is Jack Dempsey . . . disillusion him."**

I seldom uttered it to my team, and only when we had the time to discuss how it might relate to us (oh yeah, and who Jack Dempsey was). Whatever . . . it's still a great quote.

I learned (the hard way) how intimidation can affect a team during my fourth year as the Midland College coach. Cooke County was noted for creating a climate of trash-talking and other intimidating antics. In addition, their physicality intimidated us. The referees also got caught up in their intimidation. They later apologized, which rarely happens. I'm not complaining. **If you're going to be a champion, you have to overcome all types of adversity.** Cooke County was a type of team you had to be ready for. I didn't have my guys ready for the physicality and the trash talk. I learned that the preparation we needed had to begin early in the fall.

After that experience, I pledged that never again was my team going to be ill-prepared and intimidated during a silly basketball game. Never again would I sit on a bench, watching an opposing coach and his players control the atmosphere of a ballgame by actually intimidating the referees. Because of that game, future Midland College teams would be different. We also started recruiting a slightly different type of player and prepared for much more intensity. We went through the crawling and walking stages, and before long we were beginning to run.

When my Midland College team arrived at our designated motel for the 1982 NJCAA Tournament in Hutchinson, Kansas, the first player we saw was a very solidly built, six-foot-ten giant. He was an intimidating figure, but were weren't intimidated—we were certainly concerned, but not intimidated—*Big Difference.* And, I'm sure we were all thinking, "I hope we don't have to play that guy."

We didn't know it at the time, but that imposing figure was **Evon Joseph**, the starting post man for number-one-ranked, undefeated Miami Dade. The first native Haitian to play collegiate basketball in the US, Joseph later played at Georgia Tech before being drafted by the New Jersey Nets. As it turned out, we *did face him*—in the championship game.

All season long, that 1982 Chaparral squad was never noticeably intimidated by size or being considered the underdog. They were a supremely confident group of young men. The last thing we worried about was losing. Throughout the entire year, I never saw a look of fear or desperation, no matter the circumstance. **Three young men led the way: Puntus Wilson, Chester Smith, and Spud Webb.**

If you looked at any of those three during a game, you wouldn't have a clue if we were up twenty-five or down twenty-five. You're fortunate when there's one on your team—we had three. All three gave their teammates and their coach a great deal of confidence.

[Interesting, but as I have pointed out the unusual *character* that each of those three Dallas youngsters shared, I just now realize that all starting five players had the same amazing psychological makeup. The other two members—Jerome Crowe and Lance McCain—of that starting team which had been attached to the *Big Three's* hip since that disastrous tournament in November, were similar in personality.] They could be best described more as role-players, quietly doing their job on that starting five, basically unnoticed and basically unknown.

The same strategy also applies when someone is verbally razzing you from the stands. You may clearly be within the sound of his voice, but you should never acknowledge that you can hear him. It doesn't matter if you're three feet away. You are completely unaware—invisible. **Remember, those who are creating all the commotion never know for sure if you can hear them unless you react.** If you do give in, it will become three times worse.

Let it motivate you. Your *non-reaction* can turn it completely around.

The more someone yells, the better you play. Feed off of it. Again, it's a mental game.

Consider this: I can honestly say that what I achieved as a player on the road was *definitely* better than at home. My pride would boil inside me and my performance would automatically be enhanced from the moment we stepped off that yellow bus. I never could understand any teammate backing off just because Mom and Dad couldn't make it to the out-of-town game.

Likewise, if you checked my team's home and away record throughout most of my coaching career, you would find that those stats mirrored my feelings as a player.

A player's confidence trickles down from his coach. If the coach isn't confident, how can you expect the team to be?

Imagine yourself as a first-year coach. Your opponent is coached by an ex-All-American from a big university you've watched play on television. Your players would actually like to have his autograph.

You're young and even find yourself a bit intimidated. What you haven't thought about is the fact that he's young too, at least when it comes to coaching.

Analyze the situation. You've no doubt spent more hours studying the game, preparing yourself and your team. You probably relate to your players, as a coach, better than he does his. You have no need to feel inferior. **It's not what you did as a player that will win you games—it's what you've taught your players on the practice floor, as their coach.**

When I coached on the basketball court, I was in my own little world. *At that moment, I believed I was the best coach in the country. I may not have been, but I believed I was.* There's nothing wrong with feeling that way—in fact, you had better if you're going to survive in the profession (just keep it to yourself). If you believe in what you're teaching and know how to express it to your players, why shouldn't you be confident?

As a young coach, you may not view yourself with a great deal of confidence. But as the seasons roll on and you see your goals being accomplished, you'll feel differently. You'll see you deserve positive thoughts and those wonderful wins.

Sometimes it's hard to determine what motivates a player. What allows him to have a great night on the court? There are many possible answers.

Derrick Wilson, a freshman from Chicago, had to deal with an unusually difficult answer after playing for our team one night.

Our 1979–80 Midland College squad had an important conference game against Howard College. As we were getting on the bus for the one hour trip to Big Spring, I received a phone call from Derrick's grandmother in Chicago informing me that Derrick's father had passed away. I promised her that Derrick would board a plane first thing in the morning. After the game would be the best time to give Derrick the bad news.

We were supposed to be the better team, but someone forgot to tell Howard College. Throughout most of the first half, we played like an unconcerned group of children. Derrick wasn't a starter, and there were some games in which he never saw action.

He seemed to accept his backup role and contributed to the team whenever possible. With seven minutes left in the half, I was searching for something to get us going, something to change the momentum that Howard was enjoying.

Though he wasn't part of our normal rotation, I inserted Derrick. What's a bit strange is my calling on Derrick, as far as I can remember, had nothing to do with his father's passing. Something told me to sub him in, even though the timing wasn't our normal routine. Maybe it was a subconscious decision on my part. I don't know.

Call it what you will, but Derrick went nuts. He hit three long-range buckets, each time running back on defense, yelling, "I'm from Chicago." I usually tried to keep my players walking that thin line between overdoing trash talk and remaining emotionally motivated while playing. But that night, I wasn't going to interfere. Something was in the air. The night belonged to Derrick. Here's a youngster—on this night, of all nights—who hardly played, and he was winning the game for us.

He continued his excellent play throughout the evening. As far as we were concerned, it was the game of his life. As I watched his performance, I was saying to myself, *Derrick, if you only knew what you are about to face after the game.*

When we got back to our campus, I walked with him down the dark hallway away from the locker room. He immediately knew something wasn't right. I gave him the bad news and held him as he cried. **He kept repeating, "He was my *onliest* dad."**

Derrick played two years for us, helping us to establish a winning program, but never did he have another game like that night. Even though he didn't know it at the time, I can't help but believe that the magnificent game he played was anything other than a tribute to his dad.

Our team won an important game that night, but Derrick and his family back in Chicago were the ones considered responsible. There were angels flying all over that basketball court that night.

Years later, my situation was quite different. When I became the coach at Rockwall High School in 1999, there were no real expectations of winning. The thinking was, **I hope we don't**

lose. Unfortunately, that's not enough. The fear of losing is normal, but that thought should not linger. The anticipation of winning should replace it before long. The players I inherited were undisciplined and lacking in fundamentals. They had to be molded into a team, and it wasn't going to happen overnight.

As opposed to my Midland experiences, these Rockwall high school youngsters were babes in the woods. They knew nothing about the process of winning. Several changes had to be made, and, thankfully, the steps required to get there were accepted by most, but not without a struggle.

If you boil it down in simple terms, two forces were required to meet halfway: a very determined coach and a dozen kids who were sometimes reluctant to take everything thrown at them. Both forces eventually did their job.

The one positive advantage that permeated the challenge confronting me was very obvious: *I KNEW WHAT I WANTED AND WHAT I WAS DOING.* (That was certainly enjoyable.) One advantage of age is experience, which usually means that some wisdom is coming along on the journey. We made significant strides.

Expectations began to change. As the season progressed and the wins kept piling up, our confidence grew. We even managed a post-season double-overtime playoff win against Carter High School of Dallas. They were ranked third in the state. By the time we reached the regionals held at Baylor University in Waco, we had only one loss and that had come way back prior to Christmas.

We were one step away from moving on to the Texas State Final Four at the University Texas in Austin. Unfortunately, our opponent was **Klein Forrest High School from Houston**. Klein Forrest had three major-level players: a six-foot-ten center who was going to the University of Texas and a pair of guards, both headed to the Big East Conference. We were not made up of Division I players. We had only one player I would classify as even close to being a major talent. That was it. I knew it was possible to win, but the task would be difficult.

Once you convince your players (especially high schoolers) that they can win, it comes as a real disappointment to them, even a shock, when they don't. They had given their best throughout the year and provided a lot of excitement for our loyal fans, but it was suddenly time to go home.

Fast-forward to the next year. After another double-overtime sectional victory, this time against state power **Kimball High School from Dallas**, we again headed to Waco for the regionals, where we ran into another Houston area team, **Cypress Springs High School**. They too had a pair of Division I caliber guards, but this time we contained them for most of the game. However, Cypress Springs was just slightly better than us. We went to overtime before losing.

For high school guys, losing your final game brings a flood of emotion. Kids play all year with everything building toward the play-offs. When it suddenly ends, it feels like they've hit a brick wall. What they fail to realize beforehand is that sometimes the odds are against them.

Consider this: Every team in each division of the state that's involved in the post-season playoffs, *with the exception of one, ends the season with a loss.*

A veteran coach knows before each game even starts what his team's chances are. Of course, it still hurts if you lose. My Rockwall team had maxed out their effort. They had done nothing to be ashamed of. They played as hard as they could. I couldn't help thinking how far this group had come the past two years.

They had learned the power of being a team and how grand it felt being a part of it. But, again, it was time to go home.

I will always be proud of my Rockwall boys.

I recently had lunch with Josh Naylor, an ex-player, who reminded me of an incident that occurred during the fall of 2001 at the beginning of his only year at Rockwall High School. Josh was a six-foot-one point guard who moved to Rockwall specifically to play basketball. The previous year, during the Christmas break, we had played in a tournament at Round Rock High just north of Austin. Josh's dad was so impressed with our team that he wanted his son to play for us.

Moving an entire family just so someone can play a sport (I'm sure there were additional reasons) almost never works. The move is hard enough, but doing it just before your son's senior year only compounds the difficulty. Usually, a parent who will go that far is unrealistic about his child's abilities or there is something negative going on with the kid. The kid is running away from something, or the dad is living through his son's participation in sports. Whatever the reason, the move usually generates problems. Thankfully, this situation appeared to be an exception.

After watching Josh in the Round Rock Tournament, I approved the relocation. It didn't seem so risky. He had real ability. This kid with the floppy blond hair was impressive. He was a pistol, but I didn't think he was a bad kid. That's where experience helps. (If you've noticed, I'm slowly but surely inserting *experience that only comes with aging.*)

We really needed a point guard. The coaching staff (all two of us) crossed our fingers, hoping it would work out. Josh turned out to be a very good addition to the team. It was a good fit. The truth is, he came just at the right time and saved our season. We had just lost last year's solid point guard, Curt Tyszko, to graduation, and Josh stepped right in to fill the vacancy. He was an excellent player, shooter, and ball-handler. He was smart, and his teammates liked him.

Every now and then you get lucky.

Josh did have one or two minor negatives. He was an occasionally careless passer and was like typical high school players when it came to defense: he didn't take it seriously most of the time. These were fixable problems, however. **The question was: How long would it take him to buy into eliminating these negatives? In other words, was he coachable?** It usually takes a semester to adjust to a new school. It takes time to learn the new team's approach to the game. Unfortunately, we only had Josh for one year.

The incident that helped answer those questions happened during practice when we were running a drill that requires the ball-handler to go up against two defenders who are allowed to be very aggressive while guarding. The purpose of the drill is to teach ball-handlers how to remain strong and poised so they can withstand a strong defender during a game.

The drill also shows the two defenders how to trap, how to use their feet and not their hands, and how to gauge correct angles. I really liked the drill, but it was physical.

Because hacking and bumping occur during the exercise, it's tough on the offensive player with the ball. That day, after Josh had received what he considered well over his share of physical pounding, he stopped in the middle of the drill and declared, "Enough is enough." He even threw in a cuss word, something he never did. I sarcastically asked him if he couldn't handle the drill. When he mumbled something back, I told him to go sit on the side and watch the rest of the guys finish this "unbearable" task.

Since his actions were not a part of his normal demeanor, I was pretty sure Josh regretted what he did as soon as he did it. My suspicions were confirmed after practice when he came to my office and sincerely apologized for his outburst. Josh was a great kid—this was not going to be a problem. Calmly, I explained that he would not be expected to repeat something like that again.

Taking it a step further, it was important that he knew that my dealing with a player who had some fire was better than one who didn't. I told him, **"Don't lose the fire, and don't be afraid of it. Just control it."**

All of my players were not dealt with in this manner. Immature kids are usually spoiled and require some running and/or "sitting" during games to get them to understand what you want from them. Well-disciplined kids can be reasoned with.

A kid like Josh only required a brief conversation. He wasn't going to have any issues.

Years later as we were having lunch, Josh told me he was surprised at my reaction back then, and he believed the way it was handled contributed to an important "positive turning point" regarding his senior-year move.

He realized not everything was going to fall into place right away, and he would have to make adjustments quickly. He didn't want to blow it. He also said he felt he had a coach he could deal with, one who didn't make mountains out of molehills.

One of my favorite sayings is, "To teach is to touch a life forever." I believe 99 percent of coaches and teachers start out with that philosophy. (At some point, a coach's personal win-loss record and career may become more important. That's when *winning becomes everything,* meaning your goals get a little twisted). I greatly appreciated Josh's remarks. It's what coaches and teachers should want to hear.

Midland College's Herman Henry's tight defense makes things rough for South Plains' Lavell Garror in Odessa College Invitational tournament.

13
WINNING AND LOSING

*"When you win, you're not nearly
as good as you think you are.
When you lose, you're not nearly as bad."*

—Darrell Royal

When you're winning, all is right with the world, for the moment, anyway. That's why you don't overpraise a victory.** When you combine your praise with the praise from fans, parents, and girlfriends, the players may come strutting into the gym the next day. You may just have to bring them down a notch or two. Like it or not, the team must comprehend the importance of calming down and facing the reality of the next day.

Often, there's a team preparing to play you within twenty-four hours or less. Let's say they watched you play in a tournament that both of you are in. You looked real good and they didn't. **Which team do you think will be mentally ready to play tomorrow night?**

It might serve them well to remember Peanut's words (straight out of the comics): **"It doesn't matter if you win or lose . . . until you lose."**

Many people use the word "family" to describe the feeling of togetherness of a close-knit group like an athletic team. It's another term that is sometimes overused, but may certainly be accurate.

The media particularly likes it, and they don't hesitate to use it any chance they get. To some extent, all winning teams normally do feel a sense of family. It's what holds them together through thick and thin, at least for a season.

The truth is, when you're winning, things seem to click quite easily. Lose four or five games in a row and see how the "family" functions.

Wouldn't it be convenient if a coach could create that feeling on his team every year? Unfortunately, he can't. It's out of his hands. But, coaches never stop attempting to do just that. **Unfortunately, a team's chemistry has to come together on its own. It's the collective mix of everyone's personalities.** Those intangible feelings are either there or not, seemingly despite what coaches do.

One day in the dark film room, I interrupted our film viewing and slowly approached our big post man, Teviin Binns. After watching one of the many passive moves Teviin commonly demonstrated during our games, I had seen enough. Teviin was a 6-10 finesse postman who preferred to play in areas of the court where there was the least amount of contact, mainly the high post.

We were glad to have Tev at Midland Junior College, knowing full well, however, that he was a "project" that would take time to rearrange his nonaggressive personality. The truth is, skill-wise, he was more a perimeter player, as opposed to a low post area player. But, coaches tend to put players where the team needs them, at least initially. Lucky for Teviin, our offense was designed to move every player in and out—so, where you started on the floor was immaterial on our team.

Instead of dressing him down, which he was expecting,

I walked to his front-row seat, stood directly in front of him, reached out and asked him for his hands.

He didn't hesitate. For about three minutes I held both hands and softly spoke to him like a grandmother might have.

I explained that he was a good person who was on the verge of becoming a man. "You are not that tall skinny kid who used to be picked on as you were growing up. Those slender arms are now weapons. Those elbows are sharp spears that can clear out opponents while rebounding. It's time for Teviin Binns to break out and show a cocky, confident side."

There was not a peep out of the team. You could hear a pin drop.

This was the *beauty* of most of our teams at Midland College— we were together. I had several successful Division I coaches, at one time or another, tell me some very flattering things about the comradery of our teams—you can't create chemistry, but you can get close with constant "reminders" during each practice. *The secret? Don't keep people around who do not care.*

I felt everyone in that dark film room was pulling for big Tev to visualize the transition he needed to make. His problem was our problem. At no time did Teviin pull his hands away from my slight grip. It was not easy for a tall skinny kid to shake the memories of growing up in the Bronx. However, I knew he understood what I was saying. I felt he was telling me, "Keep talking, Coach, you're right on target."

He sat in that silent room surrounded by teammates who would normally have ridiculed him for his hand-holding ordeal with his coach—but not this time. This team and coach were trying to help a fellow teammate. It doesn't get any better than that. And, as we noted earlier, big Tev was one of those guys who didn't react favorably to harsh criticism. At that moment, we all got a glimpse of what "family" meant.

I have always detested the "win or lose, we're all proud of you" speech someone gives to a team before a game. Presidents of colleges are known to "help out" in this manner. They mean well and I appreciate their interest but the players don't want to hear that type speech on game day. The message unfortunately suggests that losing is acceptable. What I heard as a player was, "We're not sure if you can win, and if you don't we want you to know we still love you."

It's the kind of sentiment that should be reserved for the sports banquet after the season's completed, when it's all right to say, "Even though we fell a little short of our goal this year, I want you guys to know we're still mighty proud of you."

When I drove my Midland College team down a lonely West Texas highway, heading to or from a game, I'd occasionally have a sudden urge to talk to them. Even though some might be sleeping like babies, the bus would come to a halt wherever we were, and we all would crawl off and stretch. The real reason we stopped was to allow me to conduct a brief session of my *Basketball Brainwashing 101* one more time. I'd gather them on the side of the road and talk to them briefly. I took this opportunity to remind them of the commitments we'd all made at the beginning of the year, perhaps our goals, or simply how proud I was of them.

During these situations, the players may be sleepy and grumpy, but they will listen. **I promise you: they will remember those**

talks, if only in their subconscious—it was always a positive talk. When you gather your team up on the side of a lonesome road in West Texas, and pour your heart out, it may sound like a waste of time, but it isn't.

Of course, if you don't feel comfortable doing it, *don't*. I felt absolutely comfortable, and I'm certain the players didn't really mind. It's important to realize that young players don't have the confidence that we all want. They need constant encouragement from their coach, and they have to believe in him 100 percent.

Throughout the year, during a time-out, sometime in the last couple of minutes of a big game, it will come to them, perhaps only subconsciously. The words they have had implanted in them, not just during lonely bus rides but all year long, will come alive. It may be in the huddle, the locker room, or on the playing floor. It will give them support and make them stronger.

They will gradually believe they are the team that will win because they deserve to win. I would like playing on a team like that.

They have to get over the idea that somebody else will probably win. That has always been the mindset of many youngsters—and that's the type mentality you will begin to eliminate at your school. Understand what's going on, stop the dreaming, and start creating a winning atmosphere beginning with fall practices. Settling for second is not acceptable. Notice I didn't say striving for first and finishing second was unacceptable. *The question is, "How hard did they strive?"* There will be another day—remember how you felt and don't let it happen again.

During our preseason games and tournaments, I hoped to see signs that everything we'd put them through would produce results. At a tournament in Amarillo, we stumbled along, winning our first two games and making it to the finals. Since the players didn't expect to be there, I was curious to see how they would handle the situation. To everyone's amazement, we came from behind to defeat the tough home team and win the tournament. After receiving some individual awards along with our first-place trophy, we headed back to the motel to order some food. As the team walked through the halls to their rooms, they spontaneously chanted, "MC, MC, MC." They knew I didn't want them making a racket because of the other guests in the motel, so the chant was subdued, almost apologetic.

They weren't used to winning and were reluctant to overdo it.

Whether they understood it or not, I saw and heard real pride in this team for the first time that year. Some teams never get to that point the entire year.

The "MC" chant was music to my ears. This was just a simple example of an important step—building a winning program.

Dr. Fran Pirozzolo is a licensed consulting psychologist who works exclusively with collegiate and professional athletes. He has written several books on the mental approach to athletics and has been involved with the New York Yankees, Houston Astros, Detroit Tigers, and finally as the Mental Skills Coach for the Texas Rangers.

Dr. Pirozzolo once conducted a study to determine if top "winning" athletes at the professional level shared certain personality characteristics that seemed to result in their succeeding in the clutch. He concentrated on professional athletes who maintained amazing winning-streak performances or were constantly winning events with last-second heroics.

Three common traits always emerged:

1. They adopted a simple approach while preparing—no gimmicks, just hard work, focusing on fundamentals;
2. They had strong spiritual beliefs. They didn't feel they were alone in their sporting endeavors. The game wasn't a matter of life or death; and
3. They had a sincere desire to avoid attention, to not seek the limelight.

It's been my experience that the select group of winning athletes I've been fortunate to be involved with were very close to that. (Of course, there are always a couple of exceptions.)

Kevin Walker was in that select group of winning athletes. I'm not sure he understood why I bragged on him during and after his career at Rockwall High. If I bragged about anyone else, that player might feel full of himself and need correcting the next day. Not Kevin. He never dwelled on himself very long because he was completely unselfish, the type of young man coaches appreciate because he made things run smoother and set a terrific example for the rest of the team.

Kevin was a five-foot-seven, stocky point guard who looked more like a nose guard for a 2-A football team. He possessed average speed, quickness, and shooting ability. He was always looking to make the smart and timely pass. Among his other assets was his ability to stick to his man defensively and his desire to hit the winning basket or free throw with time running out, a shot others might avoid.

In short, he was a winner. But you would have to see him play 2 or 3 games before convincing yourself to choose him.

A guy who wins games doesn't sit around analyzing what he's going to do; he just goes out and wins games. He doesn't think, *What if I miss a shot?* He just knows, if the team is going to win, somebody needs to make a shot. He reasons, *Since I'm the one with the ball, I'm the one who has to do it. No problem.*

Though he wasn't going to get any college offers, Kevin was a pleasure to coach because of my admiration for any player who is unselfish and does everything for the good of the team. These 100-percent guys are rare. Kevin started for me for two years, doing every-thing asked of him and more. Because of his quiet consistency, he tended to go unnoticed by an outsider.

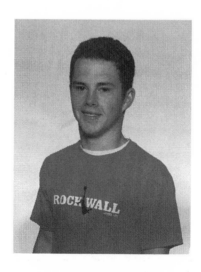

Kevin Walker

Since high school kids often do not see the big picture, his teammates probably didn't realize how valuable he was to the team. A guy like Kevin would make a good coach because he understood that nothing was given to him and much could be accomplished by pulling together. However, after a couple of years of coaching, he'd see that few players seriously love the game and the competitiveness which it requires. He'd learn that the Kevin Walkers of the world are rare indeed.

A light would come on and two thoughts would hit him: He would start to understand why Coach Stone was always bragging on him, because he would now know, first-hand, that unselfish players are rare. And concerning the team, he would tell himself, *There are going to be some changes around here.*

If you choose to be a coach, you will experience a number of contradictory situations and emotions during a season. You and your family may experience several mood swings, individually and collectively. Following a week of intensive practice, you will push your players to the peak of aggressiveness for a couple of hours during game competition, encouraging them to give everything they have to become victorious.

When the contest ends, it will be time to become gracious and humble. That switch is difficult to manage. Most young men find it almost hypocritical when it is required. Remember the saying, "Nice guys finish last"? It's often true. But there is a line that shouldn't be crossed. It's just difficult to find sometimes.

This is where a veteran coach can really help you. If you're young and just starting out in this business, perhaps you've thought about it for a long time and have a great number of ideas for developing your team. You may feel you don't need much advice from anybody. You're wrong—you do. Don't overlook the volume of good advice you can receive from a veteran coach.

When Billy Tubbs was the head coach at Oklahoma, he had his team rockin' and rollin', often averaging more than one hundred points per game. His strategy was not complicated: press, run, and bury your opponent no matter the score or the time remaining on the clock. Like it or not—if you were on the wrong end of the burial, you didn't. Billy always said, "If you ever have a similar opportunity against me, go for it." I believe he meant it, knowing full well those opportunities would be rare.

I once attended a Nike Basketball Clinic at which Billy was speaking. He was a comedian with a voice that sounded like Jack Nicholson's. Like any good comedian, there was a strong vein of truth in his humor.

One of the things he said on a serious note was, **"If there are one hundred coaches sitting out here today, there will be no more than five of you who truly believe in your chances of going all the way next year."**

Oh, so true. Think about it—if you truly believe this statement, you are way ahead of 95% of your opponents. It's like having a complete and thorough scouting report of them.

How a coach reacts to good things like winning or bad things like losing sends a strong message to his team. Periodically, coaches have to fight negative thinking too. They may not care to admit it, but a fierce competitiveness tacitly exists among them. They like to say athletics is all about the kids, but it's much more than that.

Early in the season, if you're jumping around after a victory like an NFL lineman who just made a sack at their ten-yard line, what perception are you creating? Possibly that you really didn't think your team was capable of winning?

On the other hand, if you're devastated by a loss, it might appear you have little hope for the remainder of the season.

What you do or say after a loss can affect the outcome of future games. Be smart: your players are observing you.

Winners are not mesmerized with joy when they win, nor are they racked with despair when they lose. They've learned ways of working through problems.

They have confidence they can overcome any obstacle which, in turn, gives them freedom to play. In my experience, it's seldom that a single exceptional athlete of mine did too much overthinking while playing. If you spend all your time thinking about the outcome, you miss the joy of the game. Accepting a first-place trophy is fun but not nearly as fun as playing for it.

It's kind of like the-chicken-or-the-egg scenario: **confidence creates winning, and winning builds more confidence.** A winner is a confident person. Because of his confidence, if he does lose, he honestly believes he will come out on top the next time. There's no need for tears, depression, or panic. He knows he's not going to let what happened be repeated. Two factors will emerge: he will know the opponent better and be more prepared for a possible return match, and during this preparation his concentration will be mature and very thorough.

But some years are just plain rough for a coach. When you don't have many good players, your goals have to be subtly changed. You still emphasize striving for excellent attitudes, old-fashioned hustle, and never giving up. But you don't dwell on winning so much. However, it is just as important that you continue to work on everything that gives your team a *chance* to win.

Even during this down period, you must preach a diligent work ethic. Your players may need a wakeup call or a pat on the back. There is no secret formula, but the ideal message would be something like, "You guys are the hardest-working team I've been around, and I'm very proud of you."

You may have to stretch the truth a bit, but don't feel guilty— they need to hear those very words. If Coach still believes in the team (and sometimes it's a challenge), all the work seems worthwhile. The reality is, you will occasionally have to weather the storm. **Stay strong. All coaches experience similar seasons.**

Now, all you've got to do is convince the school board.

———

I've learned that home yard work (ranking closely behind golf) is traditionally very therapeutic for all coaches that go through a rough season. Lessons learned from the past season, as well as possibilities for improvement in the coming year, flood your mind and help to deal with the hot summer task.

"Dutch" Kline, an Austin McCallum football coach during the late fifties, finished one season at 1–9. He explained how the process worked for him: **"Coaches who have great seasons are always in their front yards, working diligently. You should see my back yard—immaculate."**

"It doesn't matter if you win or lose...

until you lose."

Coaching

14
THE COACH-PLAYER RELATIONSHIP

"You don't lead by hitting people over the head—
that's assault, not leadership."

—-General Dwight D. Eisenhower

Teaching young people to play a sport is what most people view as coaching. Real coaches do much more than that. **The important questions are, "How is the student affected by this experience?** What has he gained, and will it affect him permanently?" It's not just about learning a sport, but also discovering himself and his relationships with others while moving through the entire process.

Is it like the military? Are we conducting a boot camp? No, but there should be shades of military discipline mixed in any athletic program. On many occasions, I have sat a father or mother down and asked them, "Do you really believe I can help your son grow if I can't have the freedom to push him toward a one-hundred-percent effort?

Do you understand that anything I do as a coach in an attempt to improve his maturity is for his own good and is never personal? And that someday he will be grateful for everyone's efforts on his behalf?" Seldom did Dad object. Mom often remained quiet.

Coaching for me represents all that's important. We're talking about *the power and privilege of helping young people transform* from the influence of home (whether we consider it positive or negative) to solid adulthood—a mature individual in every regard, emotionally, morally, and intellectually.

You may say, "That's not my responsibility. A school teacher or a coach can't offer all of that."

He can't? Somebody better try.

Look at it this way: I like my iced tea slightly sweet with lemon. Have you ever noticed how the flavor really kicks in after a short period of time as the ice melts? Something about the melted ice seems to blend all of the natural elements together.

But, in a manner of seconds, a waitress can unintentionally destroy what you've patiently created. Out of nowhere, she appears, refills your glass, and completes the act before you have time to explain that your tea is exactly how you like it. Now your perfect drink is no longer perfect.

The manager of an Amarillo restaurant where I was eating one day intermingled with the clientele, making sure all was well. He carried a pitcher of iced tea to refill customers' glasses. When he reached our table, he paused for a second or two, smiled, and asked, "Do you want me to refill your tea or have you got it like you want it?"

It was a simple question, but it showed the man was thinking of me, his customer. **He was paying attention to detail.**

What's interesting is this: That event occurred more than fifty years ago. I've been curious if someone would repeat it sometime. No matter where I've lived or traveled, no waiter or waitress has asked me that precise question in all of the years since—not one.

The best coaches are much like the Amarillo restaurant owner years ago—constantly communicating, and making decisions based on detailed observations.

Gregg Popovich is considered in the top three as an NBA coach. And yet he had to deal with **La Marcus Aldridge's** discontent this past season. Popovich was surprised to hear that Aldridge was not happy.

They met prior to this season, they talked, and they worked it out. Detailed observations were examined—Pop was unaware of Aldridge's legitimate concerns. Every coach (even the best) must deal with their players' concerns, those little details. All is well now. But if it can happen to Greg Popovich, it can happen to any NBA coach.

Here's the deal with coaching: you can't be a "sometime" coach. (I certainly don't consider Popovich a sometime coach. But his incident with Aldridge proves that no one is bullet-proof.) We all have to be "all in", working hard, and always consistent. That's what your players are looking for. You cannot overlook details— the details are what make the product whole. If they know you're for real, they'll feel secure because you've got their back. It's all about trust. **Real trust is discipline—real discipline is trust.** You have to remember that your players want your discipline and it has to be confirmed every day. As we keep saying, coaching isn't a part-time thing.

Discipline is something good, not bad. Discipline means, as a player, you know who you are and where you fit in. It's actually comforting.

When a coach says, "I love you guys," his players know if he's being sincere or falsely emotional. Depending on when and why it's said, players may think it's phony. It's an overused phrase. It's what they say in the movies. There's nothing wrong with saying what you feel—just be sure it's what you truly feel. If you haven't had the time to really get to know them, how can you know you love them? Your players know. They've had a close eye on you during the entire time.

Very seldom did I say "I love you guys" to a team. When I did, I meant, "I love the *effort* you guys give." John Wooden of UCLA fame used to tell us at clinics that he might love some player, but wouldn't want him marrying his daughter. Simply put, it boiled down to the players' attitudes. How hard and smart did they play? That's what mattered.

Players won't believe such sentiment until you have been through some rough times together—until you've proven you are loyal to each other. A first-day speech isn't going to cut it.

I remember one assistant from a big-time Division I program who was primed to step up to the next level.

After they won the NCAA Tournament, he got his shot at a head coaching job with a mid-major Division I school. I had known him for a few years. I privately doubted it would work out for him. The initial quotes from his new team confirmed my fears. The players told the media what a "great guy" he was and that he was a "player's coach."

Those statements, to a great extent, are red flags. How do the players know he's a "great guy" when it's the fall of his first year?

They haven't played a game yet. And what is a "player's coach"? I've never understood that label. It seems to me it can mean several things. If a new coach hears his players calling him a "player's coach" in the first semester, he should be concerned. He might need to ask himself, "Am I too buddy-buddy with them?"

I followed this coach's progress during that year. He hosted pizza nights at his home. The players really liked him and his great sense of humor. But this didn't translate very positive on the basketball court. Reality emerged quite quickly.

By the spring, he was on his way out, back to a more comfortable position as an assistant coach where he's doing well and smiling once again. I'm happy for him.

The lesson? It's always better to establish respect, not friendship, with your players. You can be friends later.

If you have a few basic, non-specific rules regarding training, you can keep from backing yourself up against a wall. **If I were required to have one and only one team rule, it would be: "Do not do anything that would embarrass you, me, or this school while you are a member of this team."** With that rule, you have all kinds of leeway.

Junior college athletes are near the eighteen year old mark or older and doors are suddenly opened to them that were closed a few months ago. Your team will be fully aware of normal co-ed activities, suddenly—like clubbing and partying—and will be tempted to join in.

As a coach, you should try to reach a happy medium and not violate your firm but fair relationship with your team.

I normally had little trouble with training rules. But the issue was jumped on as soon as their feet hit Midland, Texas soil during that first season.

They were reminded that it was not smart to be the first "violator." He would probably get the worst of it, because he would, in effect, be saying, "Ah, typical coach-talk. This guy ain't gonna stop me from having fun." They were also reminded that I had spies everywhere.

To be clear, my definition of a violator was, "If I heard about it, that meant you weren't very smart about it, so you are now a violator and now need to come see me."

Views regarding facial hair, length of hair, and a player's overall appearance tend to change. **My rule was always, "I am the judge, the only judge."**

I didn't have any length-of-hair measurement requirements. I simply said it would be up to me to determine if a particular individual looked "clean and respectful." Because my players trusted me to be fair, we never had one incident of rebellion against my judgment.

The fewer the rules you have as a coach, the better. One rule I always had was the N-word or slang names were not allowed.

Black players were not allowed to direct these words toward their black buddies, as harmless as it first appeared. What I found was when black players used the N-word, it was a red flag, a sign of immaturity, and a guarantee for trouble down the road.

To some extent, you have to view your players as the "enemy" during those first few weeks—sometimes months—because their habits are difficult to shake. You do not treat them as sub-humans, but a business-like manner is necessary. If you have a sense of humor, *use it*. But, you are not their buddy. When you act that way, you confuse them. You're supposed to be their coach.

All you need to worry about is establishing their trust and respect in a fair manner.

I had an unwritten rule regarding player-coach relationships: during the entire process of coaching, no matter the circumstances, *Never take a player's dignity away from him.*

It is one of the most important things to remember as a coach.

Of course, you push him and discipline him when necessary. Yes, at times some sarcasm is warranted, but never is he treated like a dog that the coach gets to humiliate anytime he feels like it. Resentment will build if you treat your players as sub-human.

You may try to coach like the great Green Bay Packer coach, Vince Lombardi. But remember, there was only one Lombardi. Besides, there was another side to Lombardi that often gets overlooked. **He also showed true affection for his players.** He demonstrated that on many occasions. The tough-guy coaches portrayed in sports movies are the very reason I'm reluctant to go see them. The most important factor is learning what each player can deal with. At what point does he feel he is being ridiculed instead of being coached?

I once attended a **major basketball clinic in Las Vegas** where one of the featured speakers was a Division I coach. He had recently been successful and was a bit full of himself at the time. A small college team in the Vegas area had been asked to help demonstrate various drills and schemes during the ninety-minute session. The volunteer players were hearing instruction for the first time from the guest speaker. The normal amount of confusion and hesitation was predictively taking place on the floor. The featured speaker seized upon the moment to ridicule one of the players, nonstop throughout the lecture. The audience got a kick out of it—at first.

After a while, however, it got old. I realize a college kid can take some needling, but this was, "Let me show you coaches how tough I am" at the player's expense. **At this point, I'm not being overly protective, but this is the very conduct that players truly resent.** He's got the microphone and all of the power—*he's being a bully, which isn't very smart.*

I always attempted to view the team as "my guys," not some useless bunch of delinquents. It wasn't always easy. Sometimes they received the wrath of an upset coach, no question about it, but they were always "my guys," and it took place in our own private environment, not for the enjoyment of onlookers.

You will never lead your players effectively if they believe you are unfair, or worse, a bully. They must understand that, despite everything they go through, you always have their backs.

(Having said this, do not think for one minute that you can save everyone of them—there are always exceptions, hopefully rare.)

At some point, when you're unquestionably in control, don't be surprised if your players seem settled and more confident. **The truth is, they want you in control and strong enough to lead them.**

They don't mind the perfection you demand. They just want you to remember who they are. By the second semester they will have figured it out, realizing that we are all on the same side. There will still be occasional squabbles—all families have squabbles. But, in a real sense, we will begin to think as a family.

Remember: everybody does something better than most other people. Discovering that "something" is an important step in anyone's life.

When I was in sixth grade, one of the events my coach entered me into for the citywide track meet was the seventy-five-yard dash. Placing fourth in any event for the entire city wasn't something to be ashamed of, but the one point I earned for that place didn't seem like much.

My coach reminded me, "Every point counts. You never know." His comment did little to improve my spirits.

Guess what? Our little "country school" ultimately won the meet by one point—my measly point *did* matter. This illustrated to me that, no matter how insignificant the contribution might seem at the time, everyone can contribute something to the team.

As a coach, if you have a player with a special talent, you should explain to him how the team needs that talent to secure victory. It doesn't have to be a talent that people always know about such as scoring. He might be a scrappy defensive player or a reliable spot-up shooter—or even a great practice player who brings a positive attitude to the gym every day. Let him help you win games. Brag on him some.

Get a kid to understand that he's special and he has something to offer that nobody else has and his enthusiasm will become contagious and spread to the entire team. Even the lowest man on the bench is important because, when he discovers he has something to give to the team, he becomes a contributor.

Here's the catch: YOU ARE THE KEY. Whether privately or in front of the team, you need to make every player feel important. Nobody else has the power or opportunity to control the winning atmosphere of your team.

The last guy on the team needs to know you respect him. Remember, if "a chain is as strong as its weakest link, then a team is as strong as its weakest player."

If a player feels he doesn't have your respect, he may become a traitor in your midst, causing a great deal of damage behind the scenes. Guys on the end of the bench who are ignored are prone to organize a *misery-loves-company club*. It's very easy to join.

One day, you look up and find that you have two culprits. A week later, they've been joined by another. **Be sure you keep an eye on the bench.** If things aren't right, do some adjusting, maybe some eliminating.

It ain't going to get better on its own.

The truth is, the coach and the players should learn from each other. A lot of these kids were from "the other side of the tracks." In comparison, I'd led a life coming from a small town in Kansas. I've always been grateful for the education I received from them and hoped they would some day feel equally grateful for my efforts.

You can't make snap judgments of people. The guy you figured wouldn't last two weeks sometimes becomes a solid player and a good citizen. Maybe no one ever made him do things correctly. A new start with new friends was the spark the kid needed to obtain a clear direction for the first time in his life.

On the other hand, a kid who came from a "good" family might be spoiled and unable to handle being out on his own and having the responsibility for meeting obligations such as simply washing his own clothes. Just because a prospect has great parents doesn't mean they have a great son. He might be your biggest headache.

I never quite bought into the statement, "He comes from a great family" or even, "He's always been on a winning team." I realize that may be a good sign, but what's he going to do when he looks around those first few days and realizes this is not going to be any picnic playing for this team. A coach should never assume that a recruit is going to fit right in—wait and see where the first semester leads you.

Every new level of play means tougher practices and stiffer competition. Sometimes the game that has always been so fun suddenly turns into work—when he views it as work, it can cease to be fun. That great kid from the great family might begin to show another side.

Coaches can fall short too. Some of them just don't have the strength and conviction to make winning happen—they've surrendered to the modern approach of making the game "fun". They don't want to run anybody off—they want to keep everyone happy. (Impossible.)

They "hope" they can win each game. Consequently, come game night, they might be looking up to see if the stars are aligned in a favorable way. *I really don't know what method they call upon with no visible stars during an afternoon game.*

When a young man first begins junior college or college, a vacuum exists in his life that is ready to be filled. A coach has an opportunity to help rearrange a young man's thinking at that time. He has to jump in with both feet because the window is narrow and it closes quickly.

The first two semesters will come and go in a flash. That's why I always started practices from day one of school—I wanted those kids under my thumb from the beginning.

Consider the changes they face: They're away from mama's cooking; they may have never flown on a plane; they may have never been in a disciplinary-type program before; they may never have taken their classwork or their attendance seriously; if they were black, they may never have been coached by a white guy or vice versa.

To further complicate things, when a kid is in a completely different locale, even the good kids begin to think, "Nobody knows me here."

It's actually just the opposite: new faces are noticeable. Pretty soon, trouble can follow.

Like businessmen away at a convention, they go out with some guys, and, before long, they may do something they wouldn't think of doing at home. Consequently, a coach needs to keep an eye on the new kids entering his program. He should be aware of who they are running with, what hours they keep, if they are attending classes, and if they're habitually late.

One of the most basic duties of a coach is helping his new players survive until Christmas when home sweet home awaits. This totally new environment is difficult for almost all freshmen away at school. Don't get caught off guard and discover in late December that because of some of his activities during the first semester, he won't be returning after the holiday break. The first semester is the first time a lot of these guys have been "on their own." You've got to really keep an eye on them.

To a great extent, this period in his life is monumental. If he goes back home without working through the adjustments of first semester, he will most likely regret it all of his life. When that four-week long college break finally arrives, most wounds, both physical and emotional, have time to heal. The people they've missed confirm their support for them.

They may, however, seem somewhat surprised finding themselves speaking about their first semester accomplishments with pride, unaware the feeling even existed. Before long, they're anxious to get back with the team—back to the place they've now complained about all fall, a place they consider a second home.

I remember Teviin Binns during his first year at Midland sending me a Christmas card from the Bronx, saying, "I miss you and the team and can't wait to get back," signed, "Love, Teviin." From the chaos of New York City to the sandstorms of West Texas, a kid is anxious to return after only one semester.

Incidents like these are unforgettable but not necessarily typical. The longer you coach at the junior college level, the more particular you become when choosing players. However, it's important to note that freshmen are definitely salvageable.

At my age, I'm not a dreamer. But from experience, I know that, through a game they cherish, you can get their attention and make some progress.

Their maturity level was always the most important obstacle to deal with. If anything caused an early exit, that was it. Some prospects were easily read—rigid and hopeless. In time, you learn to spot them and turn the other way before any commitments are made—let someone else sign them and produce that, "one-in-a-million" miracle.

Keeping players eligible in junior college was always a challenge. Like walking on thin ice, you never knew if or when it might bring you down. No matter what you did, you couldn't make everybody happy. The main reason these guys were in a juco wasn't because they lacked athletic ability or they were in need of some brushing up their skills but because they were academically deficient.

If you placed one of these players in easy classes and he stayed eligible for a two year period, but didn't obtain a transferable degree, you were accused of using him. Without a degree he would not be able to go on to a major university. He would be left out to dry when it came to Division I.

However, if you placed him in regular classes, including ones that were difficult for him to pass, he would probably come up short, which meant you didn't "take care of him," making everyone unhappy.

Sometimes, with college athletes, the best you could hope for was having them take some classes that varied in difficulty but not overly burdened with an unrealistic class load. If they maintained their eligibility for two years, they had a decent chance to complete their requirements during the following summer school.

That was the smartest approach. Of course, some of them were very capable of taking care of business the moment they arrived and graduated on time.

Parents are under the mistaken impression that it's the coach's job to see that their child graduates. Overzealous recruiters have helped promote this idea. How can a coach do that? He may get teachers and tutors to assist the kid in every way possible, but, in the end, it is the player who is ultimately responsible. Most kids figure this out. If they never do, their dream eventually fades away.

The school's administration may also be critical of you when you recruit borderline student-athletes. They constantly remind you what graduation rates are expected. Of course, these were the same administrators who might fire you when you don't win enough games. They like winning games with good students just like the major universities—we all do.

But it's not a realistic goal at the junior college level. I was lucky, however. There was common-sense support from my administration throughout my ten-year stint.

I always believed that college experience is positive for a kid whether he graduates or not. I saw young men mature and their outlooks brighten rather quickly in a college environment. Even their parents noticed the changes and commented on them. If discipline and character are emphasized, a team and a school can do wonders for a young man. He can get off on the right foot and make something out of his life, all the while playing a game he loves.

However, you can't help a player if he's back home hanging out with the fellas. How many excellent players have been left behind? Right now, thousands of young men throughout the country are playing in some recreational center. They're past their prime and wondering what happened. Why didn't they get to live out their dream? They're probably blaming someone besides themselves. Maybe it was just poor timing. More likely it was simply their own fault.

It could, however, be because a coach simply never demanded they play and act the right way—**I'm talking about before they even got to college.** They were never encouraged to be good citizens, especially at an early age. What was the environment at home? Who was around to mentor them?

I'm so amazed when some student counselor or dean asks me, "Coach, have you ever just sat down and talked to the kid?"

Gee, thanks—I never thought of that.

On the other hand, often leadership just happens. **A coach or a player can't simply decide someone should be a leader. It takes a set of circumstances for leadership to emerge from a player.**

If a certain player knows most teammates are not concerned with team needs (you would think most players would have these feelings, but few do), and he can't ignore it, he instinctively feels the need to straighten things out. **At that moment, he becomes a leader.** A leader doesn't spend much time thinking about his objectives; he just does them. Every true leader I've coached—even if he were the silent type—seemed totally comfortable with the role. In fact, if he took the time to reflect, he'd realize he had always been a leader.

If you feel a certain team member would or should be a good leader, it might help to have a talk with him. However, don't hold your breath. **Despite all good intentions, I have seen very few positive results from such conversations.** He may do everything he can to emulate leadership, but if he doesn't have it, it won't fly (or hunt, or whatever).

When a certain player is looked up to by everybody on the team, he becomes the leader, like it or not. He can't escape it. When Charles Barkley says NBA players aren't role models, what he means is NBA players *shouldn't have to be* role models. He believes the parents should fulfill that position.

He's right. But, I would say to Charles, "In many cases,

parents don't." Therefore, NBA players are viewed as role models, even more, like it or not. (I wonder if Charles has come to that conclusion yet? He probably has.)

Leaders come in an assortment of packages. They don't have to be rah-rah, in-your-face. They can sometimes be silent, under the radar. Most of the really good players I had the privilege to coach were quiet and soft-spoken.

You could appropriately call them silent leaders: Spud Webb, Mookie Blaylock, Charles Johnson, Puntus Wilson, Chester Smith, Cullen Mayfield, Carlos Mayes, Curtis Thompson, Rick Penny, David Grant, Chris Doyle, Larry Evans, Billy Ray Smith, Robert Tate, Todd Duncan, Justin James, Josh Naylor, and Kevin Walker. Ricky Grace was a little of both—I would call him the best "total" leader I had at Midland College. There were more. Their silence was because of their concentration during a game. But even before that, they were calm and confident. It was in their DNA. None of these players thought his game was more important than the team's game.

On the other hand, I had good players who had absolutely no problem talking, which is not to imply they were disloyal. They wanted to win as badly as anybody. I'm talking about kids with personalities, not necessarily attitudes: Lincoln Minor, Skeeter Henry, Stewart Barnett, Derrick Wilson, Tony Wright, Alex Stanwood, and Nathan Doudney. They were also leaders in their own right.

Too much chatter, however, encourages others to tune them out.

I loved them all because their common denominator was hating to lose. It was an easy formula: **if you cared about the**

game, I cared about you. We spent a great deal of time together. Their true feelings, whatever they were, couldn't escape us.

Chester Smith was one of the quiet guys. On the day of the 1982 NJCAA championship game, the question on everybody's mind was, "Can this little miracle team from Midland, Texas, win one more?" Our obstacle was Miami-Dade College from Florida, which had been ranked number one all year and was undefeated at 34–0.

Despite all the hoopla during the week, our team felt we deserved to win and would win. I'm not sure how many fans subscribed to that opinion because, on paper, it didn't quite look that way.

During our routine pregame meal, I stood up to make a couple of lowkey remarks regarding the big game we were about to play in four hours. I got about two sentences out when Chester (out of character), stood up, put his arm around me, started walking me out of the restaurant, and said, "Coach, we know what to do." Anytime a player steps up in such a sincere fashion, a coach has to be pleased. **That's exactly what you have worked for all year long.** By the way, Chester had a clutch performance that night.

Actually, they all did.

I've always felt things from my heart (I'm sure you know by now). I admire effort, pulling for the underdog and cheering for the little guy, the one nobody thought could do it. Goosebumps are common with me—sometimes tears. I'm just built that way—can't help it. Though I didn't come to this conclusion until later in life, I know it wasn't an accident that certain feelings came from deep inside me. I share these thoughts with only a few. Since most people will take a step back and give you a funny look, I've learned when and where to bring certain subjects up. I believe that's why kids have never been intimidating to me. They haven't quite learned to hide their true feelings. Most of them throw everything right at you.

Interacting with my team was the one unquestionable time I knew why I was put here—to get inside a young person's heart and mind and assure him he was good and capable of being better.

When it happened, I felt worthy. Consequently, I tried to explain my emotions to my teams before they even started early in the season, so they knew who would be coaching them every day.

They never once flinched. They learned quickly that I meant what I said and would be 100 percent sincere. What I learned quickly was that almost all young people want to do right—they just don't how to go about it. That's where you come in.

Once they see that you're for real, they don't want to disappoint you.

The explosiveness which I seemed to possess (and sometimes wished I didn't) had an important impact on my dealing with emotional players throughout my career. Knowing how they might feel made me much more patient. It became clear that it was a mistake to take some of their antics personally. They really weren't defying me, although it might seem like it to an outsider.

It was best to stay calm and let it all soak in. Walt Disney claimed Davy Crockett always suggested, **"Be sure you're right, then go ahead."** Whether that's Hollywood or not, it's always made a lot of sense to me.

Don't misunderstand: bad behavior was not ignored or tolerated. But there was always a voice (which sometimes I ignored) telling me to step back for a minute, take a deep breath and get the whole story before blurting out something prematurely that might need to be undone. As a coach who's supposed to be in control, it's better to be correct the first time you open your mouth rather than the second time when you're forced to apologize.

We had one very nice club in Midland that was the place to be it seemed. Everyone liked **Garfields**. College recruiters often went there after the games.

If you wanted to visit with your coaching friends, you went there. The problem was that the players and I did not find it enjoyable being there at the same time. We were 100 percent in agreement with that.

A plan was devised. My players were notified that *Garfields* would normally be my meeting place with the visiting coaches after our weekend games. My departure time would be no later than 11:00 p.m. *Garfields* would then become their playground from 11:00 to 2:00 a.m., when they closed.

I reminded them, "If you can't impress some gal within a three-hour time allotment, you might as well be in your room studying." Sure. I emphasized that there was no intent to encourage club-going, but if they did, we wouldn't be playing hide-and-seek in the process.

There were never more than two or three players standing outside *Garfields'* front door as we coaches headed out the door. The players and I always had a polite smile for each other as we traded places like two ships passing in the night. My guys weren't angels.

Discipline wasn't always that simple, but an attempt to be realistic and fair with the guys when possible certainly didn't hurt our relationship.

I was forced to deal with an awkward incident during the first Christmas break. A kid we were all quite fond of, Michael Smith from Florida, was on my 1986–87 Midland College team.

One Sunday evening in January, Michael was walking out of Safeway with a case of beer when he ran into Coach Stone. Neither one of us enjoyed the moment.

If one of us could have disappeared like magic, we both would have been much happier.

Drinking a beer isn't a serious crime in my mind. Drinking a lot of beer every weekend is. However, walking out of a Safeway with a case of beer in your hands where the whole world can see you is an unforgivable crime—and *it's stupid.*

It was just a case where the timing didn't favor Michael. Early on, I knew this team could get away from me. As a freshman, solid discipline had not been established yet. Had Michael not been on a team made up of several immature freshman, I would have run the dickens out of him and given him a second chance. Michael was built very stoutly, so a four-day session of extreme running wouldn't have hurt him. But, he was one of four or five questionable freshmen on that year's team.

This was the first major rule violation. If I had let him off by just running him instead of meeting the problem with some real force, I would be sending the message, "Coach Stone talks big, but he isn't going to kick anybody off this team that's any good."

Michael's roommate and best friend was Mookie Blaylock. Lucky for him—and lucky for me—Mookie wasn't around when Michael carried the beer out of the store. The truth is, being tight with Mookie didn't help Michael's cause one bit.

Mookie also needed to take note of what could happen if someone screwed up. (In case you hadn't noticed, Mookie Blaylock was very important to our success.) The entire team was watching. What was Coach Stone going to do?

I really needed to get the team's attention, so Michael had to go. *He became the sacrificial lamb of the 1986–87 team. By sending him home, it raised a big, red flag for everybody on the team to see.*

The decision may not have been fair to one guy, but it was the right thing to do for the team. **Like it or not, the team trumps the player.**

I didn't enjoy sending Michael home. He was a starter and just a few days earlier had told me he was the only person in his entire family who ever went to college. If anyone needed the Midland College experience, it was Michael Smith. It hurt him to leave, and that's why it hurts me to this day. I always wonder how he's doing.

Earlier in January of that same year, we participated in the **annual Rotary Club Invitational Tournament in Scottsdale, Arizona.** It was a nice, well-financed affair which we won every time but the first year we entered.

On the eve of the championship game of the 1987 event, all but three of my guys decided to stay out late—real late. And, of course, when that occurs there's almost certainly alcohol involved.

I found out the next morning and let everybody know they were to board the bus at 1:00 p.m. for a little workout. We arrived at the gym a half an hour later, just as the seventh-place game was being played. We went straight to the auxiliary gym and locked the door. I was not in the best of moods.

While the three kids who obeyed curfew shot baskets on the side goals, the violators ran line drills. Though the championship game was only six-and-a-half hours away, **we did a great deal of running.** I wanted to send a clear message to the team. It was a perfect win-win situation for me.

If the running wore them down to the point they had little or no production that night and resulted in a loss, then it would be all their fault. However, if they gutted up and won, it would prove to each one that they could do much more than they realized.

Either way, they would learn a lesson which could help us win in the future since conference play was about to start back in Texas.

After a lot of running, I was faced with a moment of truth when Mookie Blaylock, our All-American star player, declared, "I ain't running anymore," as he lay on the floor. He had probably gotten very little sleep the night before and was dead tired. His teammates were encouraging him to get up and finish the drill, but he was half-dazed and having nothing more to do with it.

Mookie's stunt was like a dagger in my back. He was a sophomore—he knew the drill. Everyone had to follow the rules. I told Mookie that if he didn't get up, he was history. Everyone in the gym knew from the tone of my voice that, "Coach is dead serious."

Calling out George Walker, my assistant, meant a bus trip was in store for Mr. Blaylock and he would soon be heading home. As I turned and walked toward half-court to finish our running drill, all I could think of was, "Lord, please get that boy up."

Believe me, I didn't want to lose him. However, I would have if he had given me no choice.

Then I heard the sweetest sound—it must have been three pair of gym shoes sprinting toward Mookie. **A showdown is always better if it occurs with your best player.** If the best player has to do everything right, it's fairly obvious every player on the team must fall in line.

When I turned back to the team, Mookie was wobbly but standing (more like leaning) and ready for me to give the command, "Go!"

We ended the running session shortly thereafter. (Hey, I'm not stupid.)

As the players staggered back to the bus to head for the motel, I heard a few fans say, "Hey, isn't that Midland College?" We looked like exhausted troops coming off a battlefield.

Our first ten or fifteen minutes that night wasn't pretty. We couldn't function very well. As expected, we couldn't find our legs. Our hands were a mystery, too. We missed a couple of wide-open layups. After we finally found our bearings, we ended up defeating the host team for the championship. As they held the trophy up high, I was very proud of what we had accomplished that night and what it meant for our future. (And if the truth were known, I was kinda' proud of all I had learned in the years prior. As a rookie coach, I'm not sure I would have known what to do. Experience does help.) It was a positive experience for our team, and it made us a much more tougher and confident team.

My parents, who had rarely gotten to see their son coach, had driven all the way from Kansas to see the tournament. It was nice to have them there. Winning was like icing on the cake for their trip.

After spending two years with you, success at the next level, wherever that may be, is never guaranteed. In a sense, a player has to start over after moving on to the next school.

But, if you've done your job, hopefully, they will have their head on straight and their adjustment time will be short. I'm very proud of the fact that a very high percentage of my sophomores who were signed by four-year schools did quite well with their new surroundings.

And, here's a promise: In time, they will return in some form or fashion, perhaps a letter, maybe in person, thanking you from the bottom of their hearts.

That's all you may receive—no million-dollar bonus like the fortunate few.

But, for some reason, it seems like enough.

"If a chain
is as strong as
its weakest link,
then a team
is as strong as
its weakest player."

Kent Porter/Reporter-Telegram

Mookie Blaylock slumps against a training table outside the Midland College lockerroom Monday night after a heartbreaking 103-102 loss to New Mexico Junior College in Hobbs.

Mookie Blaylock

15
THE PARENT-COACH RELATIONSHIP

"It doesn't matter if you win or lose… until you lose."
—Charles Schulz (Peanuts cartoon)

She got on a plane in Dallas to find me in Midland. She walked straight toward me and looked me square in the eye. I saw no friendly face.

When I was forced to send her son home because of disciplinary issues, one could quite naturally expect a reaction from one or both of the parents. Besides pure embarrassment, the son coming home meant the termination of his scholarship. She could have asked, "Why?" Instead, she went for the throat. This mother wasn't about to accept my decision.

We had just won a preseason tournament at home and were still standing on the court, smiling, shaking hands, and basking in the glory of the moment when she came up and verbally pounced on me, calling me a racist. I just loved hearing that. His being black had nothing to do with sending him home. Had that been the case, we wouldn't have had a team—we had one white kid on the entire roster that year.

The mother of one of my other players prevented an awkward scene by physically intercepting the irate mom. I would have talked to her, but that was certainly not the right time or place. I never heard from her again.

A coach must act in a professional manner and maintain order by staying in control when dealing with an upset

parent. If he lowers himself to the parent's argumentative level, he will become involved in an unwanted personal battle.

Nobody wins when that occurs.

Normally, when faced with unhappy parents during an otherwise peaceful environment, the first thing that came out of my mouth was, "Your son sure can be ornery, but I really like him." Such a statement usually quieted things down between me and the parents, sometimes immediately.

The normal reply was a smile and, "Boy, you've got that right."

Usually, but not always, the ice would begin to melt and we would find ourselves on the same page, trying to improve the situation. Positive results might not have lasted long—disagreements about playing time always seemed to crop up—but, if any kind of trust could be developed between us, the kid was the beneficiary.

A few years later, while visiting at Spud Webb's house, the young man I'd sent home stepped up to say hi. We had a good visit. He was very apologetic and admitted his actions had been immature while mine had been justified. I told him immaturity was totally normal at that age. It was his first time away from home. It was understandable that his mom didn't want her boy to experience failure.

On the whole, the parents of the players I coached in college weren't a problem. They tended to treat me with respect, especially since I had the ability to relieve them of the financial burden required to send their son or daughter through college.

The parents often lived a distance from the college and saw

only one or two games a year. When they showed up, they felt like visitors. They weren't around often enough to feel attached to their son's team and thereby have the right to criticize anything we were doing. If they had any negative thoughts, they kept them to themselves.

The parents of high school kids I coached were completely different.

They were more hands-on. They were the ones feeding their kid and making sure he got up in the morning. Moreover, a gradual change of attitude toward coaches has occurred over the last thirty years.

More and more, every sector of our society points elsewhere when attempting to determine, "What went wrong? Who's responsible?" It starts at the very top of the leadership board. It's actually changing us as a country; we just haven't officially recognized (or admitted) it yet. "It 'ain't my fault" has become the norm.

When I took over the Richardson High School job in the late sixties, it was obvious that some of the thirteen seniors on the squad had to go. There was no negative feedback. Today's parents wouldn't have let that slide. Any problem concerning their son or daughter would not be considered the fault of their child. The fault would be placed on the school or the coach. It's automatic.

If their boy isn't playing (and shooting), they are upset. The coach is ruining their child, now and for the future. What is best for the team doesn't concern them. Their only concern is their kid—it's serious business to them.

That's exactly why **I don't try to bond with the parents. I've**

seen very few positive results coming from "friendship" with players' parents. ("My son will be playing, right, Coach?")

It has unquestionably changed, 180 degrees, in the last twenty to thirty years. Ask any coach, in any sport, at any level.

Every year in the early fall during my high school coaching days toward the end of my career, the athletic teams would each hold a separate parent-coach get-together.

The purpose was to discuss various issues that might arise during the upcoming season. Even though I thought it did little good, it was important to communicate various team policies to the parents as soon as possible.

One of the major differences that the parents were made aware of was that the varsity team was different from the junior varsity. Immediately, their sons would be held to a higher standard. There would be no next year for their sons to prove their abilities.

Because I could sense each parent felt their son would make the team and Coach Stone's remarks weren't being directed toward them, I suggested, "Don't assume I'm talking to the parents sitting next to you." (I'm guessing they probably didn't take that to heart,either.)

You may think I'm sounding abnormally negative or sarcastic. I'm not. Today's parents are *very* protective of their kids. What we use to expect when "the kid got home" was a certain amount of support by the parents for the teacher or coach. That support isn't automatic these days.

The parent-coach meetings I had were predictable. Over the last couple of decades, parents have become more aggressive. They don't show the coaches much respect and often don't have any feeling for the"team" concept.

If you look closely at the ones who do have a good team

attitude, you'll usually find their kid is getting plenty of playing time.

Imagine that.

Parents are concerned about their children; everything else is a distant second. As the coach, you must develop a plan to tactfully deal with this situation. Parents mean no harm, initially—they just love their kids. When faced with any type of parent-coach meeting, whether it was a one on one meeting or a group session, **it always seemed to me that the their true feelings of many were:**

1. My son should be a starter.
2. He should have the freedom to shoot as often as he wants.
3. It's your obligation to assist him in getting a college basketball scholarship.
4. As his mentor, you should avoid working him too hard or criticizing him.
5. Now go get 'em, Coach—we're behind you, win or tie.

Think I'm exaggerating? I heard those thoughts quite often in different forms. As much as I wanted to be cordial and available to parents since they had a difficult time thinking objectively when it came to their sons, I found keeping my distance (short of shunning them) was the only strategy that had a chance of working. Consequently, our workouts were usually closed. When parents watch practice, they do not comprehend why you are driving their son to the point of fatigue. **When they're sitting in a booster club meeting, parents will have no problem agreeing**

hard work is what their son needs, but seeing a tough workout in person is a different story.

It's hard for parents to understand that even though a kid might have a bad day now and then, the emotional and physical stress of athletics is still very positive.

You know, *tough love.*

Young people learn so many things on the playing field that don't come up in a normal classroom setting. Not only do they learn about competition, teamwork, and how to follow instructions, they also learn about sportsmanship. The real bonus is that they discover positive things about themselves.

Years later, it's not unusual to hear ex-athletes say with great pride how tough their coach and his practice sessions were. However, if parents or coaches become "overly involved," too many negatives can blur the positives of the experience.

I expressed my feelings very bluntly with my players when it came to advice from outside sources. It was difficult trying to explain that their friends and family meant well but the team needed to let their advice go in one ear and out the other. There were no illusions on my part that they were capable of actually understanding.

(Let's face it: their response would normally be, "That's Dad giving me advice. You want me to ignore my dad?")

When a parent or friend challenged me on this, I would explain how confused the boy was going to be trying to please me along with one or two other well-intentioned people. Though the argument may have made sense to parents, it's doubtful if anything changed much. It was still their kid out there, and he was only going to be in high school one time.

My advice to young coaches meeting parents for the first time is to emulate a campaigning politician. Say "hi", but don't stop and chat very long.

Don't be rude, but avoid buddy-buddy relationships. If a dad thinks the two of you are good friends and by Christmas his son still isn't playing, the dad will feel betrayed. He'll think, *I thought we were tight*, making for an uncomfortable situation.

Still, for every rule there are wonderful exceptions. Mike and Janice Walker were both so appreciative of me just because I coached their son, Kevin, during my time in Rockwall. They were old-school, backing the coach regardless of his decisions. I'm not saying **parents shouldn't question how their child is handled in school, but they should make sure the coach's viewpoint is respectfully considered regarding any incident.**

Mike Walker was unique. He was a parent whom I could converse with throughout the season. It was enjoyable telling him almost everything. He got a kick out of getting the inside scoop. He understood that our conversations weren't going any further than where we were standing. The reason it was possible to have this kind of relationship with the parent of one of my players was because Mike wasn't looking for any favors for his son. Whether Kevin played or not, our relationship wouldn't have changed. I think this was because Mike was a college teacher and his view of kids and parents were similar to mine in many ways. Please know, there were other parents with good attitudes. Mike and Janice just seemed a comfortable fit for me.

We did a lot of laughing, which was good therapy for both of us. I wish more parents were like the Walkers.

V
OVERTIME

THE YEAR WE WON IT ALL

16
SPUD

*"Sometimes it's the people no one can imagine anything
of who do the things no one can imagine."*

—Alan Turing (The Imitation Game)

Anthony Jerome ("Spud") Webb was an unforgettable individual. He never looked directly at me, his coach, from the moment he arrived at our campus in the fall of 1981.

Not to worry—I was certain he didn't miss a word. Game time always produced the one exception: his eyes were unquestionably zeroed in on me during timeouts. He knew the importance of detail. You only had to tell him once. But even then, you might worry a little. His deadpan expression would always leave you wondering.

At the beginning of the 1981–82 season, you would not have cast Midland College as the eventual Cinderella of the 1982 NJCAA Tournament. (Back then, our Cinderella was a rather ugly child). We started the season with two wins, then headed to Barton County Community College in Great Bend, Kansas, where we went 0–3 in their annual invitational tournament. The weather was cold outside but not any colder than our shooting. Our future didn't look very promising as we dressed to head home after our final game. I was about to enter the locker room when one of the guys tried to stay positive by saying, "Come on guys. Think about the team." It sounded like **Lance McCain.**

The painful reply was, "Team? We ain't got no team." It

sounded like those words came from my five-foot-seven freshman guard from Dallas, **Spud Webb**. Hey, he wasn't going to get an argument from me.

I delayed my entry, then announced, "Let's go home."

Everyone thought it was a good idea. We hopped on the bus and drove all night.

Despite the miserable outcome of that tournament, I got to know a lot about Spud Webb. During the tail end of our final game, Spud missed an attempted layup that would have given ourselves a decent chance of winning the game. As he ran back down the court with the clock running down, he motioned to me that he had been pushed in the back during the shot.

A slight nudge can completely throw off a shooter's touch, but in my mind I thought it was a phantom push. I wasn't thrilled knowing he had come up with a juvenile excuse for missing a layup. Afterward, Spud didn't say any more about it, and my conclusion was that he'd wished he had never brought it up.

After we had returned to Midland, I took a look at the play on our game film. Wouldn't you know it? Spud was telling the truth. He didn't choose to go around crying about it. That was a big moment. It clearly showed to me that at no time was Spud untruthful. In fact, to this day, I have never known Spud Webb to be dishonest.

Today, people *admire* him for his slam dunk and basketball accomplishments on the court, but they *respect* him because of the honesty he maintains. Another incident during fall practices had already proved to me how tough Spud was.

We were running a "charge" drill where each player has to learn the right angle and timing in order to take a charge rather than be called for blocking. During the drill, Spud—all 135 pounds of him—took a solid hit right square in the mouth. The truth is he hadn't learned the finer points of this new drill, thus the blow to the mouth which resulted in biting through his lower lip.

After the loss of a lot of blood and seven stitches in his lip, Spud was back in practice the next day. Normally, we ran the charge drill every other day. But there was some curiosity on my part as to who this guy really was. Staring into the face of this charge drill the very next day might just tell me a few things about him. I was prepared to conveniently overlook him had he chosen to hang back at the end of the line for one extra day. Spud didn't even think about hiding. The little guy stepped up, stitches and all, and, without hesitation, took another heavy charge. On this occasion, his timing was better, and he managed to survive the hit without further damage. *It was another sign I had a winner.* When a player learns the mechanics of taking a charge, it's not difficult or dangerous—it's all about angles and timing. It's actually kind of fun. That '82 team took some timely charges in the championship run.

One more example of Spud's toughness occurred during the first game of the national tournament. Throughout most of the first game against Westark, the previous year's champs, we were having our way. Spud was the center of attention, and Westark was becoming annoyed.

During a sure layup from Spud, a Mac truck came out of nowhere. One of their big, strong guards just hammered Spud, both arms straight across his face—knocked him flat. By today's standards, the interpretation would be "unnecessary, excessive, and ejection," a flagrant foul—no question. Nothing was said, however. That type of play was basically part of the game in those days. Plus, this was the national tournament.

Spud just sat there for a few seconds (it had to have hurt), and with a quick rub on his head by fellow Wilmer-Hutchins teammate Chester Smith, he got up. Two free throws later, the game continued. Spud could have lay on the floor looking for sympathy (which the crowd would have gladly given), but he didn't. That was no little kid out there—that was a young man.

Spud Webb was admired by all of us. We always felt his playing ability would carry him a long way. Point guards equipped with his skills are irreplaceable. We wanted him to lead us to the promised land someday. I thought his potential leadership—as silent as it was—was unquestionably going to blossom in the near future. Fortunately for us, he answered the call his freshman year, sooner than we anticipated.

Spud didn't talk much, but when he did, we listened. **He spoke with his actions, however.** His leadership qualities emerged when he played. He became our leader because, when a close game wound down, he would say to himself, *Well, it looks like something needs to be done. I guess I'd better get going.* Whether it was scoring a couple of baskets, making a couple of steals, or blocking a shot, Spud often spoiled us by coming through.

One particular Christmas break game versus Tyler Junior College serves as a good example. We were down five points with less than a minute.

It hadn't been looking good for the "defending national champs" (a title you learn to dislike). I was just about to switch our defense from a half-court trap to a straight man and instruct our guys to foul, thereby stopping the clock. Hopefully, two or three missed free throws could give us new life with perhaps the possibility of a win.

I was a bit late. Spud had other plans. He had been positioned on the baseline in our half-court trap, and, with Tyler playing keep-away from us at the ten-second line, **he had concluded (correctly) that running the baseline on defense was not going to do him or his team any good.**

Before I knew it, my five-foot-seven point guard was (on his own) double-teaming the ball at mid-court. Two consecutive steals later, we were about to take the lead, and thirty-five seconds later, we did—plus the game.

That's a perfect example of a player on your team being allowed to use his intelligence to win a game. Within a few seconds, the deed was done. Neither one of us said a word about what had just transpired. Had I been a new uprising young coach arriving on the scene, my ego might have taken over—and it would have been a mistake. **We won because I got out of this tiny guy's way. Another victory for Midland College, thanks to Spud Webb. We were both happy—and neither cared how it happened.**

(Is this a great country, or what?)

17
THE TITLE TEAM

"Before You can win,
you have to believe you're worthy"

Mike Ditka

When you coach for any length of time, there will be teams that are special to you. For example, my first two years at Rockwall High School were just what the doctor ordered. It had been a while for me to experience winning and having a real connection to a team. Both the players and I dedicated ourselves in such a way that we went 66–5 during those two years. It was also nice to do it under the spotlight in the Metroplex of Dallas/Fort Worth. Five more years of similar success allowed me to end my career of forty-plus years in a good way.

However, nothing is more special than a team that wins a national title. Take all the factors that made up the 1981–82 Midland College basketball team, project it through the eyes of the national media, and that story would have been one that was worth remembering and repeating. One of the reasons I decided to write this book was to preserve our '82 story.

If you think I've been glorifying this little West Texas team, you'd be correct—they were a remarkable group. It's been almost thirty-five years since that Chaparral squad showed the fans what a real team could do, no matter their size.

Everyone involved with that group feels exactly as I do. They understand and share my enthusiasm. Anyone who saw this unassuming, methodical team at the National Junior College Athletic Association Tournament in 1982 hasn't forgotten it.

What made the '81–'82 Midland College Championship team so unique were the events of the two previous seasons. We were ranked one and two during most of that time and couldn't get out of Texas!

I remember driving down I-20 in West Texas, listening to the radio during the Christmas break, when radio guru **Paul Harvey** mentioned our lofty 1980–81 number-one ranking and undefeated record on his broadcast.

I almost drove off the road.

He said he previously had been to a convention held in Midland and found the West Texas hospitality delightful. He wanted to compliment the city and the success of the Midland College team. It was nice to hear.

The only thing he omitted was not mentioning Midland's dynamic young coach—but I got over it.

We maintained that number-one ranking throughout the year but ran into a tough Cooke County College of Gainesville, Texas, in the bi-regional playoff for the chance to go to Hutch. At the time, two out of every three years, the winners of Region V (West Texas and New Mexico) and Region XIV (East Texas and Louisiana) had a one-game playoff to determine who would go to the national tournament. Those were two very strong regions. In 1979–80, we were 33–0 and ranked second nationally, but had to play number-one-ranked San Jacinto College. We lost. Going one-and-done after thirty-three straight wins didn't make sense. As mentioned, it happened in the '80–'81 season, with Cooke County sending home our previously number one ranked team, with a final record of 30-3. The 1981–82 season—my fifth at Midland—started with only two sophomores: Puntus Wilson and Lance McCain.

Puntus was a six-foot-three small forward from South Oak Cliff High School in Dallas. Skinny as a rail—they nicknamed him "Stretch" during high school—he had a very quick vertical leap and needed little knee flexion to reach the heights he achieved. This ability made him perfect for the alley-oop play. Before you knew it, Puntus's nose appeared rim-high as he slammed it through with authority.

Another good quality was his shooting. He wasn't pure, but he was close. He also had what you needed in basketball: an explosive first couple of steps. He was a very smooth player.

The other sophomore was six-foot-three Lance McCain from Andrews High School in West Texas. A Midwestern State University transfer from the previous year, he started as a two guard the entire season.

We actually liked playing three guards, ideally all three being combo types, guards who were both ball-handlers and shooters. Throughout the year, we had to deal with one obvious exception, however. The only true ball handler on the team was Spud. Per my instruction, he spent half his time during the games running to get the ball from teammates.

Lance was steady, a good shooter, and a decent athlete who had some maturity. He knew how to talk to the younger guys, encouraging them as much as he could. He helped us through the early days as well as the championship run in the spring.

The rough times occurred mainly during the first semester. Besides Puntus and Lance, we had brought in sixteen new players (some were walk-ons). It wasn't until the following year that we got the assistant's pay where it needed to be. We were then able to hire Reggie Franklin in the spring of 1982, although he sat on the bench, volunteer-style, during the '82 National Tournament in Hutchinson, Kansas.

That's not a bad way to start a coaching career.

The '81–'82 season started ominously. After two wins at home, we traveled to Great Bend, Kansas, to participate in Barton County's annual invitational tournament and lost all three of our games. Barton revealed an ineligible player during the period in question.

When we arrived back home, I did the only thing that allowed us to play without embarrassing ourselves completely: I put the best five players on the floor with little regard to their normal playing positions.

Lance McCain and Puntus Wilson were off-guards—neither were true ball-handlers—and my two postmen would have to be six-foot-four Chester Smith and six-foot-three Jerome Crowe, though they were actually more comfortable on the perimeter. I had only one player, Spud Webb, my point guard, playing in his natural position. Based on this lineup, how would anyone, including their coach, have predicted the season we were about to have?

After these adjustments to our starters, it wasn't long before the squad numbers began to dwindle. By Christmas, we only had nine left. Individually, those nine weren't much to holler about. We certainly were not intimidating when we strolled onto the floor.

Because of their lack of size and numbers, those remaining Chaparrals had to stick together to succeed. It was quite obvious—they understood. By using the same starters throughout the year, chemistry between the players developed naturally. They all discovered, to our amazement, they had the right stuff. Their bonding was aided by the fact that four of the five starters were from the Dallas area and had known each other for years. It also helped that they all loved the game. Almost every one of them were what coaches want—gym rats.

The roles of each individual on the team were well-defined. We knew who should be shooting, who should have the ball at the end of the game, and who should have it when our opponent was going to press us or needed to foul us. Adjustments involving plays, press attacks, and/or certain defenses were not big problems. Talk about chemistry—we had it.

I had a friend who boxed as a young man and was fairly successful.

He used to tell me that it was the quiet ones who made him nervous. When our guys played a game, it was with a business-like attitude, a quiet manner. There was no, "me, me, me" among this group—not one ounce of jealousy to worry about.

They had confidence. As they nonchalantly walked onto the floor, they seemed to suggest, "We are not big, but we are quicker, smarter, and more skilled than you. You will have a hard time beating us."

Most of the time, our game-time M.O. had been the same: get a good lead (we were skilled offensively); get tired or bored (we played predominately five guys); allow the opponent back in (unfortunately); and finish off the game with some amazing basketball (they grew to expect victory).

We followed that pattern way too many times for my blood pressure, but there seemed to be a whisper of "destiny" with this bunch, as we came from behind time after time to win ball games throughout the year.

From mid-December 1981 through the season's end in mid-March 1982, we didn't lose a single game, progressing through conference play, winning the Region V Tournament, and earning a trip to the nationals for the first time in Midland College's history.

In 1982, the NJCAA was divided into twenty-two geographical regions in the United States. Six bi-regional playoff games were necessary to narrow the field to sixteen teams. We were fortunate that winning the regional tournament for the first time happened to be in a year that Region V didn't have to play one of those bi-regional playoff games. By winning the region, we earned the right to go straight to Hutch.

The manner in which you approach this tournament-time "new season" is so important.

As a coach, you may worry that your team has been beaten down by the rugged season and has lost some of its sharpness. The players don't know what to expect.

None had ever been to the tournament. They'd only heard about it. No need to worry. When there are only sixteen teams still playing in the US and you're one of them, everybody finds new energy.

You're not going to change your offenses and defenses. Much of your game plan will stay the same. But, as a coach, you do have to think before you speak because everything you say and do in the few days leading up to the "big trip" is magnified. **Bringing anxiety and pure excitement down to a normal level is virtually impossible. You just have to manage it.** Having your team prepared psychologically is more important than anything else. The "physical" component will take care of itself.

Here's where experience helps. Many coaches who bring a

team to Hutch are stepping onto the Sports Arena floor for the first time, just like their players. I had played on the Arena court during high school (Hutchinson High was in our conference) and had attended many Juco tournaments growing up. I, for the most part, knew what to expect.

I've never believed a group of athletes playing for a national title in any sport needed a bunch of long-winded speeches to get them ready. They already know why they're there and they've heard most every speech in their coach's arsenal. They don't need to go see a *Rocky* movie.

The bigger the game, the less a coach needs to say, but there does need to be a plan of some kind. Try to make it short and sweet. Their blood is pumping fast enough already.

If anything, the players need a sedative, not a sermon.

Playing in the national tournament is a big deal to the players. They've never been in that kind of atmosphere. Consequently, I liked to give my players occasional "reminders" nothing dramatic, but rather something that reasserts our purpose for being there. So many teams are just happy to be going to the nationals. They don't actually see themselves going to Kansas and *winning the event.* That's got to change.

I let my players know this was the time and place for which we had all been working. It was kept brief and positive with no big commotion.

They needed to be reminded that our season game plan was *right on track.* **What made it so acceptable was that they had been hearing this same message all year long.** Everything we said we were going to do, we were doing. If that were true, we should be able to operate in a relatively calm, workman-like manner.

I tried to describe what it would be like and how they might feel when they first arrived in Hutchinson.

Because of my having witnessed all the ramifications of a national tournament so often, I believe the way it was presented was very helpful. Not overdoing it was important. They needed to know what to expect so that once they were there, it wouldn't feel uncomfortable. They might be a bit nervous, but that would be all.

Because we had never deviated from our goal and had worked hard to get to where we were, deep down we had confidence. We felt like we could win it all, and, more than that, we felt we deserved to win. Was it a 100-percent feeling? No. But, we weren't shocked when it happened.

Seeing the imposing, six-foot-ten Evon Joseph that first time when we arrived at our hotel in Hutch got everyone's attention. It became clear to me they needed a little reminder of why we had made it to the nationals and what we intended to do while we were here. I asked everyone to get off the bus except the nine Chaparral players.

It was me and them—just the way I liked it.

There have been many speeches given where the coach has his fingers crossed behind his back. This wasn't one of them. I had a feeling what I was about to say was going to be good.

Sometimes you just feel the vibes.

Because of my familiarity with the surroundings, along with the team's amazing chemistry and confidence which they had shown time and time again, I believed everything I was about to tell them and they knew it.

What I told them may have been the best talk I have ever given a team. This is what they needed to hear:

1. **"The best team, not the best individual, is going to win this tournament."** (I spoke about individuals in reference to the giant we'd just seen.) If a team makes it out of the Texas Region, it deserves to be here.

2. For years, Texas teams have done very well in this tournament: San Jacinto, Western Texas, Tyler, Kilgore, etc. **You do not have to play over your head.**

3. **"By the end of the week, people are going to be talking about the Midland College team from Midland, Texas . . . especially this guy."** I pointed to Spud. One thing I knew about him was that I could brag on him and he wouldn't try to take advantage of it.

4. **"Out of the sixteen teams, eight of them won't believe deep down they're good enough to win this tournament.** Four of the remaining eight will play us tough but will not believe they can beat us. The other four will not have gone through all that we have—the workouts and the adversity. They will not be as prepared and they won't have the chemistry we have."

5. **"This one is important:** *What is required of you is constant focus.* We will be here five days playing four games. Keeping focused four games in a row is next to impossible. If you can do that, you will have a big advantage because those other teams, more than likely, will not."

6. **"Finally, take a look at your coach. Do I look rattled and unsure?** I watched this tournament as a kid many times. I played in this gym in high school. I was born and raised 110 miles from here. I have relatives living

here. This is not some magical dream we're trying to live out. We're here because we're supposed to be here."

In the ten days that followed our regional tournament victory in Big Spring, Texas, we found ourselves in Midland, Texas, with a lot of down time. Though I tried to gradually prepare the guys for the upcoming event we had dreamed about so many times, the truth was that **all our team needed to do was play the game the same way we had always played.**

That was easier said than done. It is one thing to explain how you should be thinking and quite another to have the poise to calmly carry it out. That's where experience can be your friend. Junior college kids, however, have very little experience. The most anyone of them can draw from is one year. Freshmen have none.

Back in Midland, I tried to address the issue of nerves by making a simple prediction. The day before the start of the tournament, each team received a half hour to practice in the Arena's practice gym and a half hour on the main floor. It was the only time allotted for a team to become familiar with the Sports Arena's surroundings. The players also had to be aware there would be media and college scouts present, observing their every move.

I told the team they would be so excited in that environment that, before long, they would be tackling each other, making bad passes, and shooting air balls—in other words, generally looking like they had never played the game. I told them I would have to call them in and tell them to "calm down." I made the prediction in the form of a light-hearted comment, but I was serious.

Guess what happened during our practice on the Arena floor?

Just what I had predicted back in Midland, Texas. We couldn't help ourselves.

After watching a few minutes, I called them in, "Do you guys remember what I predicted back in our gym a few days ago regarding this first practice?" Their eyes were wide open, kinda like when I'm about to feed my springer spaniel, Chelsea. But there was no response—nothing. Only one guy was smiling.

From the moment I called everyone in, Spud knew what I was going to say. We all got a laugh out of it and went forward, finishing our remaining brief time in the spotlight. That night we ate a great dinner at my cousin's house. It was a nice gesture. Everyone eating a great home-cooked meal around a big table turned out to be a perfect start on a perfect journey.

We seemed to be in the right place.

1982 Region V tournament, Spud Webb MVP

18
GETTING TO THE GAME
OF A LIFETIME

"Perseverance is not a long race,
it's many races, one after another."

—Walter Elliot

The field of sixteen for the 1982 NJCAA Tournament included:

Two undefeated teams:

> number-one ranked Miami-Dade Community College-North (30–0) and ninth-ranked Tunxis Community College (26–0) from Farmington, Connecticut.

Five former tourney winners:

> Four-time champ Moberly Junior College (30–5) from Moberly, Missouri, making its first appearance in eight years;

> Two-time champ Mercer County Community College (27–3) from Trenton, New Jersey, making its tenth trip to the tournament;

Two-time and fifteenth-ranked Vincennes University (31–4) from Vincennes, Indiana, making its thirteenth trip to Hutch, but the first under coach Dan Sparks; Seventeenth-ranked College of Southern Idaho (28–7) from Twin Falls, featuring seven-foot-one Rick Tunstall, one of two seven-footers in the event; and twelfth-ranked and defending champ Westark Community College (31–3) from Fort Smith, Arkansas, the nation's leading defensive team, giving up only 51.8 points per game.

The other ranked teams included:

> Third-ranked Henderson County Junior College (31–2) from Athens, Texas;

> Sixth-ranked Jamestown Community College (30–2) from Jamestown, New York;

> Eighth-ranked Allegany Community College (31–3) from Cumberland, Maryland; and

> Nineteenth-ranked John C. Calhoun State Community College (26–3) from Decatur, Alabama.

Midland College (30–4) was a complete unknown—no ranking, no tradition, and nothing to hang our hats on.

In some respects, that was good. We had no expectation pressure hovering over us. Every team in the tournament was ranked in the top twenty nationally—except Midland College. We came into the tournament completely under the radar.

By luck of the draw—which actually occurred shortly after the

1981 tournament concluded—our first game was in "primetime" at 7:45 Tuesday night against defending champ Westark, a squad that had brought back three of its starters, including tourney MVP DeWayne Shepard.

I had scouted the Lions a week earlier with an ex-coach who had actually won the national tournament a few years back.

After watching Westark play, my friend flatly stated there was no way we could beat them. His comment bothered me because, when you play a team only once, there's always a way to win. "Can I get an amen?"

However, I did appreciate his frankness. Had he said something like, "They shouldn't be a problem," he would have either not been very smart or would have simply been lying. Placed in a similar situation, I would probably have said, "It's going to be tough."

I did not bring those negative sentiments back home to my team in Midland. We would have had a much larger task ahead of us if I had. The players would have sniffed it out just by the way I presented the scouting report to them. I needed to keep them in a positive frame of mind.

The day we were to depart from the college campus and board our plane at the Midland Regional Airport, I got an idea. Judging from the Kansas forecast, the weather in Hutchinson was going to be definitely colder than our part of the world. We needed some kind of uniform-looking windbreaker for the team other than our regular warmup tops.

We only had enough time to check in the campus bookstore where we found some transparent, three-quarter-length rain jackets. At first glance, I wasn't sure how they would look.

The jackets turned out perfect. Their see-through design

allowed our Midland College warmups to be seen. When we walked into the Sports Arena before our first game, I was so proud. I thought we looked plain ol' classy, and the cheerleaders had pinned a flower on each player's lapel to top it off.

I watched the guys intermingle with the crowd, sitting in the stands as the game before ours was played. Though they chatted with the fans around them, they were mainly quiet—maybe a bit nervous.

Nobody, including me and my players, knew that within five days most of the entire Arena would be screaming for this unknown team from Midland, Texas.

Everyone was surprised when we took a thirteen-point, first-half lead and held a ten-point advantage at halftime for our opener against Westark. When we extended the lead to twenty-one points in the second half, it all became downright boring to the indifferent, first-day Hutchinson crowd. Let's look at the program. Who plays next?

The crowds at the NJCAA Tournament are predominately neutral (except when a Kansas team is playing) since 85 percent of their makeup are local basketball-loving fans. After we opened such a big lead, the crowd naturally became lulled, almost half asleep, assuming we had the game in hand.

On the Monday before the tournament, *The Hutchinson News* put out a special insert which included write-ups of all the teams. In the article about the Chaparrals, it mentioned we had a little bitty guy who could dunk. During practice, people would come up to me and ask, "Where is the little guy that can dunk?" When

I'd point out this five-foot-six, 135pound kid who looked as if he was in the sixth grade, they'd say, "He can dunk? Naw." Apparently, they felt it was a hoax.

During the second half lull in our opener, Spud made a steal at midcourt and decided it was time to show his stuff. We were accustomed to him preparing for a dunk by going up off one foot, layup style. This time, he slowed almost to a stop and sprang off both feet simultaneously, a much more difficult task for a little guy. Miscalculate that one and you wind up flat on your back. I was thinking, *Okay, little man. You're going to embarrass yourself this time.*

I was wrong, just like every time I ever doubted Spud Webb.

He absolutely rifled the ball through the net with a tomahawk slam. It was one of the best dunks I've ever seen him do because he actually came to a dead, standstill stop before simultaneously springing up off both feet.

Tired of hearing about Spud Webb? Well, OK—I'll give you a brief break. It's difficult. In fact . . . I don't think I can.

The place exploded. The vocal reaction was as loud as any indoor spectator sport I've ever heard—plug-your-ears loud. From the moment of "The Dunk," as people who saw it appropriately referred to it later on, a love affair began between the local fans and this fragile-looking team from Midland, Texas. Believe me, we needed that support. Spud's dunk didn't guarantee victory, though it seemed that way at the time. I'm afraid what it really did was awaken the Lions. We should have known the defending champs would not go away. Almost as soon as the crowd jumped to our side, Westark launched a come-back. Not only did they catch fire, we went in the opposite direction.

Two factors helped the Lions close the deficit: they began

hitting from long-range distances over our zone and we couldn't make a free throw to save our lives. Free throws were usually money in the bank for us. But suddenly the bank was closed—nothing would go in. Every Chaparral was affected by a virus that spread slowly, creeping into our psyche. No team at any level is fully protected from these mysterious catastrophes. In the second period, we missed fourteen of twenty-seven free shots, many of them the front end of one-and-ones. While we kept missing, I was thinking, *Come on clock. Run!* With fifteen seconds to go, Westark had pulled within one.

During those final seconds, Puntus Wilson twice missed on the front end of bonus situations that would have clinched the game. After his last miss, Westark grabbed the rebound, out-letted the ball, passed it to midcourt, and eventually got it into the hands of six-foot-one Tony Killeybrew, who took two hard dribbles on the left side of the lane and laid it up for the potential game-winning basket.

At that moment, everybody in the building—including me—felt bad for the little team from Midland who had played their hearts out, thinking Westark had demonstrated the adage "never say die" with a possible rally. At the last second, someone came out of nowhere from the right, stretched across the lane, and blocked the shot just as the horn sounded to end the game. I'm telling you, it looked like a ghost—well, some kind of spirit.

It had to be Puntus. It *couldn't* be Puntus. He was on the other end of the court.

For about five seconds, the Arena went dead silent. Was it a good block or goal-tending? The referees conferred and agreed—*good block*.

Game over.

After all the commotion, I asked some of the players, "Who (or what) blocked that shot?"

They said it was Puntus. I told them, "No, it couldn't have been him. He was on our end of the court after missing the free throw."

I was wrong.

Very few people, including me, saw the route Puntus took to cover three-quarters of the court in time to make an unbelievable, perfectly timed block that averted a one-point Westark victory and an opening loss for the Chaparrals.

After his missed free throw, Puntus actually sprinted *laterally* in an attempt to slow down Westark's pass to midcourt before making his three-quarter-court dash.

I've watched that route and block by Puntus on video many times. I am still amazed watching it. "The Block," as I like to call it, kept us in the tournament for another round.

Our St. Patrick's Day quarter-final opponent was Dixie College, from St. George, Utah, making its fourth appearance in the tournament. Because Dixie was a Mormon school, most of the players had served on a mandatory, two-year LDS mission. Consequently, the average age of the Dixie team was two years older than the other teams in the tournament. This can be a real advantage in the juco ranks since two years increases a player's size and strength, not to mention his maturity level.

But we were quicker. We led throughout the game Wednesday, though we didn't make it easy on ourselves. When we got six to ten points ahead, Dixie would battle back, tying the game twice in the second half.

Each time, we answered by opening another gap. With six seconds left, Puntus Wilson erased the memory of our opening-round nightmare at the line by sinking two free throws to ice an 85–82victory.

Puntus had another great game with twenty-five points and seventeen rebounds. Spud added sixteen points and seven assists.

However, the star of the game was Chester Smith, who scored a career-high twenty-eight, including a ten-point run that broke a fifty-all tie. In addition, Chester pulled down eight rebounds and held Chris McMullin, Dixie's leading scorer, to ten points.

The "Big Three" for Midland College were the Dallas boys: Puntus, Chester, and Spud—all three undersized, but no one could afford to underestimate them. They were excellent college basketball players. The word was spreading among the fan base: watch out for Midland.

More importantly, we now believed we belonged.

After those first two games at the national tournament, this tiny Texas dunkster and goaltender was no longer a rumor—he was real. Everyone was asking, "Have you seen this little point guard, Spud, from Texas?"

When Spud Webb was in high school, he wasn't five-foot-six. He was closer to five-foot-two or five-foot-three. When I got to know him as a freshman at Midland, he never dwelled on nor even acted like he thought about how small he was. In his mind, he was just a basketball player in love with the game.

He was the darling of the tournament. Autograph seekers were everywhere—kids and girls (and not just grade-school age girls). At home in Midland, someone had made some "I'm a Spud-

Nut" buttons, and people in Hutch were scooping them up for a good price.

The *Midland Reporter Telegram* said, "Spud Webb could be elected mayor of Hutchinson."

The first person all the media wanted to talk to in post-game inter views was Spud. Honestly, to some extent, he didn't know why. He balked at doing them, saying, "Do I have to, Coach?" He wanted nothing to do with being interviewed. I had to force him to do them. "Yes. Get over there and talk to them."

With each interview, you could see the transition. I stood close enough to recognize that my point guard was changing right before my eyes.

He began to realize, "You know what? I believe I'll play with this size thing. They seem to think it's really something." He started responding to all the fuss regarding his outstanding play despite his size. When someone asked, "What makes you want to drive right into the middle of all that traffic?" he'd reply, "Hey, that's where the basket is."

One of my favorite Spud answers was after the following question: "Do you ever wonder what you're doing out there playing with all of those big guys?"

He coolly answered, "No. They ought to start wondering why they're out there playing with me."

Spud had always been rather shy. That week he began to realize that he was actually "the man" of the tournament. Before that, he was so in love with basketball he never had a "look at me" thought. Even though, inwardly, he was one of the cockiest guys, he wasn't stuck on himself. The national tournament forced Spud to acknowledge and discuss his five-foot-six stature. He finally told himself, "If they insist, let's go with it." Toward the end of the week, his interviews were totally different, as he rattled off his comments with ease.

His change continued when he got back home to Midland after the tournament and was interviewed quite often. His transformation culminated a few years later when he won the slam dunk contest at the NBA All-Star game.

The Spud Webb love affair continues to this day. Now, everyone in the world knows he might not be very tall, but he's something special and definitely one of a kind.

He changed a lot of people's thoughts regarding height requirements when it came to playing basketball, not only for the millions of little guys just starting out, but even for the "big league" boys of the NBA.

When it came to the sudden attention we received in Hutch, I wasn't too concerned about Spud and the team. They were a close-knit group and kept to themselves. I was more concerned about our lack of manpower, and that very issue got our attention in the middle of the tournament.

Early in the week, an athletic trainer from a local school who wasn't even in the tournament noticed that Lance McCain, one of our starting wingmen, was sitting rather awkwardly in the stands, tilting his head in an unusual manner as he watched one of the games. We took him to a chiropractor who worked on him. It seemed to help and he played on Wednesday during our second game. However, the trainer remained insistent that Lance didn't look right. On Thursday, our day off before the semifinals, we took him to a doctor to be X-rayed, crossing our fingers as we did.

The news wasn't good.

They found Lance had a cracked vertebra just at the top of his spine. Apparently, he'd fractured it a couple weeks earlier during the regional tournament. That meant a neck brace and no more basketball for a few months. A few months! I was hoping to hear, "A few hours."

Great. When this team lost a starter—and one of our only two sophomores—it was serious business. We were now down to eight players, two of whom were not on scholarship. Four of the remaining eight had hardly seen the floor during the days leading up to the tournament.

Rodney McChristian, a six-foot-two freshman from Memphis, Tennessee, who had limited playing time as our sixth man, was the guy who would have to step up and replace Lance. And he did just that. You would have thought he'd started all year. He hit his first two shots, early in the game (a collective sigh-of-relief could be heard from the Midland bench). Deep down, my main worry was that I'd worked these guys too hard throughout the year and had worn them down. But when I saw Rodney's positive demeanor throughout the remainder of the tournament, I was glad we'd done it the old-school way.

During a short practice that Thursday, I told the team that Lance would not be playing and that Rodney would fill in for him. No one flinched. (I don't think any of them saw my crossed fingers.) Looking back, I believe they felt as though nothing was much different. Spud, Chester, and Puntus were still around, weren't they? OK, so what time does the game start? They were truly *that* confident. With Spud, they felt there would always be a way to pull it out.

Why not? That's what they had seen all season long.

Our semifinal opponent was Vincennes University, a regular participant in the tournament. We were concerned because, though Dan Sparks was bringing his first team to the tournament as the Trailblazers' head coach, he had won a national championship as a player for VU on this very court in 1965. Having an experienced veteran coach at the same school means a lot anytime you're involved in a play-off situation. An experienced coach can normally calm the waters when his players—first-timers to the event—are thrown by the unfamiliar environment. The Vincennes team was also known for its physicality, one thing we weren't. Thankfully, we were a disciplined and fairly smart finesse team.

Unlike our previous two games, we fell behind by five early. However, Spud, Chester and Puntus combined for seventeen points in a twenty-to-two run to put the Chaps in control as we took a ten-point advantage into the locker room at halftime.

In a repeat of our other two games, we seemed to tire in the second half, allowing our opponent to catch up. With Lance unavailable and an unproven bench, this was understandable. I could not afford to take my starters out. And if Spud made a mistake, there was nothing I could do. As I told Michael L. Johnson in his book, *The Juco Classic,* "I didn't have the luxury to take him out. Because when I took Spud out, anybody in America could press us."

On six consecutive possessions, we missed two shots and turned the ball over four times. Vincennes went on a fourteen-to-two run to take a three-point lead with just under seven minutes to go. Over the next minute and a half, Chester converted a three-point play, and Puntus nailed an eighteen-footer to put us back on top.

Then came the game-breaker. With a little more than four minutes remaining, Spud stole the ball, broke for the other end, and slammed it home. The play brought down the house. Behind Puntus's twenty-four points and Spud's twenty-one, we held on for a 71–66 victory, our twenty-third in a row—one away from the title.

The stage was set for the 1982 championship game, "the greatest NCAA Tournament title game ever played." The match-up featured a team trying to go undefeated all season against an underdog no one expected to be there. The undefeated team had progressed through the week by falling behind then coming back to pull it out at the end. The underdog had done just the opposite, building a lead, then holding on for the win. Which scenario would play out this time?

19
THE GREATEST
NJCAA CHAMPIONSHIP GAME
IN HISTORY

"Don't give up, don't ever give up."

—Jim Valvano

Miami-Dade owned an almost two-inch-per-man height advantage. This kind of disparity was normal for us. It hadn't deterred us in the past and didn't against the Falcons. It didn't hurt our confidence when Jerome Crowe, one of our six-foot-four post men, came out of nowhere to slap six-foot-ten starting center Evon Joseph's first shot into the bleachers during the first minute of the game. It was clean and rather shocking. With that swat, an attached message seemed to declare, "Hey, we're not afraid of you."

We led most of regulation play by as many as eight points. Miami-Dade didn't take its first lead of the game until just inside the ending two-minute mark, when Tracy Stringer, the Falcon's point guard, hit a jumper to give Dade a 74–73 edge.

Spud quickly gave us back the lead with a pair of free throws, his fifteenth and sixteenth in eighteen tries. After Stringer fouled out, Puntus stole the ball for an easy layup. It wasn't a sure thing. Puntus always had trouble dribbling with his right hand because he had a strong, dominant left hand. We were holding our breaths until he made the basket. During his drive to the basket, a very clear flashback hit me—all of those right-handed lay-ups after practice.

For me, watching him make a shot that was actually difficult for the soon-to-be MVP was another hopeful sign that our dream might actually come true.

We should have had the game won in regulation. Trailing by three with only twenty-five seconds to go, Miami-Dade pressed. Spud broke through, creating a three-on-one. Instead of pulling the ball back out and running time off the clock, Spud proved he wasn't infallible. He challenged the lone Falcon defender, six-foot-ten Evon Joseph, and missed the shot. Miami-Dade secured the rebound, quickly moved it up the court, and worked it inside to Joseph, who was fouled as he laid it in. The foul, a silly touch-foul was the fifth on Puntus.

This wasn't looking good. I called time to let Evon think about it, but it didn't faze him. He calmly stepped to the line and sank the free throw—nothing but net. A big guy like that wasn't supposed to hit a game-tying free throw.

We were going to overtime.

With Puntus now on the bench, we had to play cautiously in the extra period. (There was no shot clock back then.) Nobody scored until Chester's basket gave us the lead with three-and-a-half minutes left. Miami-Dade tied it up a minute and a half later when six-foot-five Emery Atkinson, their leading scorer, hit a turnaround jumper. The Falcons then took the lead when reserve Craig Jay stole the ball out front and drove for the go-ahead goal.

From the huddle our plan was to pass the ball to Spud on the wing and follow with a screen—the plan went awry. As the play developed, a walk-on let the pressure confuse him. After the pass, he cut *away* from Spud, leaving our clutch shooter standing with the ball on his own. Spud immediately but calmly realized that no screen was coming.

Five seconds, four seconds.

With a burst, he drove into the heart of the lane, pulled up, and arched the sweetest eight-foot jumper over Miami's six-foot-ten post man before the horn sounded.

Swish.

The little guy had done it again. Let the second overtime begin.

How many times can this kid bail us out?

He wasn't through, however.

From the jump-ball tip, Spud drove to the charity stripe and nailed a beautiful, arched rainbow jumper over Joseph's outstretched hand. It was very similar to the jumper he'd made earlier just to get us into the second overtime. From that point on, he took over the game. He scored again, driving the lane, beating both Joseph and Atkinson to lay in a shot high off the glass. Then he picked up a loose ball at our end, drove the length of the court, and laid it in, prudently passing up a dunk.

We led 88–83 with 2:25 remaining—an eternity for Midland, but only seconds for Miami-Dade. We were still in the lead, 89–86, when Spud picked up his fifth foul. He left the floor to a standing ovation. The question was obvious: Was the tide turning?

We prevailed at the free throw line, where we finished with twenty-nine charities—a record for a title game. Still, without Puntus and Spud on the floor, the final moments of that championship tilt were pretty nerve-racking. I had two walk-ons on that floor.

Because Dade was behind and needed to foul, the only player I really wanted to be on the free throw line was Chester Smith, the best shooter (the only shooter) we had remaining. In the final seconds, I called my last timeout.

Since we would be in bounding the ball against the Falcon's full-court press, I wanted to line up everything so Chester would receive the ball and just hold it, braced for a foul. I wanted our shooter on the free throw line. We had players on the floor who were not used to being in this situation, and I wanted everyone on the same page.

After completing my instructions, I asked Chester if he understood the play. No response.

I looked up and said, "Where's Chester?"

My manager/trainer casually informed me that Chester was at the end of the bench going through the medicine kit.

"What's the matter? Is he hurt?"

"Oh, no. He's trying to find some scissors to cut down the nets."

I looked down at the end of the bench and, sure enough, Chester was slipping scissors inside his sock.

(In your life, have you ever?)

In the meantime, the horn sounded, ending the timeout session. Chester had his scissors but didn't know the play that had been drawn up for him. To say the least, it was a bit frantic on our bench. We had no more timeouts.

"Scissors? Are you kidding me?"

I grabbed Rodney McChriston and told him to tell Chester where to line up on the throw-in and to expect contact when he caught the ball.

A Shooter's Touch

Chester got the message, caught the pass, got fouled, made two free throws, and started looking for a ladder.

We had won, 93–88.

No sweat, Coach.

At the moment we won the National Championship in 1982

at Midland College, one single, undeniable feeling engulfed me: an over-whelming feeling of joy, but not for myself. I hadn't anticipated the happiness and pride for the Midland, Texas, citizens. **Suddenly, our team and I were givers. It felt pure.**

When we won, we had been gone for seven days and knew little of the interest that had been building back home. Years later a friend told me that he and his date were about to go into The Stardust of Midland, a local country-western club, when outside in the parking area radios blared into the night. Every time we scored, the sounds of horns filled the air.

Though the championship game pushed toward 11:00 p.m., the loyal Midland College fans remained stuck in their vehicles, glued to the action, as they shared their need to pull the Chaparrals through to victory.

After two overtimes, the game finally ended and the local college was National Champs. For several minutes, horns blasted, car doors slammed, and people cheered. A spontaneous celebration—the best kind—resulted.

I didn't hear this particular story until years later—it gave me goosebumps.

Writing this book has been rewarding while reliving the events and remembering the people who shared it with me. As coaches, we fondly remember the thrill of victory, but the trials and errors involved in the quest are equally important.

The images of young men I was privileged to coach are implanted in my memory more clearly than any game.

Every season has a hundred stories, many having very little to do with the final score of a game. It's the camaraderie, the achievements, and the failures that teach us. They have much to do with who we are today.

Puntus Wilson and Spud Webb made the ten-man All-Tournament Team. Chester Smith was left out, though clearly he should not have been. However, I can understand that having one team with three All-Tourney recipients would be considered too much.

Unique to the NJCAA Tournament is the **Bud Obee Most Outstanding Small Player Award**, which goes to the player six-foot-one or under who displays "good character, leadership, and loyalty to his fellow players and coaches."

When Al Wagler, the tournament director, presented the award, he said, "Probably in all the years of this award, this is the most *difficult* decision we've had to make." Everyone in the Arena laughed. "But after long consultation, the winner of this year's award is five-foot-six from Midland, Texas—Spud Webb!"

I've described Spud as a player who really didn't think about losing. All he wanted to know was, "What needs to be done for us to win? OK, give me the ball." You could see it on his face. He finished the championship game with thirty-six points, the third largest total in an NJCAA tournament title game, and hit sixteen free throws, a tourney record for a title match. I definitely believe Spud was the MVP of the tournament.

However, since they honored Spud with the Little Man Award, Puntus Wilson was named French Most Valuable Player.

To be fair, Puntus deserved the award, too. He had an outstanding tournament and had scored just as many total points as Spud: ninety-four. He'd hit clutch shots and made game-saving plays like "The Block" against Westark. No one was complaining. We were all floating. It didn't seem real.

Were we watching a movie or what?

How many times have you heard an athlete describe an

unusual, near-perfect performance and the media comment how "calm" and "peaceful" he was? That's exactly how these Midland College Chaparrals felt. We always joked that we were so tired we didn't have enough energy to be nervous. (There was some truth to that). To the four Dallas starters who had known each other since junior high, it seemed comfortable and "meant to be."

When you are stuck to each other *every day* for most of eight months, things can wear thin for everyone involved.

That's why you see grown men hugging each other when final games finally conclude. As much as the victory is sweet, the fact we got through all of the stress and pain required just to get there is equally as satisfying.

We had started the year with a total of eighteen players; we ended with nine. Rodney McChriston filled in beautifully as a starter for Lance McCain for games three and four. The other three members, Chuck Robinson, Justin Morett, and David Thompson's playing times varied,but they each contributed. Throughout the year, they were loyal and were no less happy with the outcome than anyone else.

I thought further proof of our legitimacy as a championship team was the fact that every one (all eight) of our team members were definitely needed to see us through the two-overtime game.

Spud and Puntus had never fouled out of a Chaparral basketball game during their two years at Midland. They did that night, and two non-scholarship walk-ons completed their task.

Jerome Crowe was one of our low posts, along with Chester Smith. Jerome, Chester, Lance, Puntus, and Spud were our five starters all year long. Those nine young men will forever remember what they experienced during one week in 1982 in Hutchinson, Kansas.

I ran into Evon Joseph years later at an NCAA Final Four. He was still upset about that championship game. In his situation, I would have been too. Having gone undefeated all year long until that game must have been painful. He was very polite as we visited, but it was understandable that my reminiscence was more enjoyable than his.

It is difficult to describe how drained I felt and, at the same time, how happy and grateful we all were watching that game unfold.

Talk about surreal. This was the fulfillment of a lifetime dream: a "one-scholarship" boy *coming back to Kansas* and being in the middle of such a magnificent game.

It may sound a bit strange, but, at that moment, you are so proud, knowing most of what you've tried to teach your kids since the fall *really did work*. Our game plan was very effective throughout the tournament.

We coaches are always second-guessing ourselves. We're always wondering if we've given them too much or not quite enough. Those nine (eventually eight) youngsters went out there and did it, but I knew that all of the preparation required was an important segment in the story. We were all justifiably proud of the final outcome.

I'll say again: the story of the 1981–82 Midland College team could easily be turned into a book or put on the screen.

It is the perfect example of the little guys against the big guys. Spud's story alone would make for good reading.

Small in stature but large in heart, he has inspired many kids who have heard, "You're just too small" all their lives. From high school to junior college to NCAA Division I and on to the NBA, where he won the 1986 Slam Dunk contest, Spud Webb's story inspires everyone.

As for me, I feel gratitude in a behind-the-scenes way. I was allowed to share in the wonderful experience of winning a national championship.

You who have had a passion for competition concerning something much bigger than yourself know exactly what I'm talking about. That little Midland College team went straight through the week, attracting fans as they moved toward the finals. It was wonderful. So seldom do you get the chance to experience something that emotional. I only wish we could have returned the following year.

These are childhood dreams that overwhelm you when they occur.

20
IT WAS ALWAYS MY GAME

"What you give, you keep.
What you keep, you lose."

—Axel Munthe

When you've coached energetic athletes for more than four decades, there are endless numbers of interesting and significant memories. Remarkable games can be reflected on over and over, if only for the pure joy of reliving some of the most gratifying experiences of your life.

While attending a basketball clinic in Las Vegas in the mid-80s, I found myself sitting in a restaurant reminiscing with Boyd Grant, the Fresno State head basketball coach. We both had won a NJCAA title Midland in 1982 and Coach Grant with the College of Southern Idaho in 1976. He had also won the NIT at Fresno State in 1983.

Since he was successful at the Division I level, I would have thought that his junior college days might seem a bit trivial to him. I was wrong. As he told me about the thrill and joy of winning a national junior college championship, Coach Grant became slightly emotional. He seemed to feel the way I did about competing and winning in "the" game. It helped validate my strong inner feelings that it's OK to still be in love with a childhood game. At any level, it's really all the same.

Looking in the eyes of this man, a coach who had a reputation for being stern and stoic, I knew what he was feeling. Only those who have never dreamed of standing in the winner's circle and being handed a trophy would question the emotion. **All that's necessary for you to understand is: everything you've thought it would be falls well short of the actual experience. It seemed almost spiritual.**

It's understandable why coaches and players having just won the "Big One" usually have the same reaction: "Words can't express how I feel right now—it's like a dream."

If someone asks, "What's the big deal? It's just a game." No. It's not just a game—it's everything in your life leading up to the game, too.

The 1982–83 team, which followed the "miracle at Hutch," was anticlimactic for Midland College. Not surprisingly, it wasn't much fun. When you make it to the national tournament the first time, it becomes a totally new and different experience with which you are confronted. What is equally enlightening is the year that follows—another example of something new and different. Both must be dealt with.

We had most everyone back, with the addition of five or six new players. However, we were never able to reproduce the magical chemistry that was needed to go win another championship. We played well most of the time, but the desire to prove ourselves wasn't quite the same.

It was a very good team, reaching a top-three ranking nationally and finishing with a record of 31–4. All year long, we were "the defending national champs" and had a big bull's-eye on our backs. Every opponent was eager to come after us. We still won—sometimes it was ugly.

Yet, when it counted most, we lost to San Jacinto College, 82–69, in the interregional playoff game, missing the chance to return to Hutchinson, Kansas. They were the better team. Our season was a bit of a drag, but I wasn't disappointed with our team.

When I announced my retirement in 2007, Rockwall High School administrator/coach Lynn Nabi recognized me at the spring sports banquet. Besides his kind words, I received new golf clubs and a bag. It was a very thoughtful gesture. I didn't expect such recognition. Once again, Lynn Nabi had taken care of his head coach.

However, the setting was a bit awkward. Since it was the spring banquet, the members of the audience were tennis, golf, and soccer players, along with their parents. Teams representing schools the size of Rockwall are in their own world and have little or no identity with the other sports in the same school. I doubt if many people knew or cared what some of us were celebrating. After all, it was their spring banquet, not ours. It's possible that very few of the audience had even been to a Rockwall High basketball game.

There were many moments to reflect on and much I would have humbly wanted to say, but I was talking to the wrong people. It would have been very meaningful to me to have had friends and family present on such an occasion.

Regardless, it was very thoughtful of Lynn Nabi to give me a bit of recognition under the circumstances. All coaches that walk up and down those sidelines as much as I did deserve a pat on the back.

My career included eleven schools at all different levels, but mostly at colleges. When you move around as much as I did, you really don't have a true home base. There was no one place I could bid farewell to and celebrate with people who really knew me and knew how much the journey had meant to me.

Actually, I hope this book helps.

If I had a choice, it would have been Midland College. In fact, Midland had honored me in the past—and more than once. I was inducted into the Midland College Athletic Hall of Fame in 1997. I was honored with a special "Jerry Stone Night" on one occasion, as part of *the thousandth game of the Midland College men's basketball team.* A personal favorite was the honor of speaking at the school's 2007 All-Sports Banquet. I enjoy speaking to all of the sharply dressed student-athletes that represent a particular school.

I have received other recognitions throughout my career:

"Coach of the Tournament" at the NJCAA National Tournament in 1982 and 1987;

the National Association of Basketball Coaches Kodak Award for junior college, "National Coach of the Year" in 1987;

McMurry University Sports Hall of Fame Inductee, in 1990; Midland College Athletic Hall of Fame Inductee, in 1997;

and the Western Junior College Athletic Conference Hall of Fame inductee, in 2006.

All coaches end up with honors. The best honor of all is being called "Coach." It was a privilege to have had that honorable title for so many years.

Acknowledgements

"The mediocre teacher tells.
The good teacher explains.
The superior teacher demonstrates.
The great teacher inspires."

—William Arthur Ward

The Colorful Coaches of the NCAA

Some of the head coaches I met became friends. Most were just acquaintances I knew from recruiting. I liked them because they were genuine. They may have wanted my players, but they didn't try to blow me over. Confident people don't feel the need to impress—they just do naturally. They were delightful to be around. Their assistants (too many to mention) were equally delightful.

Some of the personalities that were enjoyable to be around: Norm Stewart at Missouri (down to earth and funny); Larry Brown at Kansas (a class act—a perfect blend of old-school and current trend); Billy Tubbs at Oklahoma (fun to be around); Nolan Richardson at Arkansas (a unique, product of the street—a serious fighter); Charlie Spoonhour at St. Louis (a country boy, comedian).

Lefty Driesell at Maryland (very likable); Bob Knight at Indiana and Texas Tech (all business and, surprisingly, a very good listener); Bill Self at Kansas (just a regular guy); Don Haskins at UTEP (gruff but tame); Tim Floyd at UTEP (a great guy); and P.J. Carlisimo at Seton Hall (very cordial and likable). There were many more. Of course, I liked them because they seemed to like me—at least, when I had players.

Abe Lemons (Texas and OCU) Always Stole the Show

Probably my favorite head coach to be around was Abe Lemons who was at Texas when I was at Midland. Many would echo that—I'm not sure Abe had any detractors (not even Eddie Sutton).

Everybody loved him. I certainly was one of his biggest fans. Abe enjoyed being a comedian probably more than being a coach. One thing I've observed, most people want to be entertained— they want to laugh. Like many Americans, I miss being tucked into bed every night by Johnny Carson because he made me happy.

Abe Lemons had that same ability. He was another Will Rogers, who was also an Oklahoman. When he spoke at clinics, finding a seat was difficult. I heard many of his "lectures," if you could call them that. I do not remember Abe ever getting past drawing a half-court diagram with a small circle representing an offensive player placed at the "elbow" of the free throw line—a popular location to have the ball for passing and scoring purposes. From that point forward, he would drift away from the "basketball clinic" and begin telling funny stories which everyone had come to hear in the first place. I heard him tell too many to relate (some wouldn't be appropriate), but here are some of my favorites:

When asked if a certain win had made him happy, Abe snapped back, "Happy? I haven't been happy since I was ten years old."

He once said, "When they finally get to the bottom of Watergate, they'll discover that it was a football coach."

Once, when his team was playing lousy, he kept them out on the floor at half-time, scrimmaging them shirts and skins.

After a losing effort one night, a reporter asked him about the poor play of one of his better players who had scored only one point. Abe replied, "Yep. He scored one more point than a dead man."

When his Texas-Pan American team didn't do well in a game against Hardin-Simmons University in Abilene, he told the media he was going to punish them by making them stay out past 11:00 pm that night. The joke was that there was nothing to do late at night in Abilene, Texas because it was noted for being "dry"—the home of three church-related colleges.

After winning the 1978 NIT championship with his Texas team, he was asked by a reporter if he liked New York City. Abe said, "Yeah, but what I really want to do is meet the chicken that laid those twenty-dollar eggs I ate for breakfast this morning."

One of the best Abe Lemons stories was told by a referee at an officials and coaches banquet. Prior to one of Abe's games, as the teams were warming up, Abe slid up to a referee who was standing at midcourt and asked him, "If I called you an SOB during the game, would you slap a technical foul on me?" The ref smiled and said, "Well yes, I'd have to, Abe." After a pause, Abe followed with, "Well, if I just thought it, would you?" Still smiling, the ref said, "Well, no—no problem with that, Abe." Abe quickly replied, "Okay. I think you're an SOB!" A technical foul immediately followed.

Prior to North Carolina State's push to get him, Spud Webb wasn't receiving many offers. I tried phoning a few coaches, asking them if they were interested in the little guy. I had known Abe Lemons for quite a while. Funny and frighteningly honest, we hit it off from the start. After his stint at Texas, he had gone back to Oklahoma City University—an NCAA Division II college with a rich basketball tradition where he had coached back in the 50s and 60s.

After asking Abe if he were interested in Spud, he said, "Interested? Tell him to forget a car, I'll give him a train!" (For the record, Abe was a straight-up guy and would never give a recruit anything.)

He always looked for shooters and playmakers and really liked Spud. He told me that assuming Spud would go to a big school (which he eventually did), he felt an inquiry would have been a waste of time. But, I can assure, had that unique coach and player teamed up for a couple of seasons, the results would have been some entertaining basketball.

When I coached at Cameron University, I used to drive the sixty miles to OCU to visit Abe. We would sit in a restaurant and talk all morning. You had to pay very close attention to his conversation because he would jump from subject to subject.

He made me feel I was one of his special friends. He made everyone feel that way. I just loved the guy. I only wish I had visited him more often.

The Western Junior College Athletic Conference—Mike and Nolan

When I landed the job at Midland College, it took me a while to get used to the explosive talent at the junior college level. Though their maturity levels varied from childlike to full manhood on any given night in the Western Junior College Athletic Conference, one could look out on the floor and see not only numerous Division I level players but also potential NBA players running right in front of you.

I learned a lot about this new juco world from a couple of WJCAC winning coaches, Mike Mitchell and Nolan Richardson during the 70s and 80s.

Mike was the head coach at Western Texas College in Snyder when I was at Tarleton State and came back to the WJCAC to coach Howard College in Big Spring toward the end of my tenure at Midland. Nolan followed Mike at Western Texas and was there until making the move to Tulsa, where he won the NIT, then at the University of Arkansas, where he won an NCAA title. Both coaches had been around juco and had won NJCAA Tournaments: Mike in 1975 and Nolan in 1980.

If you're keeping score, Nolan Richardson won three prestigious titles (the only coach in history to do it): the NJCAA, the NIT, and the NCAA Division. Both coaches were patient with me—I never did mind asking questions, the most detailed in nature. I enjoyed dealing with them, though they were hard to deal with on the basketball court.

While Nolan preferred using the full court, offensively and defensively, Mike emphasized the half-court game with plays designed for specific players.

He wanted to slow the game down in order to get a good shot, then hustle back on defense to prevent any quick transition and layups.

Both were strong coaches who demanded a lot from their players.

Whoever survived their programs knew how to win.

Hours talking to them and watching them coach helped me understand the junior college athlete, which included their ability to take a lot of hard work with little recovery time.

Both Mike and Nolan provided me with much to digest. Mike and I talked primarily about style of play, breaking things down into half-court basketball, fundamental details. As I discussed primarily in chapter 12 on race, Nolan and I, along with Andy Stoglin, talked a great deal about "black and white".

I eventually combined what I heard from them and others, with much of my own thinking, and gradually developed my own personal style of coaching. Until you've been around junior college talent a few semesters, it's really confusing as to how much leeway you should allow.

Talented players with too much freedom can prove to be a mistake. Talented players, not given enough freedom, can prove to be very frustrating for the athlete, and eventually for you.

It takes a while, but a true grasp of what you feel is appropriate will emerge. If you're not sure, latch on to an experienced coach and learn all you can from him. Don't just talk to one coach— the more you talk to, the more you may learn. The only problem is that confusion will, no doubt follow—everything looks good when you examine a winning team. Soon, however, you will settle in on a style (offensively and defensively) that suits you, and you will be off to the races.

Nolan

Some people are so unique they can be identified by using a single name: "Bear" (Coach Paul Bryant or Don Haskins), "The King" (Arnold Palmer), "The Greatest" (Muhammad Ali), "Tiger" (Tiger Woods), "MJ" or "Mike" (Michael Jordan), "Coach K" (Mike Krzyzewski), "The General" (Bobby Knight),etc.

When you say "Nolan" in basketball circles, most people know who you're talking about. Nolan's system was not complicated. His teams hounded you full-court—what he called forty minutes of hell—putting emphasis on guarding the ball and denying one pass away. His interior defense was fairly basic. The main focus was on the perimeter.

Nolan's teams were also noted for another phase of the game: they ran transition as well as any team in the country. His conditioning exercises, which were totally integrated with his practices, allowed his team to race up and down the floor without breaking a sweat.

One of the keys to determining the strength of a team is their shot selection and shot distribution. Coach Richardson's teams were overlooked with that phase of the game. He employed a very simple and effective half-court offense—their shot-selection was excellent.

I'm sure much of Nolan's basic philosophy came from his Texas Western University (UTEP today) days with Coach Don Haskins. But he had developed a love for full court basketball, offensively and defensively, separate from Haskin's control game, many years prior to his playing days at Texas Western.

After winning the NJCAA Tournament in 1982, I was a candidate for the head coaching job at Pan American University in Edinburg, Texas. I called Nolan and asked him to throw in a good word for me to the athletic director at Pan Am. Since my interview was scheduled to occur in two days, he said he'd be happy to call that very day.

After my interview at Pan American, it seemed obvious the job would not be offered to me. Turned out, they had another man in mind as their coach, anyway. Lon Kruger, now the head coach at Oklahoma University, was the man they selected. Good choice.

During the interview, I learned that Nolan had, indeed, called on my behalf the same day we'd talked. I was very appreciative that he had followed through for me. What I didn't know until a week later was that I had unknowingly asked Nolan for that favor about two hours before his Arkansas team was about to take the floor against Dean Smith's North Carolina Tar Heels in the Elite Eight that very afternoon. Interrupting any coach's NCAA March Madness drive was the last thing I would choose to do.

One more interesting note that should be pointed out was the timing of my call: Not only was Coach Richardson about to face the powerhouse North Carolina basketball team on the court, but during this time-period, he was also right in the middle of the athletics director, Frank Broyles, and Arkansas University's Chancelor, John White regarding his future continuation as the men's basketball. Although, he was surely in the midst of turmoil, he never said a word to me except, "Sure, I'll be happy to help, Jerry."

That's the Nolan Richardson some do not know: rough exterior, kind interior.

JIMMY "V"

During the spring of 1983, the Wolfpack's colorful leader, Jim Valvano, was encouraged by his assistant to fly out to West Texas in an attempt to make recruiting inroads into our junior college program.

Having just pulled off NC State's run for the NCAA title, Valvano was in high demand.

President Ronald Reagan, following tradition, offered the NCAA winners of North Carolina State to visit the White House in the spring. Somehow, Jim found time to come out and spend a day with the Midland folks and, what turned out to be, all night with me.

Looking back, I don't know how that was accomplished, but I intended to maximize my childhood hobby of trying to figure out what made coaches tick. If you can remember trying to keep up with a three-ring circus as a child, you can relate to an evening with Jim Valvano.

Like Abe Lemons, Jimmy V was a born entertainer, a stand-up comedian who could run with the big boys. He was a natural.

He was a noted motivational speaker and made frequent appearances on *The Tonight Show with Johnny Carson* and *Late Night with David Letterman*.

On Monday mornings, he'd fly from Raleigh, North Carolina, to New York City to be a regular guest on NBC's *The Today Show*. He was obviously still feeling the glow from the recent NCAA championship game, but, rest assured, Jim Valvano needed no championship to boost his confidence—no extra incentives to expend energy.

At first, I was a bit unsure who I was dealing with. I soon learned Jim was for real. I've never been around a guy like him. **He really did practice what he preached—he loved anything and everybody connected to life.** He could get on some people's nerves, but not mine. My only problem with him was trying to keep up with two or more different subjects at one time. I wondered if he ever slept—the man was intoxicating.

We talked about lots of things that night. He told me that baseball was actually his favorite sport—I can see that. He told me that I should enjoy the recent championship we had just won, more than I seemed to be. I told him I just expressed it a little differently, but there was some truth to his advice. I was always worried about the next game or the next season—it was difficult for me to think any other way. (Sometimes you get in that thought process, one that says, "You must win every game— period.")

He turned a West Texas city full of football fans into a basketball celebration at every club or pub we hit. It wasn't Vegas or New York City, but we had a blast. We ended up staying out all night. I haven't enjoyed an evening any more than that one. Jimmy V will be missed.

Hershel Kimbrell

This man has been my coach and friend for almost 60 years. He's never wavered when it comes to loyalty and friendship. His greatest single quality is his dealing honestly with an issue.

I can count on one hand (well, maybe two) the people I enjoy discussing the pros and cons of basketball with. At 90 years of age, he's one of them—still enjoys watching games and digesting them.

Dave Whitney

Coach Whitney experienced a much-traveled life, breaking down racial barriers at the collegiate level. He played basketball at Kentucky State and professional baseball in the Negro American League with the Kansas City Monarchs before settling into coaching.

In his twenty years as the head coach at Alcorn State University in Lorman, Mississippi, his teams won twelve Southwestern Athletic Conference regular-season titles.

In 2010, he was inducted into the College Basketball Hall of Fame.

He was not, however, a well-known man.

In 1976, I attended a pre-tournament dinner held by the host school, Midwestern State University in Wichita Falls, Texas. I was seated two chairs from this small frail man and notice that he was somewhat isolated in the middle of the chatter that accompanies most gatherings. Fortunately, I knew who he was. He welcomed my joining him--we were both in the mood to talk which we did while we ate for a good 45 minutes together.

As a young assistant coach at MSU, the opportunity to learn anything from a veteran coach, especially from one who was legendary, was exciting. He was typically quiet and modest—I would assume that most of the coaching staffs and boosters in attendance didn't even know who he was.

Toward the end of our visit, Coach Whitney looked at me as if to say, "Young man, don't miss what I'm about to tell you." Everyone around us was talking, so it was doubtful anyone else heard (just as long as I did). Very quietly, but with conviction, he said, "You know Coach, I just believe you can *save every boy*."

Save every boy... Dave Whitney's words shot straight to my heart. I knew exactly what and why he said what he said—I needed no interpretation.

When I occasionally speak at a clinic these days, it's next to impossible to omit words such as these—I always brace myself for the possibility of a subtle negative response from the audience, especially if they're fellow coaches.

What's interesting to me is the one thing I would prefer them to take away are words of this very nature—these are the words that give me strength and inspiration for coaching. So, while I'm standing in front of an audience, hoping that a small particle of my home-grown philosophy will connect, they, in turn, might be rolling their eyes, saying to themselves, "Coach Stone, don't get off on that emotional jargon that you seem to thrive on."

Thank goodness, I've learned to stick with what I've always heard deep inside of myself. Don't allow yourself to fall in line with what's popular at the time.

Listen to that which you know is the truth even if the "winning" coaches believe it's a bit corny and idealistic. As I have said before, don't assume that other people know more than you. To those critics I would say, "Well fellas, it must be real. I find that it's something I truly believe in, because I never get tired of hearing it or explaining why I believe in it."

If Dave Whitney had been a first-year coach, his statement would have suggested he was inexperienced and idealistic. I would have been polite but might not have engaged in further conversation with him. However, Coach Whitney wasn't a new coach and I was not so naive to think he had little to offer me.

Here was a man who would see it all for forty-plus years and those were the words he wanted to leave with me. I felt it spoke volumes and I wanted more. Some coaches are hard and bitter—some are like Dave Whitney. Two of them were spoken of very early in this writing, Merle Hinton and Dan Kahler. They fit the bill perfectly—they weren't soft—they knew when to put the hammer down. They just saw good in everyone.

Anyone involved in teaching and coaching knows that what Coach Whitney said is impossible—you really can't save them all. But isn't Coach Whitney the kind of person we want around our children?

If you have feelings like Coach Whitney, you're not a dreamer—you're a lucky man. You have the wisdom to realize that all things are possible. Having that knowledge empowers you.

As a coach, what if you are the last adult figure in the life of a young man or woman who truly has a chance to affect the way they see themselves and the world?

For years I have looked very closely at young people as they begin that first step into the real world, kinda' like from theory to reality. You know what—they're not real sure about anything. They wouldn't mind having some long meaningful talks with a

Dave Whitney now, something to anchor themselves to as they take a real look at what they're about to embark upon.

It would be nice if we could all be like Coach Whitney—his coaching philosophy is good to remember. He certainly epitomizes the words, "Leave this place in better shape than you found it."

Sometimes I wonder if I've even come close. Other times, I know I have.

Some people to thank for the development of this book:

There are many people that have encouraged me during my novice quest as an author. I appreciate their patience with the perfection side of my personality. I did actually write 90% of the text—it was tedious at times for a first-timer.

Thanks to those who helped with editing, formatting, designing, and real encouragement—especially **Michael Johnson,** of *The Juco Classic.* He was very helpful, a patient friend who held my hand as he transformed and transferred much of the early text, encouraging me to, "Please trim it up, Jerry." I learned to.

Blake Atwood picked it up in the latter stages with mainly formatting. **Melinda Martin** dealt with the cover and interior design, along with some well-timed encouragement. All were professional while working with me on a project that I felt had to be written.

A special thanks to **Bahola Edwards**, Special Assistant to President Steve Thomas of Midland College for behind the scenes gathering of photos and general information regarding MC basketball teams during my coaching years there, 1977–1987, and likewise to Ricky Penny for continued encouragement throughout its writing.

So, how does one bundle the thoughts and events of a lifetime into a single parting phrase? A favorite line of mine seems perfect:

Henry David Thoreau wrote, **"Most men lead lives of quiet desperation, and go to the grave with the song still in them."** No truer words.

This book is an attempt to heed Thoreau's words of wisdom as it relates to me. It's frustrating to spend a lifetime absorbed in an activity that teaches so many life lessons, and suddenly ends. You know the message: "Your services are no longer required." **It is my hope that my song won't end up buried somewhere. As far as I'm concerned, this writing has allowed me to sing a verse or two, while remaining on key.**

55921902R00250

Made in the USA
Columbia, SC
18 April 2019